DEUTERONOMY AND THE JUDAEAN DIASPORA

Deuteronomy and the Judaean Diaspora

ERNEST NICHOLSON

OXFORD

UNIVERSITY PRESS

OXFORD
UNIVERSITY PRESS

Great Clarendon Street, Oxford OX2 6DP,
United Kingdom

Oxford University Press is a department of the University of Oxford.
It furthers the University's objective of excellence in research, scholarship,
and education by publishing worldwide. Oxford is a registered trade mark of
Oxford University Press in the UK and in certain other countries.

Several articles are reproduced here in revised form by permission of their
original publishers. For copyright information please consult the
Publisher's Acknowledgements in the prelims.

First published 2014

Impression: 1

British Library Cataloguing in Publication Data

Data available

Library of Congress Control Number: 2013943246

ISBN 978–0–19–870273–3

As printed and bound by
CPI Group (UK) Ltd, Croydon, CR0 4YY

In memory of Peter
Filius Carissimus

Preface

This book has gone through several stages in the making. With the exception of the Introduction, the chapters in Part I began as articles published in *Zeitschrift für die alttestamentliche Wissenschaft* and in other collections of learned essays, which I list in the bibliography. Observations and constructive comments from colleagues, including notice of recent publications, have all called for an ongoing rethinking, revision, and in varying degrees expansion of some of these earlier essays, whilst at the same time signalling a need to fill out and shore up others in the interest of greater clarity. Part II, which focuses upon the nature of the so-called Deuteronomistic History, contains a reprint of my contribution to the *Festschrift* honouring Professor James Barr on the occasion of his seventieth birthday in 1994. I have included here it for convenient reference for readers, since it is immediately followed by a response to a lengthy critique of it by John Van Seters.

I am indebted to all those colleagues, both here in the UK and abroad, who have taken the time to respond so helpfully to my enquiries about some technical issues, and for their generous interest in the progress of this book. I should add that its conclusions, and with this any shortcomings, are attributable solely to myself. I am grateful also to Tom Perridge at Oxford University Press for his advice and help on various matters in the course of the publication of the book, and to Elizabeth Robottom for her very helpful assistance in the final stages of preparation for publication. I owe a special debt of gratitude to John Barton, my colleague here in Oxford, and to Andrew Mayes at Trinity College Dublin, who have read with great patience various drafts of the chapters of the book, and for their encouragement throughout. I owe them more than I can express.

Ernest Nicholson

Oriel College
Oxford

Contents

Abbreviations

ATD	Das Alte Testament Deutsch
ANET	*Ancient Near Eastern Texts Relating to the Old Testament*, 3rd edn., (ed.) James Pritchard (Princeton, 1969)
BBB	Bonner biblische Beiträge
BDB	F. Brown, S. R. Driver, and C. A. Briggs, *A Hebrew and English Lexicon of the Old Testament* (Oxford, 1907, reprinted with corrections 1953)
BeO	*Bibbia e oriente*
BETL	Bibliotheca ephemeridum theologicarum lovaniensium
BKAT	Biblische Kommentar: Altes Testament
BWANT	Beiträge zur Wissenschaft vom Alten und Neuen Testament
BZ	*Biblische Zeitschrift*
BZAW	Beiheft zur Zeitschrift für die altestamentlichen Wissenschaft
ConBOT	Coniectanea biblica: Old Testament Series
DOTT	*Documents from Old Testament Times*, (ed.) D. W. Thomas (London, 1958)
EvT	*Evangelische Theologie*
EVV	English Versions
FAT	Forschungen zum Alten Testament
FRLANT	Forschungen zur Religion und Literatur des Alten und Neuen Testaments
HKAT	Handkommentar zum Alten Testament
HSM	Harvard Semitic Monographs
ICC	International Critical Commentary
JBL	*Journal of Biblical Literature*
JCS	*Journal of Cuneiform Studies*
JNSL	*Journal of Northwest Semitic Languages*
JR	*Journal of Religion*
JSOT	*Journal for the Study of the Old Testament*
JSOTSup	*Journal for the Study of the Old Testament*, Supplement Series
JTS	*Journal of Theological Studies*
KHAT	Kurzer Hand-Commentar zum Alten Testament

NCB	New Century Bible
OBO	Orbis biblicus et orientalis
OTL	Old Testament Library
OtSt	*Oudtestamentische Studiën*
SBAB	Stuttgarter biblischer Aufsatztzbände
SBL	*Society of Biblical Literature*
SBLDS	SBL Dissertation Series
SBLMS	SBL Monograph Series
SJT	*Scottish Journal of Theology*
ThR	*Theologische Rundschau*
VT	*Vetus Testamentum*
VTSup	Supplements to *Vetus Testamentum*
WMANT	Wissenschaftliche Monographien zum Alten und Neuen Testament
ZAW	*Zeitschrift für die altestamentlichen Wissenschaft*

Publisher's Acknowledgements

The author and publisher thank the following publishers for permission to republish the author's own material in revised form.

Chapter 2, 'Josiah and the Priests of the High places (2 Kgs 23: 8a, 9)', revises and expands on material originally published in 'Josiah and the Priests of the High Places (II Reg 23, 8a, 9)', ZAW 119 (2007): 400–513 and 'Once again Josiah and the Priests of the High Places (II Reg 23, 8a, 9)', ZAW 124 (2012): 356–68. By permission of De Gruyter. www.reference-global.com.

Chapter 3, 'Deuteronomy and the Babylonian Diaspora', revises and expands on material originally published in 'Deuteronomy and the Babylonian Diaspora', in J. K. Aitken, Katherine J. Dell and Brian A. Mastin (eds.), *On Stone and Scroll: Essays in Honour of Graham Ivor Davies*, BZAW 420, Berlin 2011: 269–85. 'Reconsidering the Provenance of Deuteronomy', ZAW 124 (2012): 528–40. By permission of De Gruyter. www.reference-global.com.

Chapter 4, 'Deuteronomy, the Prophets and Scripture', includes a revision of material originally published in 'Deuteronomy 18.9–22, The Prophets and Scripture', in J. Day (ed.), *Prophecy and the Prophets in Ancient Israel*, Library of Hebrew Bible/Old Testament Studies 531, (T&T Clark , New York & London 2010): 151–71. By permission of T&T Clark, an imprint of Bloomsbury Publishing Plc.

Chapter 5, 'The Law of the King in Deuteronomy 17: 14–20', revises material originally published in D. A. Green and L. S. Lieber (eds.), *Scriptural Exegesis: The Shapes of Culture and the Religious Imagination. Essays in Honour of Michael Fishbone* (Oxford, 2009): 46–61. By permission of Oxford University Press. www.oup.com.

Chapter 6, '*Do not dare to set a foreigner over you*': The King in Deuteronomy and 'The Great King', includes a revision of material originally published in '"Do not dare to set a foreigner over you": the King in Deuteronomy and "The Great King"', ZAW 118 (2006): 46–61. By permission of De Gruyter. www.reference-global.com.

Chapter 7, 'Story and History in the Old Testament', first appeared in S. E. Ballentine. & J. Barton (eds.), *Language, Theology, and the Bible: Essays in Honour of James Barr* (Oxford, 1994): 135–150. By permission of Oxford University Press. www.oup.com.

Part I

1

Introduction

DEUTERONOMY IN OLD TESTAMENT RESEARCH: A BRIEF OVERVIEW

The modern critical study of the provenance and composition of Deuteronomy begins with W. M. L. DeWette's celebrated work published in 1805 in which he argued that 'Deuteronomy is a work that differs from the books prior to it in the Pentateuch and derives from a different author'.[1] He further related Deuteronomy to the 'book of the law' referred to in 2 Kings 22–3 as having been discovered in the Jerusalem temple in 621 BCE and on the basis of which King Josiah carried out a cultic reformation throughout Judah, and he maintained at the same time that Deuteronomy was composed not long before the events described in this narrative. Though other conclusions argued by DeWette in this short treatise were not to prevail among scholars—for example, that the Pentateuchal source P pre-dated Deuteronomy—his association of Deuteronomy with Josiah's reformation in the late seventh century BCE became established and has remained the consensus view among scholars to this day. More than that, indeed, his thesis about the origin of Deuteronomy 'provided Pentateuchal criticism with "a point of Archimedes" to which it could attach itself in order to deliver it from the bonds of church and synagogue tradition, and put in its place an alternative dating of the Pentateuch and its parts', though a

---

[1] *Dissertatio critica-exegetica, qua Deuteronomium a prioribus Pentateuchi libris diversum, alius cuiusdam recentioris auctoris opus esse monstratur*, 1805, reprinted in his *Opuscula* (Berlin, 1833); cf. also his *Beiträge zur Einleitung in das A.T.*, Vol. I (Berlin, 1833).

comprehensive working out of this was only gradually arrived at during the remainder of the nineteenth century.[2]

Such a dating of Deuteronomy did not proceed unopposed, however. As early at 1829 an exilic or even post-exilic dating was argued by C. W. P. Gramberg,[3] whose work gave rise to a so-called 'Gramberg school' among French scholars who further championed his conclusions.[4] Subsequently other leading nineteenth-century scholars adopted a similar view.[5] This view attracted further vigorous advocacy during the early decades of the twentieth century, most extensively by Gustav Hölscher, but with strong representation also among British, French, Scandinavian, and American scholars.[6] There was agreement among these scholars that the narrative in 2 Kings 22–3 *intends* the reader to identify the 'book of the law' as Deuteronomy, but this was attributed to a Deuteronomistic redactor who reworked an earlier form of this narrative to create such an impression, especially 23: 8a, 9 reporting the centralization of worship at Jerusalem. There was no agreement among them, however, as to the identity of the 'book of the law' referred to in 2 Kings 23.[7]

In contrast to such a late dating of Deuteronomy, the opening decades of the twentieth century saw a number of proposals in

[2] See O. Eissfeldt, *The Old Testament: An Introduction* (Oxford, 1965), 171. Eng. trans. by P. R. Ackroyd of the 3rd edn. of *Einleitung in das Alte Testament* (Tübingen, 1964).

[3] *Kritische Geschichte der Religionsideen des A.T.*, Vol. I (Berlin, 1829), 153 f., 305.

[4] e.g. E. Havet, G. d'Eichthal, M. Vernes, L. Horst. For a bibliography see E. W. Nicholson, *Deuteronomy and Tradition* (Oxford, 1967), 1, n. 4. See also the comprehensive survey by A. R. Siebens, *L'Origine du Code Deutéronomique* (Paris, 1929).

[5] Notably W. Vatke, *Die biblische Theologie wissenschaftlich dargestellt*, Vol. I, *Die Religion des Alten Testamentes* (Berlin, 1835), 504 f.

[6] See esp. Hölscher's 'Das Buch der Könige:Seine Quellen und seine Redaktion', in *Eucharisterion für Gunkel*, FRLANT 18 (1923), 158–213, esp. 206–13, and his 'Komposition und Ursprung des Deuteronomiums', ZAW 40 (1922), 161–255, and *Geschichte der jüdischen und israelitischen Religion* (Giessen, 1922), 130–4. An exilic or post-exilic dating had the support of a number of leading British scholars, among them R. H. Kennett, S. A. Cook, F. C. Burkitt, and J. N. Schofield, as well as A. Loisy in France, and among Scandinavian scholars Johs. Pedersen, S. Mowinckel, and E. Nielsen, and in the USA by G. R. Berry. For details, see Nicholson, *Deuteronomy and Tradition*, 4, n. 3.

[7] For bibliography, see Nicholson, *Deuteronomy and Tradition*, 7. Whilst, for example, among Hölscher's supporters G. R. Berry, 'The Code Found in the Temple', *JBL* 39 (1920), 44–51, and 'The Date of Deuteronomy', *JBL* 59 (1940), 133–9, argued that Josiah's law book was the Holiness Code (Lev. 17–26), Hölscher himself remained silent on this topic, regarding the narrative in 2 Kgs 22–3 as a Deuteronomistic redaction of an earlier, pre-exilic account of Josiah's reign which he attributed to the author of the E source in the Pentateuch.

favour of much earlier historical backgrounds to the composition of the book, ranging from the eleventh century to a time just prior to the fall of Samaria in 721 BCE,[8] with similarly widely varying suggestions as to the identity of Josiah's 'book of the law', some arguing that it was the entire Pentateuch, some that it was the so-called 'ritual decalogue (or dodecalogue)' in Exod. 34, others that it was the 'Holiness Code' in Lev. 17–26, or a collection of Jeremiah's oracles, or a general collection of prophetic oracles, or even a prophetic book.[9]

The volume and intensity of this early twentieth-century debate and the widely contrasting conclusions it yielded prompted Walter Baumgartner to give the apt title 'Der Kampf um das Deuteronomium' ('The Battle about Deuteronomy') to a survey and review of it in 1929.[10] This 'battle' soon petered out or, as some have put it, died of exhaustion,[11] and left intact the *opinio communis*—all the stronger, it seemed, for the many-sided attack it had survived—which had already established itself in the nineteenth century, of a close association between Deuteronomy and the 'book of the *torah*' discovered in the temple in Jerusalem *c*.621 BCE. Opinions varied also during these decades and beyond them as to the provenance of the book; both a northern Israel origin and a Judaean had their advocates, and various specific locations of its origin, including Jerusalem, Shechem, and Bethel were suggested.[12]

There has been wide agreement among scholars that Deuteronomy owes its present form to several stages of composition at the hands of a number of like-minded authors and redactors over a protracted period of time, beginning with an original core (the so-called *Urdeuteronomium*). For some, its original contents comprised only the central legal section in chapters 12–26, though not all of this was present, and they saw in the two main introductory discourses in chapters 1–4 and 5–11 and the diverse chapters which conclude the

---

[8] See Nicholson, *Deuteronomy and Tradition*, 37, n. 1.

[9] For detailed references see Nicholson, *Deuteronomy and Tradition*, 37, nn. 1 and 2.

[10] W. Baumgartner, 'Der Kampf um das Deuteronomium', *ThR* 1 (1929), 7–25.

[11] See N. Lohfink, '2 Kings 22–23: The State of the Question', in D. L. Christensen (ed.), *A Song of Power and the Power of Song: Essays on the Book of Deuteronomy* (Winona Lake, IN, 1993), 36–61, who comments of this 'battle over Deuteronomy' (p. 38): 'There was neither winner nor loser; the end result for all was simply exhaustion.'

[12] See Nicholson, *Deuteronomy and Tradition*, 37, n. 2, and 38, n. 1.

book (chs 27, 29–34) evidence of two originally separate editions of
the original law code that were later combined.[13] Others argued for
a supplementary theory whereby the original book was gradually
amplified by additions and expansions to reach its present form and
dimensions. In such analysis the presence and juxtaposition in
sections of the book of the singular ('thou') form of address alongside the plural ('you') form when Israel is being addressed was
viewed as evidence of such a process of supplementation.[14] This
criterion of the occurrence side by side of singular and plural forms
of address found considerable support among scholars.[15] Whilst this
variation has remained a tool in critical analysis, however, modern
commentators agree that there is probably more than one reason
for use of the two forms of address: in places it may be evidence of
secondary expansion of an earlier text (e.g. Deut. 12), but there are
other places (e.g. Deut. 4: 1–40) in which it cannot be understood in
this way, and texts where it is employed stylistically for the purpose
of emphasis.[16]

A new solution to the composition and literary growth of
Deuteronomy came with the publication in 1943 of Noth's study
of Joshua–2 Kings, and his theory, which has met with widespread
acceptance, that this corpus together with Deuteronomy itself is
properly conceived of as a 'Deuteronomistic History',[17] whose author
inherited an earlier form of the Deuteronomy (*Urdeuteronomium*)

---

[13] Notably Julius Wellhausen, *Die Composition des Hexateuchs und der historischen Bücher des AT*, 3rd edn. (Berlin, 1899), 192 n., who viewed the central 'law
section' (chs. 12–26) as the original content of the book: 'Chs i–iv and v–xi have
among other ends this one in common, to indicate a historical situation for the
Deuteronomic legislation. They are properly two different prefaces to different
editions (of the latter)'.

[14] It was first argued by C. H. Cornill, *Einleitung in das Alte Testameent* (Tübingen, 1891). It was subsequently argued independently by W. Staerk, *Das Deuteronomium: Sein Inhalt und seine literarische Form* (Leipzig, 1994), and K. Steuernagel, *Der
Rahmen des Deuteronomiums* (Halle, 1894).

[15] It gained the support of leading scholars such as J. Hempel, G. A. Smith,
G. Hölscher, M. Noth, J. H. Hospers, G. von Rad, G. Minette de Tillesse. For
bibliography, see Nicholson, *Deuteronomy and Tradition*, 23, n. 3.

[16] For an assessment of this phenomenon see A. D. H. Mayes, *Deuteronomy*,
NCB (London, 1979), 34–7; id., 'Deuteronomy 4 and the Literary Criticism of
Deuteronomy', *JBL* 100 (1981), 23–51, esp. 27–30. See also the comment of R. D.
Nelson, *Deuteronomy: A Commentary*, OTL (Louisville and London, 2002), 5–6.

[17] M. Noth, *Überlieferungsgeschichtliche Studien* (first published 1943; 2nd edn.
Tübingen, 1957); Eng. trans. by H. G. M. Williamson, *The Deuteronomistic History*,
JSOTSup 15 (Sheffield, 1981).

comprising substantially 4: 40–30: 20, which he prefaced with Deut. 1–3 as an introduction to this extensive corpus. Noth attributed the composition of this work to an exilic author who collected and wove together older sources with the purpose of providing a theodicy, that is, what Wellhausen had described as 'a great confession of sins of the exiled nation looking back on its history'.[18] The *terminus a quo* of this work was the release in 562 BCE of Jehoiachin, as recorded in the final verses of 2 Kings 25. Subsequent research has detected evidence of additional stages of redaction, one by a reviser (perhaps several) whose hand has intruded urgent summons to obedience to the *torah* in a number of contexts in Joshua and Judges, and thus described as a 'nomist' redactor and given the siglum DtrN,[19] the other, given the siglum DtrP, a redactor who has shaped the prophecy-fulfilment 'schema' in 1 and 2 Kings.[20] Among those who accept Noth's view that the corpus was composed in the exilic period, opinion remains divided as to whether its author carried out his work in Judah itself during the exilic period, as Noth maintained, or among the exiles in Babylonia.

Whilst accepting that in its present form the corpus derives from the exilic period, some commentators, notably F. M. Cross,[21] have contended for a two-stage development of its composition, a first 'edition' composed already during the late pre-exilic period and reflecting the national optimism that characterized Josiah's reign as the power of imperial Assyria declined, and affording a prominent place to the promises to the line of David. This was followed by a revision in the wake of the catastrophic events of the early sixth century and the ensuing exile, that viewed the promises to David as having been aborted by the gross apostasy of Manasseh (cf. 2 Kgs 21: 2–15).

---

[18] *Prolegomena to the History of Israel*, Eng. trans. by J. Sutherland Black and Allan Menzies (Edinburgh, 1885), 278.

[19] See R. Smend, 'Das Gesetz und die Völker. Ein Beitrag zur dtr Redaktionsgeschichte', originally published in *Probleme biblischer Theologie. Gerhard v. Rad zum 70. Geburtstag*, (ed.) H. W. Wolff (Munich, 1971), 494–507, reprinted in id., *Die Mitte des Alten Testaments* (Tübingen, 2002), 148–61.

[20] W. Dietrich, *Prophetie und Geschichte. Eine redaktionsgeschichliche Untersuchung zum dtr Geschichtswerk*, FRLANT 108 (Göttingen, 1972). For a convenient summary of the evidence for these redactions, see R. Smend, *Die Entstehung des Alten Testaments* (Stuttgart, Berlin, Cologne, and Mainz, 1978), 111–25.

[21] F. M. Cross, *Canaanite Myth and Hebrew Epic* (Cambridge, MA, 1973). See also R. D. Nelson, *The Double Redaction of the Deuteronomistic History*, JSOTSup 18 (Sheffield, 1981).

Other significant conclusions arrived at in earlier research have also been revisited, most notably the origin and nature of the concept of a covenant between YHWH and Israel, which is so central to the theology of Deuteronomy. During the middle decades of the twentieth century there was virtually a consensus that the covenant relationship was no less than a *founding* feature of Israel as a society and of its relationship with YHWH from its earliest history, and that the covenant and the obligations it placed upon Israel were the subject of annual cultic reaffirmation.[22] On this view, the authors of Deuteronomy were heirs of a long religious and cultic tradition which they sought to revive and enliven and encapsulate with other reforming measures in 'the book of the *torah*' in an endeavour to confront national apostasy that had burgeoned in the long reign of Manasseh. A close re-examination by Lothar Perlitt, however, of the relevant biblical texts yielded compelling evidence that, far from being an ancient institution, the notion of such a covenant was a creation of Deuteronomic authors no earlier than the seventh century.[23] We shall return to this feature of Deuteronomy and the rationale behind it later in this book.[24] Here two further issues that recent research has raised may also be flagged for further consideration later.

The first concerns one of the hallmarks of Deuteronomy, the centralization of the cult to one sanctuary. Although there has remained widespread agreement among commentators that this was among the reforms implemented by Josiah on the basis of the 'book of the *torah*', some have recently questioned this. Thus, for example, Reinhard Kratz has pertinently asked whether dispensing with the ancestral local sanctuaries—an action 'so special and singular in the world of the ancient Near East'[25]—could realistically have been envisaged by the state authorities in pre-exilic Judah, and suggests that such a radical shift in age-old cultic practice was more likely

---

[22] For an overview of the research that yielded this conclusion see, Ernest Nicholson, *God and His People: Covenant and Theology in the Old Testament* (Oxford, 1986), esp. ch. 2.

[23] L. Perlitt, *Bundestheologie im Alten Testament*, WMANT 36 (Neukirchen-Vluyn, 1969).

[24] See Chapter 4, 'The Legacy of the Prophets in the Deuteronomic Corpus', p. 97–8.

[25] R. G. Kratz, *The Composition of the Narrative Books of the Old Testament* (New York, 2005), 132; Eng. trans. by John Bowden from *Die Komposition der erzählenden Bücher des Alten Testaments* (Göttingen, 2000).

a reaction to the downfall of the kingdom of Judah.[26] Thus the question is thrown open for fresh discussion:[27] whence derived this institution of a centralized cult, which not only the authors of Deuteronomy but also Ezekiel in the early exilic period promote?

The second is the claim that Deut. 16: 18–18: 22 is a self-contained pericope providing an outline 'constitution' or 'polity' focusing upon the primary national offices of judge, king, priest, and prophet. Such a 'constitution', some have argued, 'conceives of Israel as a unitary realm with centralized institutions and state power to enforce obedience'.[28] Whether or not this state was that ruled over by Josiah, as Nelson, for example, suggests,[29] or was envisaged for the future by the Deuteronomic authors as a 'new social and juridical order' drawn up to replace 'the failed monarchic order' in Judah following the catastrophe of 587 BCE, as Clements, for example, argues,[30] the question arises of whether statehood, with its institutions, is at all a credible designation of the Israel which we encounter in Deuteronomy, and thus whether this pericope is properly designated as a state 'polity' or 'constitution' (see also below).

ABOUT THIS BOOK

This book makes no attempt to address all of the many complex problems that arise in the study of Deuteronomy. My main focus (Part I) is upon the provenance of Deuteronomy, and this involves two main tasks.

First, I present a re-examination (Chapter 2) of the narrative of Josiah's reforms in 2 Kings 23, with a view to reopening the question of whether these reforms included a centralization of worship to one sanctuary, the concomitant abolition of the ancient local

---

[26] See also, for example, R. E. Clements, 'The Deuteronomic Law of Centralisation and the Catastrophe of 587 B.C.E.', in J. Barton and J. Reimer (eds.), *After the Exile: Essays in Honour of Rex Mason* (Macon, GA, 1996), 5–25.

[27] See Chapter 2, 'VII', pp. 37–40; cf also Chapter 3, 'The Provenance of Deuteronomy', p. 72, n. 68.

[28] Nelson, *Deuteronomy*, 213, and for further bibliography see Chapter 5, 'Context: A Deuteronomic "Polity" for Israel (Deut. 16: 18–18: 22)', pp. 103–6.

[29] Nelson, *Deuteronomy*, 8.

[30] R. E. Clements, 'The Origins of Deuteronomy: What Are the Clues?', in 'A Dialogue with Gordon McConville on Deuteronomy', *SJT* 56 (2003), 508–16.

neighbourhood sanctuaries throughout Judah, and, as widely agreed, the relocation of their priests to employment in the Jerusalem temple, the key text in considering this being 2 Kgs 23: 8a, 9. My own re-examination of these verses has persuaded me that the widely accepted exegesis of them rests upon a misreading and that a scrutiny of their terminology points very probably to the hand of a Deuteronomistic redactor of this chapter.

Secondly (Chapter 3), I offer a reconsideration of the provenance of Deuteronomy. This calls for a fresh assessment of the character and leading features of the book: its ardent and urgent style— exhorting, cautioning, promising, threatening—which suggests a background of crisis; its pervasive preoccupation with 'encroach-ment', the lure of the worship of other gods, generated and encouraged, it seems, not by foreigners but from within the Israelite community itself; its fervent and persistent summons 'remember', 'do not forget',[31] suggesting a community whose cultural identity is imperilled; its encapsulation in a book of the founding events of Israel as the people of YHWH, a written '*torah*', a 'scripture', to be taken to heart, learned by heart, taught to the children, meditated upon day and night, given visible signs by body-marking, symbolically displayed on the doorpost of homes, publically pub-lished and made perennially accessible. Here, it seems, ancestral religion is no longer something that is socially inherited, natural, as it were, and taken for granted. Rather, circumstances have arisen which threaten its continuance, and Israel is confronted with a *choice* upon which its very survival depends; that is, the relationship with YHWH is now conceived of as a covenant. The case I seek to make in this chapter is that the exilic period, among the Judaean exiles in Babylonia, is the most likely setting in which such leading concerns and features of Deuteronomy emerged.

The conclusions of these two chapters raise still further issues, however, that call for more detailed discussion. First, Deuteronomy's passionate command that learning and meditating upon the words of 'the *torah*' should permeate daily life is indicative of the authority that these authors claimed and commanded for 'the book of the

---

[31] Jan Assmann has aptly described Deuteronomy as a book of 'memory making'. See his *Religion and Cultural Memory* (Stanford, CA, 2006), 16–21 and *passim*. Eng. trans. by R. Livingstone from *Religion und kulturelles Gedächtnis* (Munich, 2000). See also Chapter 3, 'Deuteronomy and Cultural Memory', pp. 63–6.

law', which thus acquires the significance of what we would term 'scripture'.[32] Deuteronomy also attaches manifest authority to prophecy, which it describes as founded upon a promise of YHWH to Moses at Horeb, who is here depicted as the first of the prophets (Deut. 18: 9–22), and this prompts the question of whether the author of this pericope, in describing the prophets he had in mind as successors of Moses, is referring to an emerging corpus of prophetic writings which he views as 'scripture' alongside Moses' 'book of the *torah*'. I offer a discussion of this in Chapter 4.

A further issue that arises, and to which I have already referred, is the status of kingship in Deuteronomy, and with this, whether statehood and its institutions, including a monarchy, which is ostensibly provided for in Deut. 17: 14–20, is at all a credible designation of the Israel that we encounter in Deuteronomy. Does not the minimalist role ascribed to kingship in this text rather suggest a 'depoliticized' community whose collective identity is expressed socially in terms of 'brotherhood' and defined culturally as 'the people of Yahweh', that is, a reconceptualizing of Israel as an 'internal culture' that is summoned to distance itself from engagement in the power politics of the day? This issue is discussed in Chapter 5. This so-called 'law of the king' remains the subject of Chapter 6, which focuses upon the most enigmatic clause in this short pericope, that is, v. 15b with its forceful formulation: 'Do not dare to place a foreigner over you, one who is not a brother Israelite.' Such a demand is surely unlikely to have been evoked by some passing episode or possible 'foreign' claimant to the Israelite throne, whatever or whoever that might have been.[33] It seems much more likely that behind this robust injunction is the memory of a much more severe experience of foreign governance. Might this strict prohibition have been motivated by the bitter memory of northern Israel's catastrophic vassalage to the Assyrians, followed by Judah's thraldom to this imperial power from the mid-eighth century BCE, then the short period under Egyptian hegemony in the late seventh century which led to the calamitous dealings with Babylonia issuing in the destruction of the Judaean state and exile? Might the proscription have also been partly motivated by an imposition of the worship of Assyrian deities alongside YHWH,

---

[32] On the distinction between 'scripture' and 'canon', see Chapter 4, 'Deuteronomy, the Prophets, and Scripture', p. 74, n. 2.

[33] For a discussion of various suggestions, see Chapter 6, 'Do not dare to set a foreigner over you': The King in Deuteronomy and 'The Great King', pp. 117–120.

which some scholars believe to have been Assyrian imperial policy in dealing with vassals? And might this clause also lend support to the suggestion made above that in Deuteronomy Israel is envisaged as a depoliticized 'internal culture' that has eschewed a past catastrophic history of engagement in internecine politicking and is here reconceptualized as a 'holy people', leaving the management of worldly affairs to the ruling imperial power of its era?[34] These issues will be discussed in Chapter 6.

The final two chapters (Part II) of the book centre upon what has come to be described as the 'Deuteronomistic History', a description of the corpus Deuteronomy–2 Kings, which, as briefly mentioned above, Martin Noth identified as the work of an exilic author and redactor who collected and wove together older sources, including an earlier form of Deuteronomy, with the purpose of providing a national theodicy in the wake of the calamitous events of the early sixth century BCE. In its broad outlines, this understanding of the corpus Deuteronomy–2 Kings is presupposed in the chapters that follow, my only qualification being that if, as I argue, Deuteronomy is substantially the work of exilic authors, its emergence is brought into much closer proximity to the composition of the remaining books of the Deuteronomistic corpus, priority of course belonging to Deuteronomy (*Urdeuteronomium*), which, as 'the book of the *torah*', is the keystone of this corpus.

The authors and redactors at whose hands Deuteronomy became the first chapter, so to speak, of the Deuteronomistic corpus not only provided it with a narrative framework, however; they also incorporated into Deuteronomy topics that anticipate leading themes of the subsequent long narration of this corpus. In my opinion this is so in the case of the pericope in Deut. 18: 9–22, as well as the so-called 'law of the king' (17: 14–20), both of which, as already mentioned, will be the subject of longer discussion in Chapters 4 and 5 respectively. It is also the case, however, that not all the material in Deuteronomy deriving from secondary redaction is attributable to the authors and redactors to whom we owe the expansion and incorporation of Deuteronomy into the larger narrative of the corpus to which it now belongs. This is the case, for example, with Deut. 4: 1–40, which is generally viewed as secondary,

---

[34] For this, see the discussion in Chapter 3, and especially the references there to Jan Assmann's discussion of the 'depoliticising of public life' in Deuteronomy in his *Religion and Cultural Memory*.

and which, singularly among the contents of Deuteronomy, closely echoes Deutero-Isaiah's scornful derision of the making of idols and this prophet's affirmation of the incomparability of YHWH as God alone. Rather, this text has the character of a *Fortschreibung* of Deuteronomy as 'the book of the *torah*' by a redactor anticipating not only the opening clauses of the Decalogue that follows in Deut. 5, but also one of Deuteronomy's most acute and pervasive concerns— religious encroachment.[35]

The main focus of the two chapters in Part II of this book is the genre of the Deuteronomistic corpus, which is widely identified as a theodicy. As such, it explains the devastation that befell first northern Israel in the late eighth century BCE, and subsequently Judah in the early years of the sixth century. It is not, however, an 'obituary' of the Israelite nation. Paradoxically, theodicy, an account and explanation of YHWH's judgement upon his people, is simultaneously an expression of hope on the other side of national calamity for those who will seize it, since what the Deuteronomistic writers here declare is that it is YHWH's sovereign will and not some divine or human caprice that has been at work in these events. It is upon this that these authors focus, and the description 'history' for what they wrote, though it is common place as a convenient title among Old Testament scholars for this corpus, calls for critical qualification. What these authors wrote, though 'history-like', is best described as 'story' rather than 'history'.[36] They had no interest in providing a reconstruction of past events, and their method and narrative offers no serious indication that the past was the motivation for their endeavours, even in those narratives which may be regarded as providing historically useful information. Rather, and to a significant extent, they were evidently concerned to provide patterns of God's dealings with his people in promise, fulfilment, and judgement, that is, paradigms intended for thinking about the present and hoping for the future, and thus urgently relevant to those who had suffered the devastation of their homeland and the fate of exile.

[35] A fuller discussion of this is offered in Chapter 3.

[36] For this and what follows, see James Barr, 'Story and History in Biblical Theology', *JR* 56 (1976), 1–17, repr. in id., *The Scope and Authority of the Bible*, *Explorations in Theology*, 7 (London, 1980), 1–17. Cf. also id., 'Historical Reading and the Theological Interpretation of Scripture', *Scope and Authority*, 30–51. The description 'history-like' is derived from Hans Frei, *The Eclipse of Biblical Narrative* (Newhaven and London, 1974), 10 and *passim*.

The case for classifying the work of these authors as 'story' rather than 'history' was a topic which James Barr wrote about and frequently touched upon. In a contribution to a volume of essays honouring Professor Barr upon his seventieth birthday,[37] I offered some elaboration of the reservations he had expressed concerning the description of the long narrative corpus of the Old Testament (notably Genesis–2 Kings) as 'history writing', especially the contrast he briefly drew between the character of this corpus and early Greek historiography. My discussion centred upon the Deuteronomistic corpus. In doing so, I offered a critique of John Van Seters' well-known and learned work *In Search of History*,[38] in which he argues the claim that this corpus bears significant resemblances to early Greek historiography, notably Herodotus' *Histories*. Some years after the publication of my essay Van Seters wrote a lengthy critical response to it,[39] reaffirming his view that the Deuteronomic corpus fully merits the genre description 'historiography', that its authors' purpose was to establish the beginning and cause of the destruction of Israel and Judah by a foreign power, and can, indeed, be described as 'analogue' to Herodotus' *Histories*, the main purpose of which was to establish the beginning and the cause of animosity leading to war, in this case between the Greeks and the barbarians, of which the Persian Wars is the final phase.

For easy reference to my essay in the Barr *Festschrift*, I have reprinted it as Chapter 7, followed in Chapter 8 by my response to Van Seters' critique of it.

Readers familiar with my earlier book on Deuteronomy, published in 1967, will recognize that the main conclusions of this new study represent a much-revised view of the provenance of Deuteronomy and of the leading features and themes it embodies than that earlier study maintained.[40] That is, what I have attempted here is 'revisionist'. Though the word 'revisionist', defined in the *Oxford English Dictionary* as 'one who advocates or supports revision', is

---

[37] 'Story and History in the Old Testament', in S. E. Ballentine and J. Barton (eds.), *Language, Theology, and The Bible: Essays in Honour of James Barr* (Oxford, 1994), 135–50.

[38] *In Search of History: Historiography the Ancient World and the Origins of Biblical History* (New Haven and London, 1983).

[39] 'Is There any Historiography in the Hebrew Bible? A Hebrew–Greek Comparison', *Journal of Northwest Semitic Languages*, 28: 2 (2002), 1–25.

[40] *Deuteronomy and Tradition*.

sometimes employed to express disapproval and censure, as in political dialogue and writings, there is nothing new in either the principle or the practice of revising received conclusions and opinions in humanistic studies. This is so not merely as a result of bringing to bear on the work of earlier generations fresh discoveries or insights or new methods of study, but also for its own sake, knowing that no generation is in possession of, or arrives at, all truth. This is especially the case in a field of research such as the Hebrew Bible, the complexities and problems of which conspire with the limitations of our own knowledge of such an ancient society and its culture to render the task of understanding and interpretation one that each new generation must freshly undertake. The principle of such a task was well formulated by one of the founders of modern British historiography, Bishop Stubbs (1825–1901), who wrote that: 'History knows that it can wait for more evidence and review its older verdicts; it offers an endless series of courts of appeal and is ever ready to re-open closed cases.'[41] The practice of looking again at verdicts and conclusions arrived at by scholars and subjecting them to fresh thought and revision is nothing new in biblical studies. Indeed, the modern history of the subject is one of virtually constant revision. If the present study stimulates further thinking and discussion about Deuteronomy, which all scholars and commentators agree to be central for an understanding of the history of ancient Israelite religion and the eventual emergence and development of Judaism, my endeavours will be more than adequately rewarded.

[41] Cited in J. R. Hale, *The Evolution of British Historiography from Bacon to Namier* (London, 1967), 58.

2

Josiah and the Priests of the High Places
(2 Kings 23: 8a, 9)

It is by no means the first time in the history of this much-discussed chapter in 2 Kings that these verses have been a focus of attention,[1] for among the various reforms said to have been implemented by King Josiah on the authority of the newly found 'book of the *torah*', their narration of the centralization of cultic worship provides the primary evidence[2] widely appealed to by scholars that this book was none other than the book of Deuteronomy—or an original core of it (the so-called *Urdeuteronomium*)—one of the leading demands of which is the centralization of Israel's cult to one sanctuary, 'the place which YHWH chooses'. Any challenge to this long-established view of the origin of Deuteronomy has to confront what these verses record; by eliminating them, for example, as a secondary insertion into an earlier account of Josiah's reformation that knew nothing of such a measure. Thus, as mentioned in the Introduction, in a period of intense debate about Deuteronomy in the early decades of last century Gustav Hölscher, the then leading protagonist of a post-exilic date for the composition of Deuteronomy, regarded these

---

[1] Among recent discussions and further bibliography see H. Spieckermann, *Juda unter Assur in der Sargonidenzeit*, FRLANT 129 (1982), 30–160; C. Uehlinger, 'Was There a Cult Reform under King Josiah? The Case for a Well-Grounded Minimum', in L. L. Grabbe (ed.), *Good Kings and Bad Kings*, Library of Hebrew Bible/Old Testament Studies 393 (London, 2005), 279–316.

[2] This remains the widely accepted view. See e.g. N. Lohfink, 'The Cult Reform of Josiah of Judah: 2 Kings 22–23 as a Source for the History of Israelite Religion', in J. M. Miller, P. D. Hanson, and S. D. McBride (eds.), *Ancient Israelite Religion: Essays in Honor of Frank Moore Cross* (Philadelphia, 1987), 459–75, who writes (p. 466) of the testimony of 2 Kgs 23: 8a, 9 that 'Cult centralization remains the surest reform measure to link with the Deuteronomic legislation of that [the Josianic] period'.

verses as secondary and inauthentic, the work of an editor of an original E account of Josiah's reformation that knew nothing of centralization of worship to Jerusalem.[3] Other leading scholars internationally similarly urged the dismissal of the evidence of these verses as an insertion by a Deuteronomic redactor. However, the view, already so widely accepted, of a close historical association between Deuteronomy and 'the book of the *torah*' prevailed, the testimony of 2 Kgs 23: 8a, 9 remaining key and, it seemed, unshakeable evidence in its favour.

Until recently I counted myself among this majority, since I had found nothing in recent studies of Deuteronomy to induce me to change the view I arrived at as a graduate student more than fifty years ago and that has placed me firmly throughout the time since then on the side of this consensus.[4] This remained so even in an earlier version of this essay, in which I still considered 2 Kgs 23: 8a, 9 to have belonged to the original account of Josiah's reform and to be authentic testimony to the measures enacted by him.[5] More recently, however, a fresh scrutiny of this text has led me to doubt this widely shared conclusion, and persuaded me that the evidence usually adduced from 2 Kings 23 for an association of Deuteronomy with Josiah's reformation is not as secure as I have for so long believed.

I

With variation only on some details, it is a *communis opinio* among modern commentators that these verses are to be understood as follows. Verse 8a having narrated that the king brought the country priests to Jerusalem and destroyed the altars where they had ministered, verse 9 records that these 'priests of the high places' were not, however, permitted to exercise their priestly role at the temple altar alongside the resident priests, their 'brethren'. Thus M. Cogan

---

[3] See especially his 'Das Buch der Könige: Seine Quellen und seine Redaktion', in *Gunkel Eucharisterion*, FRLANT 18 (1923), 158–213, esp. 206–13. Cf. his 'Komposition und Ursprung des Deuteronomiums', *ZAW* 40 (1922), 161–255, and *Geschichte der jüdischen und israelitischen Religion* (Giessen, 1922), 130–4.

[4] My defence of the consensus view of the relation between Deuteronomy and Josiah's reformation is contained in the first chapter of my book *Deuteronomy and Tradition* (Oxford, 1967).

[5] E. Nicholson, 'Josiah and the Priests of the High Places', *ZAW* 119 (2007), 510 f.

and H. Tadmor paraphrase verses 8a, 9 thus: 'the high places at which YHWH was worshipped were desecrated, and their priests were gathered into Jerusalem, where their service in the Temple was restricted.'[6] This is usually understood as an abrogation by the Jerusalem priesthood of the arrangements enjoined in Deut. 18: 6–8 that rural Levites who go to the central sanctuary are to enjoy the same rights there as the local priesthood. J. Milgrom, for example, puts it thus:[7] 'The Jerusalem priesthood reneged on the Deuteronomic injunction ... Not only did they not absorb their fellow priests into their order (versus Deut. 18.6–7) but they limited their sacrificial prebends to the cereal offering (versus Deut. 18.8a).' The rendering of the *New Jerusalem Bible* captures this under-standing of the verse well: 'The priests of the high places, however, did not officiate at the altar of Yahweh in Jerusalem, although they did share the unleavened bread of their brother priests.'

This theory, in addition to identifying 'their brethren' in verse 9 as the Jerusalem priests, also determines the meaning of the word מַצּוֹת on the basis of the supposed status or plight of the country priests whom Josiah brought to the city, though explanations vary in detail. Most commentators understand it to refer to a 'perquisite' granted by the Jerusalem priesthood to the newly resident country priests as a sort of 'subsistence allowance', and again they draw attention to how far this fell short of the prescriptions of Deut. 18: 8. Cogan and Tadmor, for example, suggest that the word here may be a generic term for 'grain offerings' (cf. Lev. 2: 4, 5), though, with some (see below), they also allow the possibility that it may refer to 'unleavened cakes' eaten at the Passover celebration summoned by Josiah and briefly narrated in verses 21–3.[8] Others, finding a reference to 'unleavened bread' here inappropriate, suggest that the Masoretic Text is a corruption of an original מְנָיוֹת, that is, 'portions' of the temple offerings granted by the resident priests to the newcomer priests from the erstwhile 'high places'. Still others, retaining the consonants of the Masoretic Text, suggest that it arose from a mis-reading of מִצְוֹת (from מִצְוָה 'statute') in the sense of 'statutory

[6] M. Cogan and H. Tadmor, *II Kings: A New Translation with Introduction and Commentary* (New York, 1988), 297.

[7] J. Milgrom, *Leviticus 1–16: A New Translation with Introduction and Commentary* (New York, 1991), 187.

[8] Cogan and Tadmor, *II Kings*, 287. But see the comment on R. de Vaux's view below.

perquisites'.[9] The Hebrew text is, however, supported by all the ancient versions, and the comment is justified that 'such an early corruption of the familiar word is unaccountable, unless by intentional perversion'.[10]

An alternative suggestion is that the word refers to the 'unleavened bread' eaten at the Passover celebration summoned by Josiah and described later in the narrative (vv. 21–3). Representative of such an understanding of v. 9b is Roland de Vaux's comment: 'the mention of unleavened bread is no doubt a reference to the great Passover which closed the reform.'[11] It is doubtful, however, whether v. 9b can be uncoupled in such a way from v. 9a; the clause כִּי אִם does not suggest a forward reference to vv. 21–3 but relates what follows in the verse to what precedes. That is, the clause כִּי אִם is an 'exceptive' clause here, limiting what is stated in the first half of the verse in some such way as is suggested by the rendering preferred by the *New Jerusalem Bible* noted above. Alternatively, the clause may have the sense of 'but rather', thus introducing a contrast to what is described in the first half of the verse: the priests did not go up to the altar of YHWH in Jerusalem, 'but rather/instead ate unleavened bread among their brethren'.[12]

A further and more significant objection to such a view arises from the syntax of the sentence in which the verb 'they ate' (אָכְלוּ) occurs, since the frequentative use of the imperfect 'to go up' (יַעֲלוּ) in the first half of the verse, indicating a continuous condition or action, whether in the past or ongoing, entails that 'they ate' should in this context be similarly understood as frequentative, as, indeed, it has been by most commentators. That is, 'they ate' does not describe a solitary occurrence such as the eating of 'unleavened bread' at the famous Passover celebration, which is described as a separate event marking the culmination of Josiah's reformation; both parts of the verse refer to the manner of life of these 'priests of the high places' now dispossessed of their neighbourhood altars.

---

[9] See, most recently, J. Gray, *1 and 2 Kings: A Commentary* (London, 1964), 730–1.

[10] J. A. Montgomery and H. S. Gehman, *A Critical and Exegetical Commentary on the Books of Kings*, ICC (Edinburgh, 1951), 532, 539.

[11] R. de Vaux, *Ancient Israel: Its Life and Institutions* (London, 1961), 363, Eng. trans. by John McHugh of *Les Institutions de l'Ancien Testament*, Vols. I–II (Paris, 1958, 1960).

[12] For both these uses of the clause כִּי אִם see BDB 474–5.

Yet another understanding of מצות has been suggested by
H. Spieckermann,[13] for whom also the eating of 'unleavened bread'
reflects the plight of the country priests at the hands of their
Jerusalem colleagues. Like others, he regards the arrangements laid
down in Deut. 18: 6–8 as the necessary background for understanding what is narrated in 2 Kgs 23: 9. Thus he takes v. 9a to
indicate the refusal of the Jerusalem priesthood to permit the priests
from the countryside towns and villages to officiate at the altar in the
temple, as provided for in Deut. 18: 7, and the statement in v. 9b that
these priests 'ate unleavened bread' to mean that neither did their
Jerusalem colleagues stand by the arrangement laid down in Deut.
18: 8 that such priests should have equal share with the Jerusalem
priesthood of the offerings brought to the temple. He reads this verse
as signifying that the temple priestly authorities felt no obligation of
care and support for these priests, denying them any part of the
offerings, with the result that, now deprived of their ancestral means
of livelihood, 'they had to make do with the most meagre means
of survival'.[14] 'Unleavened bread' in this verse should therefore be
understood on the analogy of its use in Deut. 16: 3, that is, לחם עני
'bread of affliction', though of course for a different reason. On
such an understanding, the very word 'brethren' is a mismatch for
the rather less than 'brotherly' treatment these priests received at the
hands their Jerusalem colleagues.

The question arises, however, of how plausible it is to construe in
such a way what is narrated in 2 Kgs 23: 9 with what is enjoined
in Deut. 18: 6–8.[15] Although in Deuteronomy all Levites are eligible
as priests,[16] this text makes no mention of a concentration of the
priesthood at the central sanctuary. What it rules is that any
individual Levite 'from any of your towns' who wishes to exercise the
office of priest at the central sanctuary and seeks to do so 'with
eagerness of heart'—from a sense of 'vocation', we might say—shall
be received by the priests at the central sanctuary on an equal
basis with themselves and shall share all the rights and privileges that

---

[13] H. Spieckermann, *Juda unter Assur in der Sargonidenzeit*, 96–7.

[14] *Juda unter Assur in der Sargonidenzeit*, 97.

[15] See the apt comment by A. D. H. Mayes, *Deuteronomy*, NCB (London, 1979),
278–9.

[16] Against the view that in Deuteronomy only some Levites were eligible to serve at
the altar whilst others were not, see the examination of the evidence by J. A. Emerton,
'Priests and Levites in Deuteronomy', *VT* xii (1962), 129–38.

pertain to them. To claim, as Spieckermann and many others do, that the background of 2 Kgs 23: 9 was a refusal on the part of the resident Jerusalem priesthood to implement the requirements of Deut. 18: 6–8 thus begs the question of whether this injunction could have been construed as providing for or warranting a mass immigration of 'all the priests of the cities of Judah from Geba to Beersheba' to the Jerusalem temple.

This supposed tension between what is enjoined in Deut. 18: 6–8 and what 2 Kgs 23: 9 is usually believed to narrate has prompted an alternative solution, one which dissolves the problem by suggesting that Deut. 18: 6–8 was absent from Josiah's 'book of the law' and was therefore unknown to the Jerusalem priesthood in their treatment of the newly arrived rural priests brought to the city and temple by Josiah.[17] Against such a drastic suggestion, since the provision enjoined in Deut. 18: 6–8 arises directly from the centralization of the cult and its consequences for the rural priesthood, it seems more likely that it belonged to the same stage in the composition of Deuteronomy as the demand for the centralization of worship than that it was an afterthought.[18] Quite apart from this, however, the premise of this suggestion is open to the same objection as the view of Spieckermann and others mentioned above: that Deut. 18: 6–8 does not envisage a mass importation of the rural priesthood to the central sanctuary as 2 Kgs 23: 9, as usually understood, implies.

I shall return later to the relevance of the provisions in Deut. 18: 6–8 for an understanding of 2 Kgs 23: 8a, 9. A more immediate question is raised, however, by these discussions of a supposed tension between these two texts. Spieckermann writes for all who share the common interpretation of 2 Kgs 23: 8a, 9 when he states that it is an *inference* that Josiah brought 'all the priests from all the cities of Judah' to Jerusalem: 'though this is not said *expressis verbis*, it

---

[17] See e.g. N. Lohfink, 'Die Sicherung der Wirksamkeit des Gotteswortes durch das Prinzip der Gewaltenteilung nach den Ämtergesetzen des Buches Deuteronomium (Dt 16, 18–18, 22)', in *Studien zum Deuteronomium und zur deuteronomistischen Literatur* I, SBAB 8 (1990), 305–23, esp. 314; Eng. trans. 'Distribution of the Functions of Power: The Laws Concerning Public Offices in Deuteronomy 16: 18–18: 22', in D. L. Christensen (ed.), *A Song of Power and the Power of Song* (Winona Lake, IN, 1993), 336–52. Cf. id., 'The Cult Reform of Josiah of Judah', 474 n. 37.

[18] For a critique of recent arguments that Deut. 18: 6–8 is a late Deuteronomistic or even post-Deuteronomistic addition, see J. Schaper, *Priester und Leviten im achämenidischen Juda: Studien zur Kult- und Sozialgeschichte Israels in persischer Zeit*, Forschung zum Alten Testament 31 (2000), 27–32, 86–8.

is nevertheless clear to all readers',[19] because, first, since Josiah is the subject of the verb ויבא מן in v. 8a, it is a plausible inference that he brought these priests from their home cities and towns to the capital, and second, because in any event, as commentators acknowledge, v. 9a presupposes that they had been settled in Jerusalem where, as the text is usually understood, they were barred from officiating at the temple altar. Two clauses are of special significance in discussing these commonly agreed conclusions: first the phrase in v. 8a ויבא את כל הכהנים מערי יהודה usually translated 'he brought all the priests from the cities of Judah', and the first half of v. 9, especially the clause לא יעלו ... אל מזבח יהוה 'they [these priests] did not go up to the altar of YHWH in Jerusalem', which has been of key importance in understanding the fate of the rural priests in Jerusalem.

I shall return to a consideration of this phrase below. Here questions of a practical nature are in place concerning the commonly received understanding of 2 Kgs 23: 8a, 9 outlined above. As far as I am aware, none among the very many commentaries and studies sharing the view that this text narrates a relocation of Judah's rural priests to Jerusalem has raised the question of the logistics of such an operation. Since estimates of the population of Judah in the final decades of the seventh century remain only tentative—a figure of 200,000 has recently been cautiously suggested[20]—we can only conjecture how many of these priests there would have been in the final decades of the seventh century. But their numbers 'from Geba to Beersheba' would surely have been many hundreds, probably, indeed, on such an estimate of the population, rather more. The question is justified of how credible is the widely supported claim that these numerous neighbourhood priests, together with, we must assume, wives and families, would have been accommodated and in other ways provided for in Jerusalem. Similarly, and related to this, how realistic is it to imagine that this mass incursion of priests, whose numbers would have substantially exceeded the resident temple priesthood, believed themselves to be entitled to officiate at the temple altar, as, on the usual understanding of it, v. 9 supposedly

---

[19] Spieckermann, *Juda unter Assur in der Sargonidenzeit*, 92.

[20] For a discussion, see J. Blenkinsopp, 'The Age of the Exile', in John Barton (ed.), *The Biblical World*, Vol. I (London and New York, 2002), esp. 416–20. Blenkinsopp, 'allowing for a reasonable margin of error', tentatively suggests a total population of Judah in the final decades of its independence at about 200,000.

implies? Further, on the commonly accepted view that these new-comers, upon taking up residence in Jerusalem, were 'downgraded', what nevertheless would the temple revenues have had to be to enable the authorities to sustain the 'prebend' or 'perquisite' due, on the usual view of v. 9b, to each and all of these many priests and assumed by commentators to be what is here expressed as 'eating unleavened bread among their (Jerusalem) brethren'?

Considerations such as these themselves prompt a fresh attempt to understand what the key text 2 Kgs 23: 8a, 9 was intended to convey, and whether further scrutiny might yield an alternative interpretation, and, if so, what repercussions this might have for the widely accepted view of the origin of Deuteronomy that scholars have erected mainly upon the supposed testimony of these verses.

II

The verse 2 Kgs 23: 9 has been crucial for all commentators alike in understanding Josiah's action described in v. 8aα. As noted above, in the clause אל מזבח יהוה ... לא יעלו 'they [these priests] did not go up to the altar of YHWH in Jerusalem', the verb with its accompanying preposition (אל + עלה) 'to go up to' has commonly been understood to mean that the priests of the high places whom Josiah is said to have brought to Jerusalem were not permitted to officiate at the altar in the temple. Though the verb עלה is employed elsewhere in texts narrating the action of a priest or a king stationing himself at an altar to carry out a ritual, however, it is in all such incidences coupled with the preposition על and never with אל. The relevant texts are: Exod. 20: 26 banning priests from officiating at an altar on a dais raised on a progression of steps;[21] 1 Sam. 2: 28, narrating YHWH's choice of Eli's ancestor as priest; 1 Kgs 12: 32, 33, of Jeroboam officiating at the altar on the occasion of the new feast instituted by him; it is similarly used of Ahaz in 2 Kgs 16: 12–13 and of Solomon in 2 Chron. 1: 6.

---

[21] The meaning of this, probably ancient, statute has been much discussed (cf. e.g. B. S. Childs, *Exodus* (Louisville, KY, 1974), 466–7). Whatever may have been its original rationale, the sense is that a priest is prohibited from officiating at an altar on a dais on a flight of steps.

In 2 Kgs 23: 9, however, the preposition employed is not על but
אל. Other texts employing the collocation of עלה with אל 'to go up
to' do so, however, not in any technical sense, as in the case of עלה
על מזבח 'to officiate at an altar', but straightforwardly of the movement of persons from one place to another. Thus in Gen. 44: 17
Joseph in Egypt commands his brothers to 'go up to (עלו אל)' their
father in peace; Deut. 17: 8 enjoins that in legal cases too complex
for local resolution, the disputants are 'to go up to' (עלית אל) the
central sanctuary for final arbitration; in Isa. 2: 2–4 (=Mic. 4: 1–3)
the prophet announces of 'the mountain of the house of the Lord'
that 'in days to come . . . many nations will stream to it (נהרו אליו)
and many peoples shall come and say: "Come, let us go up to
(נעלה אל) the mountain of the Lord, to the house of the God of
Jacob (אל בית אלהי יעקב)"'; in Jer. 31: 6 the prophet speaks of a
future when 'the watchmen on Ephraim's hills will call out, "Come,
let us go up (נעלה) to Zion, to (אל) the Lord our God"'. Though
it does not employ the verb עלה, Ps. 43: 3–4, which refers to a
worshipper coming to (אל) the altar at the temple in Jerusalem,
provides a supporting analogy. Here a petitioner prays to God to
send forth his 'light and his truth . . . and let them lead me, let them
guide me (*hiphʿil* of בוא) to (אל) your holy hill . . . that I may come
to the altar of God (ואבואה אל מזבח אלהים), to God my joy and
my delight'.

In brief: one might 'approach or draw near to (קרב אל or נגש אל)
an altar' (e.g. Lev. 9: 7, 8; 21: 23), one might 'go up to the altar
(עלה אל) of YHWH in Jerusalem' (2 Kgs 23: 9), or, like the pilgrim
petitioner of Ps. 43: 3–4, one might 'come to (בוא אל) the altar of
God'. But all these are distinct from the priestly ritual action
of officiating at an altar for which the technical term is consistently
עלה על מזבח.

It might be objected that too much should not be made of the
preposition employed with עלה in 2 Kgs 23: 9, since elsewhere,
including, indeed, the books of Kings, there is evidence not only of
transcriptional errors between אל and על but also that they could be
interchanged.[22] As far as I am aware, however, there is no manuscript
evidence that the preposition אל in this verse is a scribal error for

[22] See BDB 41, and, for example, C. F. Burney, *Notes on the Hebrew Text of the
Books of Kings* (Oxford, 1903), 72, 184, 201, 228, 297.

an original עַל—and no commentator, again as far as I am aware, has suggested that it is an error. Other considerations rule out any possibility that the use of אֵל here is an example of the inter-change between this preposition and עַל attested elsewhere. First, it is evident that the phrase עלה על מזבח is a liturgical technical term for a priest or a king stationing himself at an altar to carry out a ritual. The phrase is idiomatic. More specifically, in the modern study of language עלה על in this context would be classified as a 'phrasal verb' with the characteristics of such: the meaning it conveys is different from its grammatical or logical significance; it is understood by its cultural users but difficult for foreigners.[23] Put differently, the phrase is opaque—a literal translation of it ('to go up upon an altar') makes no sense[24]—whilst, by contrast, the collocation עלה אל המזבח ('he went up to the altar') is trans-parent, just as, for example, 'approach or draw near to (נגש אל or קרב אל) an altar' or 'come to (בוא אל) the altar of God' are transparent. In short, the preposition אל is manifestly not inter-changeable with עַל in the use of the liturgical phrase עלה על מזבח 'to officiate at an altar', and the one could not have been substituted for the other in 2 Kgs 23: 9 without completely altering the meaning; עלה אל מזבח and עלה על מזבח are semantically discrete phrases.

In addition, not only does the LXX support the reading of the Masoretic Text of 2 Kgs 23: 9a, translating οὐκ ἀνέβησαν. . .πρὸς τὸ θυσιαστήριον κυρίου ἐν Ιερουσαλημ; it also consistently preserves elsewhere the same distinction as the Masoretic Text between the two semantic units עלה אל and עלה על. Thus in the texts cited above[25] employing עלה על for priests or kings officiating at an altar, the LXX translates with ἀναβαίνω ἐπὶ τὸ θυσιαστήριον—transcribing the idiom quite literally—whilst in the case of the texts employing עלה אל the LXX translates with ἀναβαίνω + πρὸς or εἰς.

---

[23] Examples in English are *bring off* ('he tried but couldn't bring it off (= did not succeed)'); *drop off* ('he tossed and turned on the bed for hours before dropping off (= falling asleep)'); *write off* ('he wrote off (= wrecked) his car the afternoon he bought it'); *fell on* ('the troops fell on (= attacked) the enemy'). See R. W. Burchfield (ed.), *The New Fowler's Modern English Usage*, 3rd edn. (Oxford, 1996), 594–5.

[24] Thus BDB 756 under 'to go up upon' with 'altar' has to explain it: 'i.e. to a ledge beside it'.

[25] With the exception of 2 Chron. 1: 6 where the LXX understands both occurrences of ויעל as 'bring' and 'offer' sacrifices respectively.

What emerges from this evidence may be put thus. The pre-supposition of the widely accepted understanding of 2 Kgs 23: 9 is that 'all the priests from the cities of Judah' were relocated to Jerusalem as the central sanctuary and sole place of sacrifice. However, the collocation of the preposition אל with עלה in this verse renders such a presupposition inadmissible, since the action indicated by the verb and its preposition is not the cultic procedure of taking up position at an altar *in loco*, so to speak, but of going to where the altar is, that is, 'in Jerusalem' (בירושלים). Thus, contrary to the accepted interpretation, the presupposition of this clause is that these priests were not relocated to Jerusalem but remained where they were, in their home towns and villages.[26]

III

In the light of this, our attention is again directed to the clause in v. 8aα, which, according to the testimony of v. 9a, properly understood, cannot mean that Josiah transported these priests[27] en masse to Jerusalem. If this is so, how is the statement in v. 8aα to be construed?

The Vulgate's rendering of the clause is itself an acknowledgement of the problem that a correct understanding of v. 9a poses for an understanding of Josiah's action stated in v. 8aα. In v. 9a, this translator correctly employs the Latin past continuous tense in rendering the Hebrew frequentative of both verbs (*ascendebant* and *comedebant*). He also employs the Vulgate's usual terminology

---

[26] In an oft-quoted passage referring to 2 Kgs 23: 9 and with Ezek. 44: 6–16 also in mind Julius Wellhausen famously wrote of the fate of the rural priests: 'It is an extraordinary sort of justice when the priests of the abolished Bamoth are punished simply for having been so, and conversely the priests of the temple at Jerusalem rewarded for this; the fault of the former and the merit of the latter consist in their existence. In other words, Ezekiel merely drapes the logic of facts with a mantle of morality.' (*Prolegomena to the History of Israel*, Eng. trans. by J. Sutherland Black and Allan Menzies (Edinburgh, 1885), 123–4.) If the new reading of 2 Kgs 23: 9 proposed above carries conviction, however, this verse can no longer be cited as recording the origin of the post-exilic two-tiered priesthood at the Jerusalem temple which Ezek. 44: 6–16 draped 'with a mantle of morality'.

[27] That the priests referred to in v. 8a and v. 9a are one and the same body of priests is clear, for what other group of priests would be described as not going up to Jerusalem to the altar there if it was not those whose altars had been destroyed, as v. 8aβ narrates?

ascendere + *ad* for the Hebrew עלה אל 'to go, travel *to* a place', not confusing this phrase with the technical term for presiding at an altar (עלה על מזבח), for which it employs *ascendere altare/ascendere super altare*.[28] That is, there can be no doubt that this translator did not understand ויבא את כל הכהנים מערי יהודה to state that Josiah brought these priests to Jerusalem. It seems, however, that he consequently found it difficult to make out what Josiah's action here referred to. Elsewhere in a number of texts narrating the bringing of people from one place to another (1 Sam. 15: 15 (cf. v. 20); 2 Kgs 17: 24; Isa. 66: 20), each of which, like 2 Kgs 23: 8a, employs the *hiph'il* (causative form) of בוא, the Vulgate translates with *adducare de* 'to bring *or* lead from'. In 2 Kgs 23: 8a, however, ויבא מן is rendered by *congregavitque* 'and he *assembled* all the priests from (*de*) the cities of Judah', without any indication of where King Josiah assembled these priests, or of why and for what purpose this was deemed necessary, though presumably it was a temporary arrangement, since v. 9 describes these priests as living in their local neighbourhoods 'among their brethren' (*in medio fratrum suorum*; see below). Such a rendering serves to highlight the crux that v. 9, properly understood, poses for an understanding of v. 8aα, which the author of v. 9 cannot have understood to mean that the king relocated these priests to Jerusalem. Is there an alternative way of understanding the *hiph'il* ויבא in this context?

IV

Verse 9a has the character of a parenthetic statement about 'the priests of the high places'. Its opening and arresting אך 'however', 'nevertheless'—in older English 'howbeit'—signals a qualification or limiting clause emphasizing what follows, but also by implication

[28] The Vulgate consistently employs the preposition *ad* with *ascendere* (*abire* Gen. 47.17) in the texts cited above in which אל is used with עלה for movement of people from one place to another. For עלה על מזבח Vulgate translates *ascendere altare* (1 Sam. 2: 28; 1 Kgs 12: 32) and *ascendere super altare* (1 Kgs 12: 33; 2 Kgs 16: 12), but puzzlingly, in view of this, at 1 Chron. 1: 6 translates *ascenditque Solomon ad altare*. At Exod. 20: 26 the translator apparently understood the issue to be the means of climbing the altar rather than presiding ritually at (עלה על) an altar on a dais elevated by a stair (see n. 15), and so renders *non ascendes per gradus ad altare meum*. For the LXX translation see n. 28.

drawing a contrast with something that precedes. That is, it reads like
a reservation excluding something which might otherwise have been
expected. Put differently: why make such note of what these priests
did not do unless there was a possibility that they might have acted
differently? Was there perhaps something in Josiah's actions towards
them that required such a rider?

Turning to the crux clause in v. 8aα ויבא את כל הכהנים מערי
יהודה, it is well known that the *hiph'il* of בוא can be employed with
the sense of 'allowing something or someone to come', 'to grant
something to someone'. For example, in Gen. 18: 19 YHWH declares
his confidence in Abraham so to teach his children and household
to 'keep the way of the Lord' that YHWH will 'grant, allow to come
(למען הביא)' to Abraham the blessings he had earlier spoken
concerning him; the Psalmist writes that God 'granted (יביא להם)'
to the Israelites in the wilderness 'what they craved (תאותם)'
(Ps. 78: 29); similarly, 'God granted to Jabez what he asked
(ויבא אלהים את אשר שאל)' (1 Chron. 4: 10); still more pertinent
for our present purposes, in Esther 5: 12 Haman reports that Queen
Esther 'did not allow anyone to come (לא הביאה)' with the king
to the banquet . . . except me' (כי אם אותי); in Num. 14: 24 Caleb is
set apart from his untrusting generation as the only one whom
YHWH will 'allow to come (הביאתיו)' into the land to which he had
(previously) come (as one of the spies)'.

On the basis of this evidence, a new understanding of the clause in
2 Kgs 23: 8a may be suggested, and the text translated: 'and he
allowed (ויבא) any of the priests of the towns of Judah to come
[sc. to the Jerusalem temple]'.[29] Such a reading suggests that Josiah's
treatment of these priests acknowledged their entitlement under
the provisions set out in 'the book of the *torah*' (Deut. 18: 6–8) to
come to the temple in Jerusalem—the same verb 'to come (בוא)' is
used twice in Deut. 18: 6—if any of them so wished, to officiate at

---

[29] LXX follows MT literally, translating ויבא with ἀνήγαγεν 'he brought'. In view
of its translation of v. 9a (see above), the translator cannot gave intended his use of
this verb to imply that Josiah *conveyed* these priests to Jerusalem. Since the LXX offers
some examples of a permissive nuance in the use of some verbs (e.g. ἔπταισεν ἡμᾶς
= 'he allowed us to fall' (1 Sam. 4: 3); ζησόν/ζήσεις με 'let me live' (Pss. 118 (119):
37; 142 (143): 11)), is it possible that ἀνήγαγεν has such a permissive nuance, as here
proposed in the case of the Hebrew word which it translates? For these examples see J.
Lust, E. Eynikel, and K. Hauspie, *A Greek–English Lexicon of the Septuagint*, Vol. I
(Stuttgart, 1992), Vol. II (Stuttgart, 1996), under ζάω and πταίω.

the altar there.[30] It also suggests that though depriving them of their age-old means of livelihood, Josiah's action towards them was not punitive or intended to humiliate these priests (see below).

V

Such a reading of 2 Kgs 23: 8a directs us afresh to v. 9 and raises two issues: (1) what is meant by 'unleavened bread' in this context, since, from the new reading of the first half of the verse suggested above, this cannot be understood as a reference to a share or perquisite of the offerings at the Jerusalem temple; and, pursuant to this, (2) who are the 'brethren' among whom these priests 'ate unleavened bread', since, again on such a revised reading of v. 9a, they cannot have been the priests of the Jerusalem temple?

To consider first the latter issue, the Levites are depicted in Deuteronomy as living among 'their brethren' the Israelites, and dependent upon them, since they are without 'share or hereditary possession'; that is, they are landless 'among their brethren' (Deut. 10: 9; 18: 2). Because of this they are included among those whom the community is enjoined to provide for—the fatherless, the widow, and the resident alien (גר) (Deut. 12: 12, 18, 19; 14: 27, 29; 16: 11, 14; 26: 11, 12, 13). Israelites are solemnly charged to 'take care not to forsake the Levite as long as you live in your land' (12: 19; cf. 14: 27).

It is these arrangements for the care and well-being of the Levites, which are given such attention and emphasis in Deuteronomy, that offer a background for an understanding of the statement in 2 Kgs 23: 9 concerning the outcome of Josiah's reformation for 'all

---

[30] Whilst arguing that these verses are from a Deuteronomistic hand, Hölscher ('Komposition und Ursprung', 201 f.), adhering to the usual reading of them, had to conclude that what they narrate is at odds with the provisions of Deut. 18: 6–8, which does not envisage a concentration of the rural priests in Jerusalem, and, contrary to what is (supposedly) described in 2 Kgs 23: 9, confers full rights upon any of these priests who chooses to come to the central sanctuary. Others find such a contradiction between Deut. 18: 6–8 and 2 Kgs 23: 8a, 9, for example Lohfink, 'The Cult Reform of Josiah of Judah', 474, n. 37, who suggests that Josiah's 'book of the *torah*' may not yet have contained Deut. 18: 6–8. No such 'contradiction' or tension between Deut. 18: 6–8 and 2 Kgs 23: 8aα, 9 arises, however, when the latter is understood as suggested above.

the priests of the cities of Judah', that is, 'the priests of the high places' whose ancient means of livelihood at the ancestral local altars throughout the land had now, as narrated in v. 8bβ, been swept away. If such is the background, the 'brethren' among whom these priests now lived in the new circumstances brought about by the reformation were their *fellow Israelites* in the communities where they resided throughout the land. What is striking about this is that one of the most distinctive features of Deuteronomy is its coinage of the term 'brethren' (אחים) to describe Israel as a society and community (Deut. 1: 16, 28; 3: 18, 20; 10: 9; 15: 2, 3, 7, 9, 11, 12; 17: 15, 20; 18: 2, 7, 15, 18; 19: 18, 19; 20: 8; 22: 1–4; 23: 19–20; 24: 7; 25: 1–3).[31] Given this, its usage in 2 Kgs 23: 9 surely carries the hallmark of a Deuteronomistic editor and casts doubt upon this verse as belonging to an original account of Josiah's reform measures.[32]

What, then, is meant by the phrase 'they ate unleavened bread'? Since these priests were not transported to Jerusalem, it cannot refer to supposed harsh treatment ('bread of affliction') they had to endure under conditions imposed by the official priesthood there, as Spieckermann suggests.[33] In any event, 'affliction' as associated with the eating of unleavened bread in Deut. 16: 3, where it is not suffering or hardship presently born but a way of remembering Israel's bondage in Egypt and simultaneously giving thanks for their deliverance, has manifestly a wholly different motivation and connotation from the restrictive terms of employment supposedly imposed by the Jerusalem priesthood upon these priests. Further, and of more general significance, against any such association of 'eating unleavened bread' with suffering hardship, the eating of un-leavened bread in the Hebrew Bible seems to have wholly favourable and positive contexts and connotations. Three narratives describe the provision of a meal including 'unleavened bread/cakes'. In all

---

[31] On the distinctiveness of this description of Israel, see L. Perlitt, ' "Ein einzig Volk von Brüdern": Zur deuteronomischen Herkunft der biblischen Bezeichnung "Bruder" ', in id., *Deuteronomium-Studien*, FAT 8 (1994), 50–73. Cf G. Braulik, *Das Buch Deuteronomium*, in *Studien zum Deuteronomium und seiner Nachgeschiche*, SBAB 33 (2001), 28–9.

[32] Most of the texts here cited are usually attributed to later, Deuteronomistic, stages in the composition of Deuteronomy. On Deut. 14: 14–20 (the 'law of the king') and 18: 9–22 (on prophecy) as Deuteronomistic, see Chapter 4, 'The Background to the Composition of Deuteronomy 18: 9–22', pp. 90–3 and Chapter 5, 'Deuteronomy 17: 14–20 as a Critique of Kingship', pp. 107–16.

[33] See Chapter 2, 'I', p. 20.

three texts the guests are of honoured status—divine messengers in Gen. 19: 1–29, 'the messenger of YHWH' in Judg. 6: 11–24, and King Saul in 1 Sam. 28: 3–25—and the impression given is that 'unleavened bread' signals the appropriate hospitality for such guests. Elsewhere the eating of 'unleavened bread' is associated with the cultic festivals of Passover and Unleavened Bread, where again it has a wholly positive connotation, and also with other offerings at the altar. In the case of the latter, offerings of unleavened bread, when not required to be burned upon the altar, are the preserve of the priests (Lev. 2; 6: 14–18; 7: 9–10, 11–13; 8: 2, 26, 31). Both the narratives and especially the cultic contexts in which it is mentioned indicate the distinctive status of this bread.[34] The use of unleavened bread is a mark of the holiness and separateness of the altar and of the priesthood who serve at it. When, therefore, 2 Kgs 23: 9 narrates that the priests now dispossessed of their livelihood at the sanctuaries throughout Judah 'ate unleavened bread among their brethren', it means nothing more than that these now 'altarless' priests received the support appropriate to their status deriving from their priestly pedigree.

A further consideration lends support to such a benign reading of 2 Kgs 23: 9b. There is no suggestion that these priests were subject to any punitive action on the part of Josiah; as noted above, what is related about them in v. 8a leaves no impression of any intention to debase or humiliate them. They are clearly distinguished from the 'idolatrous priests' (הכמרים) mentioned in 2 Kgs 23: 5,[35] and from the priests of the 'high places' in the cities of Samaria whom, we are told (v. 20), Josiah 'slaughtered' (ויזבח) upon their altars. Neither, again as we have seen, can the eating of 'unleavened bread' here be interpreted as referring to the Passover feast that marked the culmination of Josiah's reformation. Rather, 'they ate unleavened bread' is more plausibly understood as referring to the requirements

---

[34] It is possible that the original rationale for the special relationship of such bread with offerings at the altar was that leavened bread, i.e. bread made with yeast, was associated with fermentation, i.e. decay, and therefore unfit for the sphere of the holy and those who were specially associated with it, most notably the priests. For a discussion of this see Milgrom, *Leviticus 1–16*, 189–90.

[35] The כמרים seem to have been a specific group, attested only from the eighth century until the late seventh, and exclusively concerned with the cult of astral deities. They cannot plausibly therefore be identified with 'the priests of the cities of Judah from Geba to Beersheba' in v. 8a or with 'the priests of the high places' in v. 9. For this, see Uehlinger, 'Was There a Cult Reform under King Josiah?', 303–5.

of life that these priests received 'among their brethren', their fellow
Israelites, in the new conditions which the abolition of the local
sanctuaries brought about for the rural priests. In short, this phrase
describes these priests in terms of the provision for the Levite
commanded and exhorted in the book of Deuteronomy.

From such considerations, it seems clear that v. 9 does not represent a secondary scribal correction of what is stated in v. 8a, as
this verse is usually understood; that is, it is not a glossator's blunt
denial of a supposed mass relocation of the rural priesthood to
Jerusalem. Such a reading would not in any case explain its author's
use of the frequentative tense of the verbs,[36] which indicates that he
did not understand Josiah's action described in v.8aα as such a one-
off measure, but rather, we must presume, as making provision for
these now 'altarless' priests to exercise their priestly office at the altar
in Jerusalem, should any of them wish to do so.

Understood newly in this way, the text 2 Kgs 23: 8aα, 9 displays a
positive attitude towards the priests to whom it refers. Evidently no
opprobrium is attached to them, as some, on the basis of the usual
understanding of these verses, have suggested; for example, that they
were brought to Jerusalem not only for 'stipend' but also for
'restraint'.[37] The most plausible explanation of this concurrence
between v. 8aα and v. 9 is that, since the one (v. 8aα) alludes to the
provision of Deut. 18: 6–8 and the other (v. 9) tellingly employs
the distinctively Deuteronomistic appellation 'brethren' for the
people of Israel, and likewise reflects Deuteronomy's insistence
upon the people's duty of care for the Levites, they belong to a
Deuteronomistic redaction of an earlier account of Josiah's reform
measures.

Is v. 8a a unity, however? Obviously, what is described in v. 8aα
presupposes 8aβ, without which it hangs in the air and loses context,
since the disbandment of the 'high places' narrated in v. 8aβ provides
the grounds for Josiah's action on behalf of the 'altarless' priests as
reported in v. 8aα. Manifestly also, the latter understands the priests
referred to in v. 8aβ as being identical with the 'priests from the

---

[36] Had a redactor wished to state that these priests refused to be relocated from
their local communities to Jerusalem, we would expect the text to read לא עלו rather
than לא יעלו.

[37] See Montgomery and Gehman, *A Critical and Exegetical Commentary on the
Books of Kings*, 53.

cities of Judah' to whom it refers, that is, priests of YHWH now to be deprived of their altars. Probability thus lies in favour of the unity of v. 8a: v. 8aβ 'and he defiled the high places where the priests had burned incense, from Geba to Beersheba' cannot convincingly be disengaged from v. 8aα and could not have alone been the original content of v. 8a, since without v. 8aα's 'all the priests from the cities of Judah', v. 8aβ's bald 'the priests' loses context, 'the priests' whom it mentions having no identity as to the cult they served. Both clauses in v. 8a cohere together and have a degree of literary interrelation-ship.[38] Thus the nationwide scope of Josiah's dissolution of the 'high places' where the priests referred to in v. 8aβ burned incense 'from Geba to Beersheba' parallels the national scale of his action in relation to 'all the priests from the cities of Judah' in v. 8aα and suggests unity of authorship. More importantly, however, v. 8aβ shares the same non-hostile attitude as v. 8aα towards the priests here mentioned. There is no accusation or suggestion that these priests who 'burned incense' at 'the high places from Geba to Beersheba' were, like the כמרים mentioned in v.5, engaged in non-YHWH cults. The statement that they 'burned incense' is no evidence against this; there was nothing heterodox in 'burning incense', which was no less an activity of the priests of YHWH than of priests of foreign cults. Neither is the reference to these priests as 'priests of the high places' here derogatory or pejorative;[39] as we have seen, the writer of v. 9 (correctly understood), which refers to these same priests, manifestly did not understand it so. It seems from this that the objective of Josiah's actions as narrated in v. 8aβ was the dissolution of the local YHWH sanctuaries rather than any censure or denunciation of the priests who ministered at them.

How, then, are we to understand v. 9 in relation to v. 8aα and especially to Deut. 18: 6–8, which prescribes that any Levite may have access to the altar at the central sanctuary, and which, it need not be doubted, lies behind what Josiah is said in 2 Kgs 23: 8aα to have granted the priests whose altars he is about to disband? As noted above, that these priests are described in v. 9b as living among their brother Israelites conforms to the social standing ascribed to the Levites in Deuteronomy, including Deut. 18: 6–8, which portrays

---

[38] It would be in contrast to the כמרים priests referred to in v. 5 (see n. 35) with its reference to the cults of various astral deities whom they served.

[39] Against Spieckermann, *Juda unter Assur in der Sargonidenzeit*, 98.

them as resident throughout the towns and cities of the land, dependent upon their local communities for their well-being. But what of the first clause (v. 9a), which states that these priests 'do not go up to [*continuous past tense*] the altar of YHWH in Jerusalem'?

The key text in elucidating this is Deut. 18: 6–8, the rationale of which is that all priests are Levites but not all Levites exercise a specifically priestly cultic function, that is, 'preside at an altar', which is reserved only for those who 'minister in the name of YHWH' at the central sanctuary and, as prescribed in this text, any Levite resident elsewhere in the land who comes to 'the place which YHWH chooses' desiring to do so. Evidently, however, no mass take-up of the provision set out in this text is in mind. Rather, access to the altar at the central sanctuary is here portrayed as altogether exceptional and occasional, and not an option normally taken up by members of the Levite priestly caste resident throughout the land. The provision is framed in such a manner as to suggest that such access is in reality intended to be limited or only sparingly sought and gained, that a Levite 'from any of your towns' seeking access to the altar at the central sanctuary must be one who fulfils the condition that he comes 'with all the desire of his soul'.[40] It is in the light of this that the authorization said in 2 Kgs 23: 8aα to have been granted by Josiah to the priests of the decommissioned high places, and the statement in v. 9a that these priests 'do not go up to the altar of YHWH in Jerusalem', are to be understood. Verse 9 is not intended as a comment upon v. 8aα to the effect that, for a reason or reasons not stated, these priests were prevented from gaining access to the altar in Jerusalem, and so could not exercise the option provided by Josiah. Rather, taken together vv. 8a and 9 narrate that both Josiah and these priests acted in accordance with the prescriptions of 'the book of the *torah*', both the recurring command to care for the Levites 'who have no share or heredity possession' and the arrangement set out in Deut. 18: 6–8.

---

[40] It is not clear whether such a priest is then entitled to permanent attachment to the priesthood at the central sanctuary or is expected to return to his home community where he normally resides. (See R. D. Nelson, *Deuteronomy: A Commentary*, OTL (Louisville and London, 2002), 229.) This will depend partly upon how the verb גר in v. 6 is read, that is, 'resides' (cf. Judg. 17: 7; 19: 1; see S. R. Driver, *Deuteronomy*, ICC, 3rd edn. (Edinburgh, 1902), 217, or 'resided', 'had been residing'.

VI

A summary of the essence of the preceding analysis of 2 Kgs 23: 8a, 9 will serve to introduce some concluding observations.

(a) It cannot plausibly be questioned that the referent of 'priests of the high places' in v. 9 is identical with that of this same clause half a verse earlier in v. 8aβ, for who, if not those referred to in the latter as priests now dispossessed of their local altars, could the author of v. 9 have had in mind as similarly 'altarless'?

(b) It is clear also that this verse presupposes the centralization of the cult to the Jerusalem temple, and, still more significant, that it also implies that the priests to whom it refers, 'the priests of the high places', have an *entitlement* to access to the altar there.

(c) Syntactically, the arresting opening word of the verse, אַךְ, 'however', 'nevertheless', is here employed in its restrictive sense, stating a contrast to, or qualification of, something that has been stated concerning these priests in the preceding account of Josiah's reforms. This can only be v. 8aα, understood, obviously not as narrating a relocation of these priests to Jerusalem,[41] but as an entitlement granted by Josiah to 'any of the priests of the towns of Judah', 'the priests of the high places' (v. 8aβ) now dispossessed of their ancestral altars, to exercise their priestly office at the 'altar of YHWH in Jerusalem', if they so wished. There is no compelling reason for disengaging v. 9 from v. 8aα.

(d) Neither is there any compelling reason for uncoupling v. 8aα from v. 8aβ as deriving from different redactors. V. 8aα complements v. 8aβ, the 'priests from all the towns of Judah' in the former giving identity to the otherwise nondescript 'priests' of the latter. Further, v. 8aα's 'all the towns of Judah' parallels v. 8aβ's report of the nationwide desecration of all the local 'high places from Geba to Beersheba'.

(e) The description 'brethren' of the fellow Israelites among whom the priests of the high places 'ate unleavened bread' (v. 9) is a distinctively Deuteronomic usage, and this suggests that the text 2 Kgs 23: 8a, 9 derives from a Deuteronomistic redactor of an earlier

---

[41] It is only on the basis of what v. 9 is commonly (but erroneously) believed to record that commentators have read v. 8aα to mean that Josiah relocated 'the priests from every town of Judah' to Jerusalem.

account of Josiah's reform measures. Coinage of the word 'brethren' as a way of expressing Israel's social identity, a 'brotherhood', alongside Deuteronomy's cultural identity of this society as 'the people of YHWH', suggest circumstances in which both social and cultural identity were imperilled. I shall argue in the following chapter that such circumstances are most plausibly identified as the devastation and loss of homeland and the exile that followed, with the threat to social cohesion and erosion of cultural moorings which this would have occasioned.

Arising from the foregoing discussion of 2 Kgs 23: 8a, 9 however, a feature of this text, already referred to above, provides some further evidence that it is a redactional addition to an earlier account of Josiah's reform measures. This is that there is something of a misfit between what these verses recount and their narrative context. It is apparent that, as newly understood above, nothing is mentioned or implied in this text that censures the priests referred to on the grounds that the places where they ministered were centres of apostasy such as is associated with the other cultic locations referred to in the narrative, including, conspicuously indeed, Jerusalem and the temple itself and its precincts. The king's favourable action towards these priests, indicated in v. 8aα, again as here newly understood, confirms this, as does the depiction in v. 9b of their standing and well-being among the people, their 'brethren', which, as noted above, closely resembles Deuteronomy's commendation of the Levites to the care of their local communities. It seems that the sole ground on which these priests are the subject of the royal action described in v. 8aβ is that they exercised their priestly ministry— 'burned incense' (v. 8a)—at these sanctuaries, from which it follows that, though now to be proscribed and disbanded, these sanctuaries themselves seem likewise to have been free from the apostate and idolatrous cults which had established themselves elsewhere and which the king had set about purging.

In such a way, 2 Kgs 23: 8a, 9 introduces an element of incoherence into a narrative that otherwise describes a royally driven, national cultic reform, which included Jerusalem itself and the temple as a prime target for purging—rigorous purging, to judge from the narrator's forceful vocabulary[42]—of multiple apostate cults and

---

[42] 'Burn (to ashes)' (שרף), 'pulverize into dust' (*hiph.* דקק), 'demolish' (*piel* נתץ), 'exterminate, destroy' (*hiph.* שבת), 'break in pieces' (*piel* שבר), 'cut down' (כרת),

rituals. With the presence of this text the narrative becomes one of a nationwide group of sanctuaries which, though apparently not indicted of the apostate offences of the other cultic foundations and sites listed, now underwent dissolution and the disenfranchisement of their priesthood in favour of a centralized cult at Jerusalem, which, we read, had been a centre of apostasy on an endemic scale that had evidently been tolerated by a resident priesthood which was now to be entrusted with the safeguard and conduct of the national cult.

If such a consideration is justified, it provides additional evidence of the intrusive nature of 2 Kgs 23: 8a, 9, which, at the cost of a degree of incongruity with the surrounding narrative, derives from a hand intent upon associating Josiah's reformation with the requirements of Deuteronomy. At an earlier stage in its composition the narrative of Josiah's reformation contained no mention of a centralization of the cult—and this surely casts doubt on a dependence of the measures implemented by the king upon the demands of the book of Deuteronomy. Without the intrusion of vv. 8a, 9, Josiah's reform measures are more credibly viewed as an expression of new national self-assertion against the waning power of Assyria in the late seventh century BCE, a suggestion strengthened by the inclusion in the purge of local, west-Semitic versions of east-Semitic cults.[43]

VII

The question immediately arises, however: if centralization of the cult was no part of Josiah's reformation, whence derived this institution, with which the central law section in Deuteronomy begins? The book of Ezekiel provides testimony that already in the early decades of the sixth century this prophet took it for granted

'crush in pieces', the latter based on emending וירץ משם (v. 12) to read וירצם שם 'and he pounded them to dust there' as from the verb רץץ (Pi.). Of these verbs, Deut. 12: 2–3 employs שבר,שרף, נתץ. See Montgomery and Gehman, *A Critical and Exegetical Commentary on the Books of Kings*, 540.

[43] Theodor Oestreicher suggested this in his *Das Deuteronomische Grundgesetz* (Gütersloh, 1923), and a number of contemporary scholars (e.g. Lohfink, 'The Cult Reform of Josiah of Judah', 466–7) describe some of Josiah's reforms as expressions of growing disengagement from Assyrian sovereignty which was now seen to be in terminal decline.

that Jerusalem was the only valid place of worship, and this has usually been explained by an appeal to Josiah's 'deuteronomic' reformation which the prophet would have known of. If the conclusions argued above are justified, however, such an explanation is no longer admissible. The result is that, unless an alternative—but surely implausible—claim is made that Ezekiel derived the notion of a centralized cult from a reported but short-lived centralization of worship by Hezekiah more than a century earlier (2 Kgs 18: 4, 22), it is the testimony of Ezekiel's preaching that provides the first dependable evidence of the notion of a centralized cult. And there is, indeed, no need to look beyond Ezekiel and the priestly tradition to which he belonged to explain this. In his commentary on Ezekiel, Paul Joyce, writing about the centrality of the Jerusalem temple in Ezekiel's thinking, remarks that 'we should not overestimate the need for dependence on deuteronomistic influence here', adding pertinently that, 'indeed more generally the deuteronomistic element in Ezekiel is relatively muted, and certainly less important than the priestly background'.[44] He quotes with approval Andrew Mein's observation that 'the centrality of the Jerusalem sanctuary is an immovable datum of the religion' in the context of priestly as well as deuteronomistic theology.[45] Mein, drawing attention to close parallels between Ezek. 6 and Lev. 26, argues that 'it seems reasonable to deduce that Ezekiel's polemic [against the 'high places' (*bamoth*)] is taken from the milieu of priestly rather than Deuteronomistic theology'. Since the centralization of the cult in Jerusalem meant the centralization of the *sacrificial* cult, it is a reasonable conjecture that it was an initiative of the Jerusalem priesthood to whose numbers Ezekiel belonged. That the authors of the Priestly material in the Pentateuch likewise presupposed that there was only one place of worship lends support to this.

There are strong indications that such an elevation and promotion of Jerusalem as the only valid place of the sacrificial cult would have found a natural acceptance among the Judaean exiles generally in Babylon. It is no mere surmise that Jerusalem's status and its claim to a special relation with YHWH was a 'given' of Judaean religious tradition and piety before the cataclysmic events that brought Judah and Jerusalem with its temple to destruction in the early

---

[44] Paul M. Joyce, *Ezekiel: A Commentary* (New York and London, 2007), 38.
[45] Andrew Mein, *Ezekiel and the Ethics of Exile* (Oxford, 2001), 115.

sixth century BCE. That such pre-eminence of Jerusalem endured throughout the exilic period and was a leading source of hope and a focus of devotion among the exiles, even as the temple lay in ruins, is well attested. The significance of Jerusalem/Zion in the preaching of Deutero-Isaiah, whose 'thoughts dwell continually on Zion',[46] witnesses to the vitality of the Zion tradition among the exiles, as does the eschatological vision of the restoration of the temple and of the city of God in the preaching of Zechariah and his contemporary Haggai in the immediate post-exilic period, both of whom have been described as 'true successors of Ezekiel'.[47] The Deuteronomistic 'prayer of Solomon' (1 Kgs 8: 14–53) is further evidence, depicting the exiles as praying towards the temple. That this reflects devout custom among the exiles—its refrain petitioning that YHWH would hear 'from heaven' may reflect a liturgical form with a *Sitz im Leben* in community worship—and cannot seriously be put down to a fictitious invention of Deuteronomistic piety is widely agreed.

On such evidence, the centralization of the cult in Deuteronomy thus reflects a watershed in the arrangement of the cult envisaged and planned by Jerusalem priestly circles in exile, to which Ezekiel belonged, and would have been wholly of a piece with the enhanced significance attached among the exiles to Jerusalem[48] and its temple.

If in this matter, however, the authors and redactors of Deuteronomy adopted such an initiative of priestly circles during the exilic period, the long-acknowledged fact remains that there is little family resemblance, so to speak, between Deuteronomy and the Priestly material in the Pentateuch, with which for these purposes we can couple the book of Ezekiel, which shares with this material a distinctly sacral and priestly ethos. In Deuteronomy sacrifice and ritual and cultic institutions are given a low profile and there is an

---

[46] See G. von Rad, *Old Testament Theology*, Vol. II (Edinburgh, 1965), 239–40, Eng. trans. by D. M. Stalker from *Theologie des Alten Testaments*, Vol. II (Munich, 1960).

[47] See e.g. O. Eissfeldt, *The Old Testament: An Introduction* (Oxford, 1965), 433–4, Eng. trans. by P. R. Ackroyd of the 3rd edn. of *Einleitung in das Alte Testament* (Tübingen, 1964).

[48] It is of interest in this connection that there is now evidence of a city in the vicinity of Nippur bearing the hitherto unattested place-name āl-Yāhūdu 'Judah city', which some suggest was 'Babylonian Jerusalem'. See M. Weippert in E. Ebeling *et al.* (eds.), *Reallexikon der Assyriologie*, 11 vols. (Berlin and New York, 1976–), v. 200, and W. G. Lambert, 'A Document from a Community of Exiles in Babylonia', in Meir Lubetski (ed.), *New Seals and Inscriptions, Hebrew, Idumean, and Cuneiform* (Sheffield, 2007), 201–5, esp. 205. See also Chapter 3, 'Deuteronomy and the Babylonian Diaspora', pp. 42–3.

absence of any 'sacerdotal' element proper resembling what we encounter in P or in Ezekiel. There is not the same engagement with the sacrificial cult, which, indeed, is treated minimally, and nothing about the sanctuary designated by the phrase 'the place which YHWH will choose', or its 'furniture'; there is likewise only a minimal indication of the office and functions of the priesthood. Indeed, as a number of scholars have suggested, the book displays a marked degree of 'desacralizing',[49] a shift away from ritual to ethics seen, for example, in the way in which ancient cultic festivals such as the festivals of Weeks and Booths (Deut. 16: 9–15), each of which would originally have had its own distinctive sacral identity and purpose, its own cult 'legend', are both now reinterpreted in terms of providing for the vulnerable and underprivileged elements in society.[50] The claim is justified that in Deuteronomy 'religion changes from a matter of cultic purity to one of learning and education', and Israel is characterized 'as a community of learning and remembering';[51] 'remember and forget not' epitomizes the thrust of the book, which is aptly described as 'oppositional' literature, born of circumstances of social and cultural crisis.[52] An ethos of encroachment pervades the book, and an anxiety for group survival in an environment that threatens a loss of cultural memory and national self-identity. It is to such features of Deuteronomy and the indications they may offer as to the provenance of the book that I now turn.

---

[49] See M. Weinfeld, *Deuteronomy and the Deuteronomic School* (Oxford, 1972), 191–243, who writes of 'secularisation' as a marked feature of the book.

[50] The 'desacralizing' tendency of Deuteronomy and the shift it shows from ritual to ethics can be an indication of social upheaval and radical change in a community. For this see Mary Douglas, *Natural Symbols: Explorations in Cosmology*, Penguin edn. (Harmondsworth, 1978; first pub. 1970).

[51] J. Assmann, *Religion and Cultural Memory* (Stanford, CA, 2006), Eng. trans. by R. Livingstone from *Religion und kulturelles Gedächtnis* (Munich, 2000). The reference here is to the English translation, p. 19.

[52] See esp. Assmann's discussion of this under the subtitle 'Counterfactual Memory and the Normative Past: Deuteronomy', *Religion and Cultural Memory*, 14–21.

3

Deuteronomy and the Babylonian Diaspora

THE JUDAEAN EXILES

It is history that the exiles deported to Babylonia in the early sixth century were destined to live out their lives there, like Jehoiachin and the members of his family deported with him (2 Kgs 25: 27–30), to be succeeded by a generation which had never lived in or even set foot in the homeland. Further, although under Persian rule in the late sixth century some of their descendants returned to the homeland, numerous others did not but remained in the towns where they had been born, grew up, worked and pursued their livelihood, married and raised their families, buried their grandparents and parents.[1] In this they were no different from immigrants generally throughout history for whom, after the first generation or two, the land to which they had emigrated becomes their home, whatever affection they may retain for the ancestral homeland.

The letter in Jeremiah 29 (esp. vv. 4–7) offering advice to those recently exiled to Babylonia is a vignette of the social reality which before long the Judaean deportees faced: advising that the might of Babylonia was in no imminent danger of being overthrown, and that there was thus no realistic alternative to settling down where they had been transported and securing as best they could their community and providing for their families. The letter assumes a prolonged sojourn, long enough for population increase of the exiled communities and the development of means of livelihood in their new environment; long enough, it envisages, for second and third

---

[1] See the discussion of this by B. Becking, ' "We All Returned as One!": Critical Notes on the Myth of the Mass Return', in O. Lipschits and M. Oeming (eds.), *Judah and the Judaeans in the Persian Period* (Winona Lake, IN, 2006), 3–18.

generations to be born;[2] the letter implies also the opportunity of living peacefully and thriving economically alongside the native citizenry, and of benefiting from the prosperity of the indigenous population, for which the deportees are exhorted to pray. The letter thus considers the community to which it is addressed to be sufficiently permanent in its new location as to take on, over time, a new life of its own.

The prospects for, and opportunities open to, the Judaean exiles as briefly stated in this text are confirmed by the evidence of cuneiform sources from the Neo-Babylonian and Achaemenid periods. That many exiles of Judaean descent remained in Babylonia and were still there in the Achaemenid period, as, for example, Ezra–Nehemiah records, is attested in texts of the Murašû archive from Nippur and other towns in its vicinity and extending over the second half of the fifth century BCE. These texts contain western Semitic names, numbers of them compounded with the theophoric element YHWH. More recently an archive of approximately one hundred similar cuneiform texts dating from the early sixth to the fifth centuries has yielded further information about the Judaean exiles in the Neo-Babylonian period itself, including some that shed light upon the earlier years of the sixth century BCE and not long after the fall of Jerusalem in 587 BCE.[3] The texts in this archive derive from two locations, one of which, āl-Našar, has been known for some time, the other, where most of these texts were written, a town somewhere near Nippur bearing the hitherto unattested place-name āl-Yāhūdu, 'Judah city', which, it seems likely, was 'Babylonian Jerusalem'.[4] According to Laurie Pearce, the name in one of its earliest appearances, which she dates to 572 BCE, is written with a

[2] On the LXX of v. 6, see W. McKane, *A Critical and Exegetical Commentary on Jeremiah*, Vol. II, ICC (Edinburgh, 1996), 728.

[3] These texts are being prepared for publication by L. E. Pearce and C. Wunsch. For this archive and a preliminary description of the information it yields see L. E. Pearce, 'New Evidence for Judaeans in Babylonia', in Lipschits and Oeming, *Judah and the Judaeans in the Persian Period* 399–411. Three of the texts are discussed by F. Joannès and A. Lemaire 'Trois tablettes cunéiformes à l'onomastique ouest-sémitique', *Transeuphratène*, 17 (1999), 17–33. See also W. G. Lambert, 'A Document from a Community of Exiles in Babylonia', in Meir Lubetski (ed.), *New Seals and Inscriptions, Hebrew, Idumean, and Cuneiform* (Sheffield, 2007), 201–5.

[4] On the appropriateness of the name 'Jerusalem' see Lambert, 'A Document', 5, whose observations are in support of the suggestion originally made by M. Weippert in E. Ebeling *et al.* (eds.), *Reallexikon der Assyriologie*, 11 vols. (Berlin and New York, 1976–), v. 200.

gentilic ending (*ālu ša* ^{lú}*Yāhūdāia*),[5] indicating that the city was so named after groups who came from Judah and thus was at first known as 'the city of the Judaeans'. Pearce also finds, however, that before long this ending is dropped and the city is known simply by the toponym 'the city Judah' (^{uru}(*ša*) *Yāhūdu*), thus suggesting that 'the Judaean deportees and their descendants were sufficiently established in the social and economic life of Babylonia for their town to be referred to simply as "Judah-ville" or the like' (p. 402). She believes that this may have already been how the town's name was newly signified as early as the third decade of the sixth century BCE (p. 402).

Našar town and Yāhūdu and other places mentioned in association with them in this corpus were, like Nippur, located in southern Mesopotamia.[6] This new archive reveals the participation of the Judaean exiles in legal, commercial, and administrative matters as early as 572 BCE, that is, a mere fifteen years after the destruction of Jerusalem. They thus confirm that the exiles did indeed, as the letter from Jeremiah exhorts, adapt to their new situation, engaging in various occupations and even, it seems, holding minor local administrative office.[7] The activity is evidenced in receipts for payments, debt notes for commodities owed, sales of livestock, leasing of houses, and so on.[8] It seems also that Judaeans were officially entrusted with a measure of fiscal administration relating to their community, and there is some evidence of an officially organized Babylonian administrative district of a mainly Judaean population, a *hatru*.[9] In short, there is sufficient evidence 'to show that the Judaean exiles . . . were not isolated from the world of their Babylonian masters, indeed could have been exposed to a variety of

---

[5] Pearce, 'New Evidence', 401, n. 7 lists nine orthographies of the city, including this, which is the final one in her list.

[6] It has been estimated that there were altogether 28 such settlements for Judaeans, out of a total of 200, distributed over the whole region of Nippur. See E. J. Bickerman, 'The Babylonian Captivity' in W. D. Davies and L. Finkelstein (eds.), *The Cambridge History of Judaism*, Vol. I (Cambridge, 1984), 342–58, esp. 346.

[7] Pearce, 'New Evidence', 405–6, and on the status and degree of integration of the Judaean exiles into the Babylonian state structure and practices see id., ' "Judaean": A Special Status in Neo-Babylonian and Achemenid Babylonia?', in O. Lipschits, G. N. Knoppers, and M. Oeming (eds.), *Judah and the Judaeans in the Achaemenid Period: Negotiating Identity in an International Context* (Winona Lake, IN, 2011), 265–77.

[8] Pearce, 'New Evidence', 405.

[9] Pearce, 'New Evidence', 405 f.

its facets, social, economic, political, and cultural'.[10] It shows also that the Judaean immigrant population of Našar and Yāhūdu and other places in their vicinity were not sitting upon their hands waiting for news of an imminent return home.

We know too of other minority ethnic groups who had been uprooted by the Babylonians from their native lands and cities, mostly in the west of the region, and settled in areas of Babylonia. Legal and economic documents from the Murašû archive record toponyms in the vicinity of Nippur all of which are of western origin: there is reference to a canal (*nār Milidu*) near which people deported from Milid in Asia Minor were settled, and of communities from Phoenicia, Syria, Philistia (including Ashkelon and Gaza), deportees from towns in Syria, and mention of Arab exiles; another canal is referred to as 'the Egyptians' Canal' (*nāru ša* ^{lú}*Misiraia*), reminiscent of the Judaean community among whom Ezekiel lived in the town 'Tell Aviv' by the *nār Kabāru*-canal, which ran through or close by Nippur. Another toponym refers simply to ^{uru}*Galûtu* 'exile city', thus signalling, as in the case of Yāhūdu, the origin of its inhabitants and how they came to be there.[11]

What may we deduce from such evidence concerning the conditions in which the Judaean exiles lived in their different settlements in Babylonia, where they were caught up in the legal, commercial, and economic affairs of everyday life? The settlements named after the different population groups mentioned above indicate that the Babylonian authorities did not seek to assimilate these groups of deportees into their own native population or to intermingle them with each other. There was, that is, a degree of segregation, but there is no evidence that the settlements were ghetto-like, and no reason to believe that access to each other or communication between them was in any way restricted; neither is there any evidence of persecution by the state authorities. The settlements, which were on crown lands, were especially in rural

---

[10] For a cautious sketch see P. Machinist, 'Mesopotamian Imperialism and Israelite Religion: A Case Study from the Second Isaiah', in W. G. Dever and S. Gitin (eds.), *Symbiosis, Symbolism, and the Power of the Past: Canaan, Ancient Israel, and their Neighbours from the Late Bronze Age through Roman Palestine* (Winona Lake, IN, 2003), 237–64, esp. 255–6; the quotation is on p. 256.

[11] See I. Eph'al, 'On the Political and Social Organization of the Jews in Babylonian Exile', in *Zeitschrift der Deutschen Morgenländischen Gesellschaft*, Supplement Vol. V: *Deutscher Orientalistentag XXI 1980* (1983), 106–12.

areas, but some were also close to cities such as Borsippa and Uruk or near cities such as Nippur and in Babylon itself, where Jehoiachin and his family and entourage were brought and maintained by the Babylonian court. These various ethnic population groups were free to manage their lives and livelihood and to worship their national gods.

That there was a process of acculturation is in no doubt, however, including the adoption of the worship of Babylonian deities. Thus, among the Babylonian personal names of Judaeans evidenced in the Murašû texts and in the Yāhūdu/Našar corpus some contain theophoric elements of the names of Babylonian gods. The evidence suggests[12] that Judaean fathers with Babylonian religious names could give their sons names containing the theophoric element of their ancestral God YHWH, whilst in other cases the patronyms of sons bearing Babylonian names were Judaean and comprised the theophoric element YHWH.[13] It seems, on this evidence, that some Judaean exiles worshipped Babylonian deities as well as continuing the worship of YHWH.[14] This much, indeed, can already be inferred from various texts in the Hebrew Bible. Deut. 4: 28 'foretells' the worship by Israelite exiles of gods 'of wood and stone that neither see, nor hear, nor eat nor smell'; Jeremiah, as narrated in Jer. 5: 19; 16: 13, prophesies that the exiles of Judah will 'serve other gods day

---

[12] On the basis of Pearce's preliminary comments (in 'New Evidence'), P.-A. Beaulieu, 'Yahwistic Names in Light of Late Babylonian Onomastics', in Lipschits, Knoppers, and Oeming, *Judah and the Judaeans in the Achaemenid Period*, 245–66, estimates (p. 251) that of 55 pairs of names of Judaeans in the Yahudu and Našar corpus, 35 pairs mention fathers with West Semitic names whose sons have Babylonian names, and 20 pairs mentioning fathers with Babylonian names whose sons have West Semitic names, adding that the Murašû archive reveals a similar pattern. The projected full publication of the Yahudu/Našar texts will enable a more detailed study of such name giving among the Judaean exiles and their descendants.

[13] Some Judaean leaders who bore Babylonian names (e.g. Zerubbabel), including names with theophoric elements of Babylonian deities (e.g. Sheshbazzar, Shenazzar), were most likely assigned them by the Babylonian authorities. See Machinist, 'Mesopotamian Imperialism and Israelite Religion', 256, following R. Zadok, *The Earliest Diaspora: Israelites and Judaeans in Pre-Hellenistic Mesopotamia*, Publications of the Diaspora Research Institute, 151 (Tel Aviv, 2002), 57. The names of the Judaean exiles participating in legal, commercial, and administrative matters in the Murašû and Yāhūdu/Našar texts would of course have been freely chosen and not imposed externally.

[14] For a fuller discussion see Bickerman, 'The Babylonian Captivity', 352–4; and his 'The Generation of Ezra and Nehemiah', first published in *Proceedings of the American Academy of Jewish Research*, 45 (1978), 1–18, repr. in his *Studies in Jewish and Christian History*, Vol. II (Leiden and Boston, 2007), 975–99, esp. 989–93.

and night' in a foreign land; evidently some elders among the deportees of 597 BCE, who had decided to follow 'the nations and tribes of other lands' and 'worship wood and stone', came to consult the prophet Ezekiel (20: 32; cf. 14: 1–3), the inference being that such worship would be in addition to their own ancestral worship of YHWH; Deutero-Isaiah (48: 5) declared in advance to fellow Judaeans what YHWH was about to do for his people, lest when it happens they should boast that it was the work of their 'idols'.[15] The 'spectrum' of worship among the exiles thus seems to have included those who worshipped YHWH alone, and some who lost faith in YHWH (cf. e.g. Isa. 40: 27) and adapted to the local culture and religion and for whom local deities gradually became all that counted,[16] whilst for others, encroachment of the indigenous culture would have yielded, not a systematized theology, and probably not participation in the official imperial cult, but a form of, as it were,

---

[15] Beaulieu, 'Yahwistic Names in Light of Late Babylonian Onomastics', whilst acknowledging that names 'may reveal changes in preference for one deity or the other' (p. 245), questions whether the fact that some Judaeans in exile bore names containing such theophoric elements as Markuk, Nanaya, Bel, Nabû indicates that they worshipped these gods alongside YHWH. He asks whether 'these people were truly less Yahwistic than others?', suggesting as 'more likely' that they 'just adopt[ed] fashionable names of their new homeland, names that sounded right and gave them the impression of participating more fully in the ambient culture and society' (p. 253). Whilst perhaps such an explanation of these names cannot be excluded, these biblical texts from the exilic/early post-exilic period, of which Beaulieu makes no mention, lend manifest support to what such names *prima facie* suggest: that some Judaeans in exile did indeed adopt the worship of local deities. That this was so is surely the background of, for example, significant texts and themes in Isa. 40–55. No doubt, as Beaulieu suggests (p. 259), those who adopted such names would still have regarded themselves as Judaean, but for others among them there was more to their identity than ethnicity. J. Blenkinsopp 'The Age of the Exile', 417 states that we cannot 'be sure that individuals bearing Judaean names belonged to the families and descendants of Judaeans deported by the Babylonians'. Why, however, would a Babylonian citizen or a member of some other ethnic community exiled from its homeland have chosen to revere the name YHWH in such a way? It strains credibility to imagine that these individuals of non-Judaean descent would have 'converted' to the worship of YHWH—the god whose land had been ravaged and whose worshippers were defeated and in exile. If, on the other hand, those who bore such names were children of mixed marriages, whether the Judaean was the husband or the spouse, this in itself would be evidence of the threat of encroachment that is such a characteristic of Deuteronomy.

[16] R. Albertz, *Israel in Exile: The History and Literature of the Sixth Century B.C.E.* (Atlanta, GA, 2003), Eng. trans. by David Green from *Die Exilzeit: 6 Jahrhundert v. Christ* (Stuttgart, 2001). Albertz writes (p. 105) of 'the temptingly easy possibility' of Judaeans 'immersing themselves in the ethnic mosaic of the Babylonian Empire. Undoubtedly, not a few chose this path.'

'homespun' syncretism which would have included devotion to Babylonian deities alongside their ancestral God YHWH.[17]

These short Akkadian commercial and legal texts from the sixth and fifth centuries BCE merely underline the problem that the historian faces when attempting to write a history of the Judaeans in exile in the sixth century BCE. They indicate an assiduous engagement by exiles for means of livelihood in their places of settlement allotted to them by the Babylonian crown authorities, and their onomastics shows a degree of adaptation to their new ambient culture and religion. But this falls well short of conveying the extent and the acuteness of the challenge that would have confronted these Judaean exiles of the early sixth century BCE, whose erstwhile societal structures and communal bonds had been disrupted, whose faith in YHWH and his promises had wavered or failed, and numbers of whom sought blessing from local deities or conjoined their ancestral worship of YHWH with local cults, and all of whom faced 'the temptingly easy possibility' of 'ridding themselves of all their burdensome problems at a stroke by turning their backs on the muddled history of their own people and immersing themselves in the ethnic mosaic of the Babylonian Empire'.[18]

The historian of the period wants to know how and by what means these Judaean exiles were to retain and sustain their own national, cultural, and religious identity among the ethnically and culturally mixed populace of Babylonia, which, in addition to its ruling, native population, was home to many other minority ethnic communities, each with its own religious and cultural heritage. We know that a substantial body of them succeeded: the return by some to the homeland in the late sixth century and by others subsequently under Ezra and Nehemiah, and not least the Judaean/Jewish Diaspora community that continued to reside in Mesopotamia

---

[17] Cf. W. G. Lambert: 'The city cults were the preserve of the official priesthood, of the ruler, and perhaps the upper classes. Ordinary people might share in the spirit of the more important annual festivals, but the city temple was not a place of their devotions. For them the niche at home or the street corner shrine was the place of religion.' 'The Historical Development of the Mesopotamian Pantheon: A Study in Sophisticated Polytheism', in H. Goedicke and J. J. M. Roberts (eds.), *Unity and Diversity: Essays in the History, Literature, and Religion of the Ancient Near East* (Baltimore and London, 1975), 191–200 (the quotation is from p. 191).

[18] Albertz, *Israel in Exile*, 105.

throughout the Achaemenid period and beyond, evidence this.[19] It is the case also that the other ethnic minorities mentioned above maintained their national identity throughout decades in exile in Babylonia; this was not, therefore, a phenomenon peculiar to the Judaean communities. The fact is, however, that apart from those who returned under Persian rule to their homelands, all of these other ethnic groups eventually disappeared from Babylonian society, that is, were assimilated. Drawing attention to this, Israel Eph'al has pertinently observed: 'The outstanding survival of the Jews in Babylonia as an entity-in-exile in the subsequent period . . . remains, however, a problem demanding further explanation.'[20] By what means, religious and social, therefore, were the Judaean exiles enabled to maintain their ethnic, communal, and religious identity?

It might be thought that the much more substantial biblical texts from the exilic period would yield fuller information about this. We are not well served, however, by our Old Testament sources for any attempt to write a history or even a historical sketch of the exilic period, whether of conditions in Judah itself or among the Judaeans deported to Babylonia. In the Hebrew Bible, the period in Judah is treated as an interim in which those who remained there seem to count for nothing, while history awaits the return of the exiles who count for all, whether in Ezekiel or the book of Jeremiah or in Deutero-Isaiah.[21] Of the exiles themselves, Ezekiel announces the promise of YHWH's presence with them in Babylonia 'for a short time' or 'in a small measure' (Ezek. 11: 16), a temporary blessing pending a return to the land. Such a promise is simultaneously and importantly also a declaration of YHWH's power in the face of the exiles' experience of the apparent defeat of their God, and thus of loss of faith, and, related to this declaration, the prophet's mocking onslaught upon Israel's historic idolatry is as much a statement of

---

[19] Bickerman, 'The Generation of Ezra and Nehemiah', finds evidence of a heightened use of names compounded of YHWH among the Babylonian Judaean community in the second half of the 5th century BCE, suggesting perhaps a fresh interest and pride in their ancestral Judaean and religious roots.

[20] See his 'The Western Minorities of Babylonia in the 6th and 5th Centuries B.C.', *Orientalia*, 47 (1978), 74–90, esp. 88.

[21] On the relative neglect among scholars of conditions in Judah itself in the exilic period see Hans M. Barstad, *History and the Hebrew Bible: Studies in Ancient Israelite and Ancient Near Eastern Historiography*, FAT 61 (Tübingen, 2008), 'The Myth of the Empty Land' (pp. 90–134), and 'Judah in the Neo-Babylonian Period' (pp. 135–59).

the powerlessness of the 'gods of wood and stone' to whom, we are told, leaders among the community are turning (e.g. Ezek. 14: 1–11; 18: 1–32; 20: 32–44).[22] In such a way the prophet proclaims the power and presence of YHWH among his people in exile, and defines the distinctiveness of Israel. A return to the land, however, with a 'blueprint' for the new temple and its priestly cult remains a focus of the book, and we are told little or nothing of how and in what ways, in an environment of ever-threatening encroachment, these exiles were in the meantime to sustain their national and cultural identity.

Jeremiah's letter to the exiles (Jer. 29, esp. vv. 4–7), mentioned above, exhorts them to take a long-term view of their deportation to Babylonia, and to 'plan on this assumption both for the welfare and continuance of their own community and for the prosperity of the Babylonian communities from which their own highest interests cannot be dissociated'. Here at least we encounter some counsel in the face of the new historical and social reality that faced the exiles. For all the wise counsel the letter offers them, however, about integrating peacefully[23] with their exilic environment and finding prosperity, again nothing is said of how and in what ways they were to maintain their social, religious, and cultural identity.

The promise and expectation of a return home reaches its climax in Isa. 40–55 at the close of the exilic age, proclaiming the imminent release of the exiles under Cyrus. The prophet declares the incomparability of YHWH, and, like Ezekiel, though differently expressed, he proclaims the power and kingship of YHWH by parodying and thus 'delegitimizing' as delusory and powerless the local hand-made, lifeless idols to whom some among the exiles have turned (Isa. 40: 18–20; 42: 17; 43: 12; 44: 9–29; 48: 3–5).[24] The prophet's robust declaration of YHWH's control of historical events and his sheer intellectual confidence are themselves conspicuous testimony to a vigorous survival of Judaean cultural and religious heritage. No more than from the books of Ezekiel and Jeremiah, however, can we gain an outline of religious and cultural resistance

---

[22] On the ideological and iconographic background of Ezekiel's depiction of YHWH's departure from Jerusalem and promised return to the land of Israel, as well as motive for the ridicule with which he describes cultic images, see N. B. Levtow, *Images of Others: Iconic Politics in Ancient Israel* (Winona Lake, IN, 2008).

[23] McKane, *Jeremiah*, Vol. II 742 f. aptly describes the advice in these verses 'build, plant, marry' as paradigms of 'integration'.

[24] On the genre of 'icon parody', which he suggests is an innovation of the exilic age, see Levtow, *Images of Others*, esp. ch. 2.

over the previous sixty years, of how and in what ways this prophet's Judaean forebears in exile had maintained their national and religious identity when it might otherwise have gradually faded with the passing of the years, or through a process of acculturation to local religious and cultic practice mutated into a sort of Babylonian sub-cult embodying elements of east- and west-Semitic cults.

The Deuteronomic corpus, the present form of which is usually dated substantially to the exilic period, concludes with a notice of the fate of Jehoiachin at the Babylonian court and implies that he is dead (2 Kgs 25: 27–30), but offers no narrative of the conditions of the exiles during the decades of exile that preceded this, though the narrative of the dedication of Solomon's temple allows us a glimpse of how they prayed towards Jerusalem (1 Kgs 8: 14–53).

Historians of this period have endeavoured to fill the gap in our knowledge. On the one hand, insights derived from sociological and anthropological studies have been used to shed light upon the experience of the exiles, of their status and treatment, and of their social and cultural resources and means of resistance.[25] On the other, attention is drawn to this and that institution—observance of the Sabbath, circumcision, praying towards Jerusalem, and so forth—as measures, sometimes described as 'survival strategies',[26] adopted to maintain social cohesion and survival. But these offer but glimpses of how the Judaean exiles met and endeavoured to overcome the pressing challenges with which their new social, cultural, and religious environment confronted them.

The inference is warranted that an 'agenda' would soon have emerged among leading Yahwistic circles directed at the conditions and challenges of exile in Babylonia, one that would gradually have focused more and more upon present realities, acknowledging that exile would not be a brief sojourn and that hopes for a future return home which became increasingly far off could not substitute for new thinking and initiatives, social, ethical, and theological, to defend and reinforce national identity and community survival against ethnic, cultural, and religious assimilation and gradual extinction.

My contention is that the authors and redactors to whom we owe the book of Deuteronomy addressed themselves to just such needs of

---

[25] See e.g. D. L. Smith, *The Religion of the Landless: The Social Context of the Babylonian Exile* (Bloomington, IN, 1989); D. L. Smith-Christopher, *A Biblical Theology of Exile* (Minneapolis, 2002).

[26] Albertz, *Israel in Exile*, 98–111.

the exiles, and that in such a way they gave thought and taught and wrote, not for an interim situation requiring 'survival strategies', but for a new age in the history of their people, who were now no longer identified simply as the resident population of the ancestral home-land, but embraced also what we have come to describe as the Diaspora, in this instance specifically the Babylonian Diaspora.

It might immediately be objected that the Israel to whom Deuteronomy is addressed was a monarchical state rather than a community of stateless exiles. After all, Deuteronomy alone among the legal corpora of the Pentateuch makes provision for a monarchy (Deut. 17: 14–20), and some scholars view this passage as part of a larger pericope (16: 18–18: 22) providing an outline 'constitution' or 'polity' focusing upon the primary state offices of judge, king, priest, and prophet.[27] It seems unlikely, however, that at any stage of its composition Deuteronomy was intended as state law to be imple-mented under royal prerogative and supervision, as proposed by a number of scholars with Judah under Josiah in mind,[28] or that the book's authors had in mind a newly constituted state following the destruction of the kingdom of Judah.[29] Against such views, which will be the subject of closer critique in an ensuing chapter,[30] outside

---

[27] N. Lohfink, 'Die Sicherung der Wirksamkeit des Gotteswortes durch das Prinzip der Gewaltenteilung nach den Ämtergesetzen des Buches Deuteronomium (Dt 16, 18–18, 22)', in H. Wolter (ed.), *Testimonium Veritati* (Festschrift Wilhelm Kempf), Frankfurter theologische Studien, 7 (Frankfurt a.M, 1971), 144–55, repr. in N. Lohfink, *Studien zum Deuteronomium und zur deuteronomistischen Literatur* I, SBAB 8 (Stuttgart, 1990), 305–23, Eng. trans. 'Distribution of the Functions of Power: The Laws Concerning Public Offices in Deuteronomy 16: 18–18: 22', in D. L. Christensen (ed.) *A Song of Power and the Power of Song* (Winona Lake, IN, 1993), 336–52; B. Halpern, *The Constitution of the Monarchy in Israel*, HSM, 25 (Chico, CA, 1981); S. Dean McBride, 'Polity of the Covenant People: The Book of Deuteronomy', *Interpretation*, 41 (1987), 229–44; U. Rüterswörden, *Von der politischen Gemeinschaft zur Gemeinde: Studien zu Dt 16,18–18,22*, BBB 65 (Frankfurt a.M., 1987); B. M. Levinson, 'The Reconceptualization of Kingship in Deuteronomy and the Deuteronomistic History's Transformation of Torah', *VT* 51 (2001), 511–34; R. D. Nelson, *Deuteronomy: A Commentary*, OTL (London, 2002), 210–36.

[28] See e.g. R. H. Lowery, *The Reforming Kings: Cults and Society in First Temple Judah*, JSOTSup 120 (Sheffield, 1991).

[29] See e.g. R. E. Clements, 'The Origins of Deuteronomy: What Are the Clues?', in 'A Dialogue with Gordon McConville on Deuteronomy', *SJT* 56 (2003), 508–16, who suggests that Deuteronomy was intended as 'written book of polity for a state' offering a 'new social and juridical order' to replace 'the failed monarchic order' in Judah following the catastrophe of 587 BCE.

[30] See Chapter 5, 'Context: A Deuteronomic "Polity" for Israel (Deut. 16: 18–18: 22)?', pp. 103–6.

Deut. 17: 14–20 the king plays no role in the institutions of the Israel envisaged in Deuteronomy; there is a striking absence of anything to do with the nature and essence of 'kingship' (מלוכה) or 'kingdom', 'sovereignty' (ממלכה) in the book. In short, no state with a monarch, even a titular one, is seriously provided for in the book, neither is any other temporal ruler of the state mentioned.[31] Indeed, a contrary impression is given: in Deuteronomy Israel is a 'depoliticzsed' society whose collective identity is expressed socially in terms of 'brotherhood' and defined culturally as 'the people of Yahweh' whose leaders (ראשים cf. Deut. 1: 13) are locally appointed 'wise, understanding, and experienced men'.[32] The Israel that had been constituted as a state or two states with appropriate political institutions has been eclipsed, and here replaced by a collective identity and self-awareness that is distinctively different. At the same time, Deuteronomy presupposes a jarring disjuncture between its vision of 'the people of Yahweh' and the social reality that is 'Israel', which is portrayed as a nation prone to idolatry and imperilled by encroachment (see below). Such a portrayal of Israel represents its authors' response to a time of drastic change which brought not only political but also social and cultural jeopardy. We shall return to this below.

This prompts a further comment upon the long-accepted view of a close relationship between the origin of Deuteronomy and Josiah's reform of the late seventh century BCE. Scholars find evidence that Josiah's reign from a relatively early stage became a time of mounting national revival and optimism as the power of Assyria began to crumble, and that Judah's regained sovereignty and a new-found self-confidence among the ruling and leading parties regenerated faith in the promises to the house of David, inspiring hope for a recovery and reconstitution of the Davidic state that would reincorporate the territory of the erstwhile Northern Kingdom. It is then frequently argued that Josiah's 'Deuteronomic' reform was

---

[31] See esp. the acute observations of L. Perlitt, 'Der Staatsgedanke im Deuteronomium', in S. E. Ballentine and J. Barton (eds.), *Language, Theology, and the Bible: Essays in Honour of James Barr* (Oxford, 1994), 182–98.

[32] On the meaning and significance of such a description, see the observations below on Jan Assmann's discussion of the 'depoliticising of public life' in Deuteronomy in his *Religion and Cultural Memory* (Stanford, 2006); references here are to the Eng. trans. by Rodney Livingstone from *Religion und kulturelles Gedächtnis* (Munich, 2000), esp. ch. 3, 'Five Stages on the Road to Canon: Tradition and Written Culture in Ancient Israel and Early Judaism'.

carried through on this tide of regained sovereign independence and nationalistic renewal and confidence.[33] Against this latter suggestion, however, and by contrast, the tone and thrust of Deuteronomy, as suggested above, is redolent of a historical context of menacingly ominous rather than buoyant, hopeful change, just as the narrative framework of the book depicts (see below) a situation of national peril rather than auspicious national renaissance. The question suggests itself: is not the period following the collapse and dissolution of the Judaean state a more likely *terminus a quo* for the emergence of the character and leading concerns of Deuteronomy, of those features of the book that, as we may put it, make Deuteronomy Deuteronomy?

DEUTERONOMY AS COUNTERFACTUAL LITERATURE

I share the view of scholars generally that Deuteronomy was not written at one sitting, but emerged through various stages of composition and redaction. It is widely agreed that in its present form it derives from the exilic period, with allowance also, however, for some still later, post-exilic additions. Most scholars also agree, though with significant variation in detail, that the book is part of a larger corpus comprising also Joshua–2 Kings and usually described as a 'Deuteronomistic History', and that the authors and redactors of this corpus contributed significantly to the literary growth from earlier to later stages of Deuteronomy itself. However, although there is every indication that the book underwent such a more or less protracted period of composition at the hands of successive authors and redactors, who further enriched its contents and contributed to its teaching and claims, Deuteronomy retains a striking homogeneity, not only in its instantly recognizable style, which is pervasive, but also in its intense 'mono-Yahwism' and, accompanying this, its fierce

---

[33] R. Albertz, *A History of Israelite Religion in the Old Testament Period*, Vol. I (London, 1994), 201–4, Eng. trans. by John Bowden from *Religionsgeschichte Israels in alttestamentlicher Zeit*, Vol. I (Göttingen, 1992); N. Lohfink, 'The Cult Reform of Josiah of Judah: 2 Kings 22–23 as a Source for the History of Israelite Religion', in J. M. Miller, P. D. Hanson, and S. D. McBride (eds.), *Ancient Israelite Religion: Essays in Honor of Frank Moore Cross* (Philadelphia, 1987), 459–75, who describes (p. 467) some of Josiah's reforms as expressions of growing disengagement from Assyrian sovereignty which was now seen to be in terminal decline.

iconoclasm, its preoccupation with religious encroachment, and in its vision of Israel as 'the people of Yahweh' and as a community of 'brothers', and the choice they are summoned to make for or against YHWH, between blessing and curse, life or death.

Deuteronomy is a pseudepigraph ascribed to Moses, who is said to have delivered its contents in a series of addresses—more strictly, a string of speeches—to the Israelites on the plains of Moab as they were about to cross the Jordan into the land of Canaan. The distinctive literary style of the book already signals its character—an urgent hortatory style that exhorts, cautions, promises, threatens. In the fiction of the book, life in the land which the people are about to enter is depicted as one that will be fraught with danger of forsaking YHWH, and from this the inference suggests itself that the historical context in which the book's authors and redactors lived and worked was one of apprehension for continued fidelity to YHWH, which evidently could not be taken for granted. The ardour with which the these authors appeal for faithfulness to YHWH, the passion, even vehemence, with which they warn against apostasy, the book's threats of curse, including of loss of land and nationhood—these and other prominent features stamp Deuteronomy as literature born of crisis.

Thus, for example, Deuteronomy's 'mono-Yahwism' is all-pervasive, declared as the first of the Decalogue commandments spoken directly by YHWH to the assembled people at Horeb/Sinai (Deut. 5: 6–7) and, closely following this, encapsulated in the *Shem'a* (Deut. 6: 4–5).[34] The context of these declarations is described as one of imminent drastic change fraught with the peril that in the land now to be entered Israel will forget all that has happened, what their eyes have seen and their ears have heard in the events of exodus and the covenant at Horeb:

Only take heed, and keep your soul diligently, lest you forget the things which your eyes have seen, and lest they depart from your heart all the days of your life; make them known to your children and your children's children. (Deut. 4: 9)

And when the Lord your God brings you into the land which he swore to your fathers . . . then take heed lest you forget the Lord, who brought you

[34] I side with those scholars who consider it more likely that in the *Shem'a* the word אחד should be understood as 'alone' rather than 'one'. Such a reading of the word is more coherent with the command that follows to love YHWH with heart, and soul, and strength. See A. D. H. Mayes, NCB, *Deuteronomy* (London, 1979), 176, and, for further discussion and bibliography, Nelson, *Deuteronomy*, 89–91.

out of the land of Egypt, out of the house of bondage. You shall fear the Lord your God; you shall serve him, and swear by his name. You shall not go after other gods, of the gods of the peoples who are round about you; for the Lord your God in the midst of you is a jealous God; lest the anger of the Lord your God be kindled against you, and he destroy you from off the face of the earth. (Deut. 6: 10–15)

Here, as commentators have long observed, is already struck one of the most acute concerns of Deuteronomy—encroachment. Thus S. R. Driver wrote of the encroachment of other religions as 'the pressing danger of the age', which 'the author strove to resist by every means in his power. Not only does he repeatedly declare, in solemn terms, that if allowed to prevail, they will ultimately involve Israel in national ruin; but a large number of provisions—much larger than in the Book of the Covenant—are aimed directly against them.'[35] We can, indeed, speak of an 'ethos of encroachment' pervading the book, of an 'in-group–out-group' culture born of an anxiety for group survival.[36] It is not 'foreigners', however, who pose a direct threat to Israel's well-being and imperil its religious and moral boundaries.[37] Rather, 'the most profound threat to Israel's survival . . . is posed not by enemies who live far away but by "indigenous outsiders", that is, "bad insiders" '.[38]

Louis Stulman analyses a number of texts in Deuteronomy dealing with capital crimes against the community. The crimes are various, including enticement to apostasy, a prophet speaking falsely in God's name, premeditated murder, a rebellious son, harlotry, adultery, rape, and abducting and selling a brother Israelite into slavery. Of these, enticement to apostasy is my main interest here. Stulman draws attention to four texts: 13: 2–6; 13: 7–12; 13: 13–19; 17: 2–7. Of these, the first two relate to enticement by a prophet or 'dreamer of dreams' and by one's own kin or an intimate friend, the third to 'miscreant' co-citizens ('sons of Belial'), the fourth, in 17: 2–7, to any apostate individual, man or woman. Capital punishment is prescribed, with

---

[35] S. R. Driver, *Deuteronomy*, ICC, 3rd edn. (Edinburgh, 1902), pp. xxxi f.

[36] See L. Stulman, 'Encroachment in Deuteronomy: An Analysis of the Social World of the D Code', *JBL* 109 (1990), 613–32.

[37] On the much-debated issue of whether the Assyrian's imposed their national cult upon client states or provinces, Stephen Holloway's expansive study, *Aššur is King! Aššur is King! Religion in the Exercise of Power in the Neo-Assyrian Empire* (Leiden, Boston, and Cologne, 2002), shifts the balance of probability to the view that they did not. See Chapter 6, 'V', pp. 123–31.

[38] Stulman, 'Encroachment in Deuteronomy', 615.

the object of 'purging the evil from [Israel's] midst'. Stulman's study shows that the percentage of statutes pertaining to apostasy is much higher than in the Book of the Covenant and, indeed, than in other ancient Near Eastern legal code.

From his analysis of such texts, Stulman concludes that these ordinances carrying the death penalty in Deuteronomy reflect 'a great deal of internal anxiety and a marked sense of vulnerability. The world of D[euteronomy] is fragile and fraught with danger, and Israel's survival is perceived to be in jeopardy' (p. 626). That Deuteronomy dwells so anxiously upon encroachment, providing no less than four separate formulations of the danger it poses, and stressing that it comes not only from leaders in the community (prophets and 'dreamers of dreams') and deviant groups but also from one's nearest and dearest—brother, son, daughter, beloved wife, cherished friend—makes good sense against such a social and religious background. These formulations show no dependence upon earlier statutory ordinances, and are aptly described as 'legal homilies'.[39]

These texts do not stand alone, however, and here I draw attention to a further text that shares a similarly anxious concern with encroachment and that unquestionably presupposes an exilic background for its composition. It is usually regarded as belonging to the later stages in the literary growth of the book. As such, however, it offers further evidence that recognizably secondary texts in Deuteronomy were by no means all directed towards serving its incorporation into the Deuteronomistic corpus, but that an equal driving force in the growth of the book was the development of Deuteronomy as 'the book of the *torah*', a designation to which I shall return below.

---

[39] There is an obvious air of unreality in these texts, strikingly so in 13: 12–18, which envisages the razing of whole cities and the annihilation of their populations and livestock, though without any indication of the authority under which such action, which would have had to be national, and implemented (establishing guilt and marshalling a task-force to mount an assault on the city and carry out the mass executions, followed by the destruction of the city, reducing it to a desolate tell forever). It is no objection to a Babylonian setting for the composition of these texts, therefore, to say that such actions could not have been sanctioned under Babylonian law, since they would have been equally unrealistic measures in the homeland, whether during the monarchical or exilic periods. In short, the texts have much more to do with the rhetoric of persuasion than with legal reality.

This text is Deut. 4: 1–40, which was probably a still later addition to Deuteronomy than the Decalogue pericope which follows in 5: 1–27[40] and of which it may be described as a sort of prefatory extrapolation. It dwells upon various leading motifs and themes of the Decalogue pericope (see below), but pride of place is given to solemn and repeated warnings against the making of any image (vv. 15–31), combined with a scornful polemic against idols described as 'wood and stone, the work of men's hands, that neither see, nor hear, nor eat, nor smell' (v. 28), a depiction that is strikingly reminiscent of the mockery of idols and those who carve them in Deutero-Isaiah (Isa. 40: 18–20; 44: 9–20; 46: 5–7). Such a strong echo of the Deutero-Isaiah's biting derision suggests an exilic background for the composition of Deut. 4: 1–40.[41] This is confirmed by the equally striking similarities in thought between v. 32, with its allusion to creation—only here in Deuteronomy—and such passages as Isa. 45: 18 ff.; 46: 9 f., and by the declarations in vv. 35 and 39 ('know therefore this day, and lay it to your heart, that the Lord is God in heaven above and on the earth beneath; there is no other') and the affirmations in such passages as Isa. 43: 10–13; 44: 6–8; 45: 6–7, 22.[42]

Though it places on Moses' lips a solemn threat of exile (vv. 26–8), this text is not primarily intended as having been an 'early warning' justifying God's present judgement upon his people and composed with this broad theme of the Deuteronomistic corpus in mind. Rather, its author intended it much more as part of Deuteronomy as *torah*. Its marked hortatory, 'sermonic' nature holds the key to its primary purpose as exhortation and instruction. Thus, its solemn warnings virtually run into each other: 'take heed . . . take good heed to yourselves . . . beware lest you act corruptly by making an image . . . lest you lift up your eyes to . . . the sun and the moon and the stars, all the host of heaven [cf. 17: 2 f.] . . . take heed to yourselves, lest you forget the covenant . . . and make an image . . . if you act corruptly by making an image . . . I call heaven and earth to witness against you this day, that you will soon utterly perish from the land.' In short, in tone the passage is shot through with an

---

[40] See Mayes, *Deuteronomy*, 161, and id. 'Deuteronomy 4 and the Literary Criticism of Deuteronomy', *JBL* 100 (1981), 23–51.

[41] For the rationale and significance of such derision, see Levtow's observations noted below.

[42] Mayes, *Deuteronomy*, 153–7.

anxious and urgent need to meet a present danger that threatens the
future of the community to whom it was addressed in the later exilic
period or the early post-exilic, surely most probably the community
of the Babylonian exiles. And no less than in the case of the 'legal
homilies' of Deut. 13, such unremitting warning and exhortation was
directed at a community whose survival is threatened, not by foreign,
cultural enemies, but from within itself.

Support for such a setting is offered by Levtow's study, referred to
earlier, of political and social aspects of iconography in the ancient
Near East, who observes, citing Deut. 4 as an example, that 'exilic
strata of Deuteronomistic literature promote a most extreme form
of oppositional iconic rhetoric, wherein a normative Yahwistic ritual
and social order is defined through categorical opposition to all
anthropomorphic and theriomorphic cultic imagery'.[43] This and
other texts, for example the Decalogue command prohibiting the
making of images (Exod. 20: 4–5; Deut. 5: 7–8),[44] and the opening
verses of the central law code of Deuteronomy (Deut. 12: 2–3),[45]
promote 'a distinct vision of Israelite identity . . . through a binary
system of classification that distinguishes between "the Israelite
way" and "the Canaanite way"'.[46] Set in the historical context of
the foundation of Israelite society, when the menace and challenge
of encounter with 'Canaanite' culture lay immediately ahead, such
texts, Levtow suggests, testify in reality to an endeavour to delineate,
assert, and sustain the distinctiveness of the Judaean exilic communities in circumstances of ever-threatening encroachment.

Such texts, with their warnings and threats of vehement punishment and wholesale annihilation of cities, and their mocking
derision of idols, which, manifestly, is directed not at the Canaanite
or other foreign clients of such cults but at Israelites who have
adopted them, display a fundamental feature of Deuteronomy: a

---

[43] Levtow, *Images of Others*, 150–1.

[44] On this see F.-L. Hossfeld, *Der Dekalog: Seine späten Fassungen, die originale Komposition und seine Vorstufen*, OBO 45 (Göttingen, 1982), especially his discussion of the prohibition on the making of images (pp. 258–62); C. Dohmen, *Das Bilderverbot: Seine Entstehung und seine Entwicklung im Alten Testament*, BBB 62 (Frankfurt a.M., 1987), who argues (pp. 211–30) that the texts forbidding the making of images have undergone exilic redaction, mainly at the hands of Deuteronomistic editors.

[45] Deut. 12: 2–3 employs 'utterly destroy, wipe out (cultic sites)', 'blot out (the names of idols)' (*piel* אבד), 'demolish, raze to the ground' (*piel* נתץ), 'smash in pieces' (*piel* שבר), 'Burn (to ashes)' (*piel* שרף), 'hew down' (*piel* גדע).

[46] Levtow, *Images of Others*, 148–9.

sharp dissonance between its authors' vision of Israel and the social reality of their time, which was evidently a context of far-reaching national, social, and political upheaval corrosive of cultural identity and cohesion, which they viewed as being in peril of disintegration and oblivion. Evidently the book presupposes a time that can aptly be described as one of one of national 'forgetting',[47] just as Moses 'anticipated' (Deut. 4: 9; 6: 10–15), and in the face of which these authors strove to recall their contemporaries to the events, the experiences, and the commitments that defined their identity as 'the people of Yahweh', to construct, that is, a counter-culture to one that their contemporaries were forging in conditions of drastic change and that threatened national and social survival. Viewed in such a way, Deuteronomy may be described as 'counterfactual' or 'oppositional' literature.[48]

The Decalogue (Deut. 5: 6–21) here calls for attention, since its opening declaration, 'I am the Lord your God who brought you out of the land of Egypt, out of the house of bondage' and its commands ('the ten words') are here presented as foundational of Israel's identity as 'the people of Yahweh', and it also relates a 'normative past', the constant remembering of which makes for cultural survival and consolidates social cohesion against a prevailing 'forgetting' that bodes national extinction. There are also good reasons for believing that, like other texts considered above, this text was composed in the exilic period, though drawing upon earlier custom and tradition.[49]

There is no mistaking the primal significance that Deuteronomy attaches to the Decalogue, the 'ten words' (5: 6–21), which are said to have been spoken directly by YHWH to Israel, crowning the theophany at the primordial assembly of the people at Horeb/Sinai. These commandments, inscribed on two tables of stone by God's own hand and placed in 'the ark of the covenant' (10: 1–5), are thereby designated the quintessential terms of the covenant and

---

[47] On 'forgetting' and 'remembering' as a central theme and motivation of the authors of Deuteronomy, see Assmann, *Religion and Cultural Memory, passim*; he describes Deuteronomy 'the only one of the Five Books of Moses that is dedicated to the themes of remembering and forgetting' (p. 55).

[48] For this, see Assmann, *Religion and Cultural Memory*, 16–21, and see also below on Deuteronomy and cultural memory.

[49] For details see Hossfeld, *Der Dekalog*, especially his discussion of the prohibition on the making of images (pp. 258–62), the misuse of the name of YHWH (pp. 243–7), the Sabbath commandment (pp. 247–52), and the command to honour parents (pp. 252–9).

normative for the ordering of Israel's life before God. They are headed by a declaration of YHWH's intimate relationship with Israel wrought in the deliverance from bondage (v. 6)—'election'—and by two commandments, the one (v. 7) outlawing the worship of other gods, the other (v. 8) forbidding the making of any divine image. The positioning of vv. 9–10, which refer back to 'other gods' in v. 7, has the effect of bracketing the two commandments together, and, indeed, together they are of the essence of 'Yahwism'.[50]

Among indications of the background to Deut. 5.6–21, the commandment for the observance of the Sabbath day (vv. 12–15), upon which Deuteronomy's presentation of the Decalogue places special emphasis,[51] has every appearance of having been conceived among the exiles as a distinctive way of expressing and conserving the community's religious and cultural identity, and there is much agreement among commentators about this.[52] A range of texts, all of them deriving from the exilic or early post-exilic period (Lev. 23; Isa. 56: 2, 4, 6; 58: 13; 66: 23; Jer. 17: 19–27; Ezek. 20: 12 f., 16: 20, 21, 24; 22: 8, 26; 23: 38; 44:24; 46: 1, 3, 4, 12), lends support to this view. There has been growing agreement also that the conception of the weekly Sabbath drew upon an ancient new-moon Sabbath festival mentioned in such texts as 2 Kgs 4: 23; Isa. 1: 13; Hos. 2: 13; Amos 8: 5, as well as upon customary law reflected in Exod. 23: 12 and 34: 21 commanding rest from labour on the seventh day of the week (in each of these texts the verb 'to rest' (*šābath*) but not the noun 'Sabbath' is employed).

That the ordinance 'to hallow' (לקדשׁ) the Sabbath, which is 'the Lord's Sabbath', may indicate not only desisting from work but also some form of liturgical act, though any suggestion that it marked the beginning of synagogue worship is conjectural. It is striking, however, that the Decalogue, though an ostensibly foundational declaration of YHWH's will for his people at Horeb/Sinai, contains

---

[50] Hossfeld, *Der Dekalog*, 282 writes of the framework of vv. 6–16 as offering 'eine Kurz-Theologie von Jahwe in Tat und Wesen'.

[51] See N. Lohfink, 'Zur Dekalogfassung von Dt 5', *BZ* 9 (1965), 17–32 who argues that the structure of the Decalogue in Deut. 5 has the effect of presenting the Sabbath command as central to the Decalogue and not simply as its fourth commandment. Cf. also Mayes, *Deuteronomy*, 164–5.

[52] For a discussion of its origin and its relation to earlier cultic and social institutions see Hossfeld, *Der Dekalog*, 247–52. For a summary of the issues see Albertz, *A History of Israelite Religion in the Old Testament Period*, Vol. II (London, 1994), 408–11.

not the merest mention of altar or sacrifice,[53] and the surmise is prompted that, quite apart from the injunction that sacrificial worship is confined to 'the place which Yahweh chooses', that is, Jerusalem, the newly conceived and instituted weekly Sabbath consecrated to YHWH was marked by some kind of family or possibly communal act of worship.

The commandment honouring parents (v. 16) has no earlier formulation or 'proto-text' in the Hebrew Bible which might have been a source for the author of this clause, though respect and submission to parental authority is a familiar topic in the wisdom literature (Prov. 1: 8; 13: 1; 19: 26; etc.). Since the combination of a prescription with the promise of blessing is familiar in Deuteronomy (e.g. Deut. 4: 40; 5: 33; 6: 2; 11: 9; 22: 7; 30: 18; 32: 47), there is no need to question the unity of this clause and its Deuteronomic authorship. The importance attached to honouring parents is of a piece with the emphasis among the exiles upon family and family associations ('fathers' house') as the main social entity. Commentators also draw a close association between the inclusion of such a clause in the Decalogue and the injunction, which occurs a number of times in Deuteronomy (4: 9–10; 6: 7–10, 20–1; 11: 18–21; 31: 13; 33: 46), requiring parents to instruct their children in the *torah*,[54] and they consider the primary intention of the commandment to be that of maintaining and fortifying the role of parents in the transmission and teaching of the law, which is probably a development of the exilic period. The easy-to-learn nature of the Decalogue, with its mnemonic number ten, may thus not have been the least consideration among the intentions of those who drafted this text.

The Decalogue's emphasis upon the quintessentially distinctive features of 'Yahwism' and its requirement of Israel's monolatrous faithfulness, its accent upon the family as the primary entity in its society and the font of social control as well as the context in which the *torah* is taught and learned (see below), the injunction 'hallowing' the seventh day as 'YHWH's Sabbath'—such contents and emphases would surely have had conspicuous pertinence to a

---

[53] The 'Book of the Covenant', by contrast, contains the altar law in Exod. 20: 24; the provision for sacrifice and cultic festivals in Exod. 34: 17–25 provides a further contrast.

[54] See Mayes, *Deuteronomy*, 161 f., and for fuller discussion Hossfeld, *Der Dekalog*, 254–9.

community uprooted and exiled from its ancient religious and cultic, social and cultural moorings and transplanted into an environment of ever-present encroachment.

DEUTERONOMY AND CULTURAL MEMORY

The significance attached to the *torah* in the broader theologically apologetic context of the Deuteronomistic History is surely matched by the remarkable conjoining of the 'book of the *torah*' with the conduct of family life in which the *torah* is to be both learned by parents and also taught by them to their children, and incessantly so, as commanded by Moses (4: 9–10; 6: 7–10, 20–1; 11: 18–21; 31: 13; 33: 46): 'You shall therefore lay up these words of mine in your heart and in your soul; and you shall bind them as a sign upon your hand, and they shall be as frontlets between your eyes. And you shall teach them to your children, talking of them when you are sitting in your house, and when you are walking by the way, and when you lie down, and when you rise. And you shall write them upon the doorposts of your house and upon your gates' (Deut. 11: 18–20). Those to whom such command and exhortation is addressed are now and newly conceived of as 'the people of the book'.

Herein resides the character of Deuteronomy which Assmann aptly describes as a book of 'memory making',[55] 'memory making' in the face of a prevailing state of 'forgetting' on the part of those to whom these teachers and authors addressed themselves and for whom the circumstances of life had evidently drastically changed. He describes this 'memory' as 'counterfactual': it introduces 'into the present something distant and alien for which there is no room in everyday life and which therefore has to be ritually imagined at regular intervals, in order to maintain a context that is threatened by disintegration and oblivion' (p. 16). 'That is the exceptional situation of a counterfactual memory. It keeps present to the mind a yesterday that conflicts with every today' (p. 53). This 'yesterday' comprises the story of the nation's 'normative past' in the deliverance from

---

[55] *Religion and Cultural Memory* 16–21 and *passim*. He describes Deuteronomy as 'the only one of the Five Books of Moses that is dedicated to the themes of remembering and forgetting' (p. 55).

bondage in Egypt and of Israel's immemorial covenantal commitment to God at Horeb.

This collective memory is bonding memory: it restores a lost unity or recovers one that is threatened, for collective memory is simultaneously 'connective' memory; that is, it is memory that builds community and thus sustains national identity in an environment that threatens its survival. 'When collectives "remember," they thereby secure a unifying, "connective" semantics that "holds them inwardly together" and reintegrates their individual "members" so that they possess a common point of view' (p. 11). Thus, Assmann argues, the core command of Deuteronomy, and what fired the teachers and authors from whom it derived, can be aptly epitomized as ' "thou shalt not forget" means "thou shalt not become assimilated" ' (p. 54).

To this end, Assmann suggests, Deuteronomy provides an elaborate 'memory technique' which is employed to salvage memory from oblivion by elevating the experiences of exodus, revelation, and the wilderness 'to the status of a normative past for all future generations'.[56] The procedures adopted intend that this foundation story and its normative role in fashioning and bonding is all-pervasive in the community: it is to be taken to heart, learned by heart, taught to the children, meditated upon day and night, given visible signs by body-marking, symbolically displayed on the door-post of homes, publically published and made perennially accessible; the annual pilgrim festivals (Deut. 16: 1–15) are to be occasions of collective remembering.

This foundation story and its normative role in fashioning and bonding the community is enshrined in the description of Deuteronomy as 'the/this *torah*' or 'this book of the *torah*' (1: 5; 4: 8, 44; 17: 18, 19; 27: 3, 8, 26; 28: 58, 61; 29: 20, 28 (EVV 21: 29); 30: 10; 31: 9, 11, 12, 24, 26; 32: 46). In such a description of 'the words that Moses spoke to all Israel beyond the Jordan' (Deut. 1: 1, cf. v. 5) is reflected for the first time the concept of an authoritative 'scripture' in prescribing and guiding Israel's relationship with YHWH. By this means Israel is constructed 'as a community of learning and remembering ... Here religion changes from a matter of cultic

---

[56] See esp. his section under the subtitle 'Counterfactual Memory and the Normative Past: Deuteronomy', *Religion and Cultural Memory*, 14–21.

purity to one of learning and education'.[57] It marks a shift in
religious action from temple, altar, and sacrifice and the offices that
went with these to family life as the institution which, it seems, is
now charged with conserving and inculcating the commandments in
obedience to which lies blessing. And the conviction and the passion,
indeed, with which these authors lodge and impel this zealous teaching of the *torah* within the family and promote its visible symbolical
representation throughout the community is manifest. It is the *torah*,
to be read and meditated upon, that establishes and perpetuates
the cultural memory of Israel which can withstand changing
circumstances—' "Thou shalt not forget" means "thou shalt not be
assimilated" '.

Assmann thus views Deuteronomy as a first step on the way to the
formation of a canon,[58] and he tentatively links this beginning to
the reign of Josiah at the end of the seventh century. He finds a
second step in the period of the Babylonian exile, and a third stage,
which he associates with the mission and work of Ezra, in the time
of the Persian empire. It is to this latter stage that he attributes
the 'depoliticizing' of public life which is a leading feature of
Deuteronomy, commenting (p. 72) that 'only in Israel was religion
able to crystallize into a definite and distinctive alternative method
of establishing a collective entity. Only here had a "nation" emerged
that was able to separate itself from the outside world and create
an internal community entirely independently of political and
territorial ties, namely, simply through its adherence to "the law and
the prophets." ' With the post-exilic Province of Judah in mind,
which had become part of the satrapy of Transeuphratene, he means
that the Israelite 'nation' now becomes an 'internal culture' within
the larger framework of the Persian empire, and now constitutes
a society whose collective identity is expressed socially in terms of
'brotherhood' and theologically defined as 'the people of YHWH',
titles that have the appearance of being intended to supplant the
older designations of Israel as a society of tribes and subsequently
monarchically ordered states. This newly restored and 'depoliticized'
society, referred to also as a 'holy people' and YHWH's 'inheritance',
was 'concerned with purity of life, teaching, and interpretation,

---

[57] *Religion and Cultural Memory*, 19.
[58] See esp. *Religion and Cultural Memory*, ch. 3: 'Five Stages on the Road to the
Canon: Tradition and Written Culture in Ancient Israel and Early Judaism'.

whilst delegating the management of worldly affairs to the Persian occupying power' (p. 72).

Of the beginnings and earlier development of Deuteronomy, Assmann agrees with the view, shared by many scholars, that Josiah's reformation was politically as well as religiously motivated and driven, suggesting that 'the turning point of Josiah's reign' came in the 'brief moment of respite, autonomy, and memory' between the crumbling rule of Assyria and the subsequent suzerainty of the Babylonians—a turning point characterized by 'a revolutionary, national liberation movement whose semantics were typical of such movements in the sense that it combined the memory of a forgotten tradition of one's own with an exclusion of outsiders that was justified with reference to that memory' (p. 68). It was in this historical context that laws and normative traditions were 'not simply collected, but comprehensively codified and put into effect, and . . . with considerable revolutionary force'.

It might be objected that since, in the world to which Josiah's kingdom belonged, law-making and putting it into effect was quintessentially a central role of the king, this rules out such a period for the appearance of Deuteronomy, in which, Assmann argues, 'torah replaces the ancient Oriental law-making king' (p. 66). Perhaps, he concedes, the episode of the finding of the 'book of the law' may be considered 'a reconstruction inspired by the exile situation, in which there was no longer any king to personify the law and put it into effect' (p. 68). Whilst acknowledging such a possibility, however, he leans towards the alternative and generally accepted view that Deuteronomy supplied at least part of Josiah's reforming agenda, supporting this on the grounds that although kingship is not abolished in Deuteronomy, 'it is domesticated and reined in by religiously based norms that have always been associated with the name of Moses and which now—around 622 or after 587—were codified, perhaps for the first time, in a comprehensive book' (p. 69).[59] From now onwards, he argues, that is, from the appearance of 'the book of the law', '[h]istory frames, or rather

---

[59] On the issue whether 'the monotheistic and theocratic idea of a covenant and chosenness belongs to the basic core of normative and formative knowledge of Israel, that is, of its cultural memory, and whether it can actually be traced back to the religious and political conflicts in Egypt and the Late Bronze Age', see his comments on p. 100, where he suggests that 'it quite conceivably is an ancient, primordial memory'.

"determines," the law' in the sense of a 'normative' past; in 'the Torah the law is ... recontextualised since it is inserted into the determining framework of a history, in other words, a framework that gives it meaning. Its embodiment in a king is replaced by its anchoring in a history' (p. 67).

Against Assmann, however, there is no evidence that Josiah—or any of his successors—abdicated any of his traditional roles as monarch; indeed, quite the contrary is surely the case. In the narrative of 2 Kgs 22–3 he is centre-stage in his role as king: it is he who commands the reform measures and is the agent of the various verbs listing these reforms, all of this wholly in keeping with the exercise of the role of the monarch as leader and custodian of the national cult; and typically he also conducts and endeavours to effect state policy, as for example in the invasion and seizure of territory of northern Israel, which for a century or so had been constituted as a province of the Assyrian empire, and, fatefully, in waging war against Pharaoh Necho, who had allied himself with the fading rule of Assyria against the mounting power of Babylonia. In this narrative monarchical authority is scarcely 'domesticated' and 'reined in'. Nor, in any case, are such terms an adequate account of how monarchy is viewed in Deuteronomy, where the institution is tamed beyond historical recognition by a mainly negative formulation far removed from the sacral ideology, well attested elsewhere in the Hebrew Bible, that consecrated and surrounded kingship in Judah. The Josiah whom we encounter in the narrative of 2 Kgs 22–3 does not resemble the rather 'unkinged' figure of Deut. 17: 14–20.[60] It may be agreed with Assmann that Deuteronomy narrates a 'normative past' as a determining framework of history for the giving of the *torah*, and that this *torah* replaced the law-giving role and agency of the king. It seems more likely, however, that the independence of the *torah* from the law-giving role of the monarchy presupposes a situation in which, as Assmann puts it (p. 68), 'there was no longer any king to personify the law and put it into effect', that is, the exilic period.

---

[60] A fuller discussion of the law of the king in Deut. 17: 14–20 is provided in Chapters 5 and 6.

THE PROVENANCE OF DEUTERONOMY

Assmann himself writes of the exile of the Judaean Diaspora as a significant time in the emergence of Deuteronomy, which took place in the context of 'the hegemony of Babylonian culture'.[61] The upheaval of deportation, the breach in societal bonds, the threat of a disintegration of tradition understood as 'lived knowledge . . . that is passed on in active association with others . . . a form of knowledge that is largely self-evident and that has become unconscious and implicit' (p. 69)—in such a situation, he argues, in which 'the contact with living models is broken, people turn to the texts in their search for guidance'. In circumstances like these, he suggests, 'we find not only that new texts emerge, but also that already existing texts are given an enhanced normative value' (p. 69). In such conditions, he argues, the 'written tradition cannot simply be experienced, it has to be studied . . . The normative status of the texts has to be scrutinised and established so that people can have something they can rely upon'. This entails an endeavour to learn by heart this written knowledge, internalizing it and thus 'reconverting writing into lived knowledge', an endeavour upon which Deuteronomy places special emphasis (p. 70): 'The words of the Torah shall "not depart out of thy mouth, but thou shalt meditate therein day and night," they shall "be upon thy heart," "thou shalt teach them diligently to thy children," and "talk of them when thou sittest in thine house. And when thou walkest by the way."' (citing Josh. 1: 8; Deut. 6: 6; 6: 7 (cf. 11: 19)).

Assmann offers no indication, however, of what redaction the 'book of the *torah*' of Josiah's reformation underwent during this period of the hegemony of Babylonian culture, and offers no comment on whether the character of Deuteronomy, which he himself so persuasively epitomizes as a book of 'memory making', may reflect the threat to the survival of national identity that exile and life in the

---

[61] He quotes as offering an analogy an observation by Helmut Lethen about the period between the two world wars: *Verhaltenslehren der Kälte. Lebensversuche zwischen den Kriegen* (Frankfurt a.M., 1994), 7: 'In such disorganized times, when the fabric of tradition disintegrates, and morality loses its persuasive force, codes of conduct are required that enable people to distinguish between what belongs to them and to others, between inside and outside. They make it possible to distinguish zones in which people can feel confidence from those where they feel distrust, and help them to establish their identity.'

environment of Babylonian would have occasioned. The book's 'counterfactual' or 'oppositional' character and its preoccupation with Israel's 'cultural memory', to which he draws special attention, its brooding fear of encroachment—these and other features of the book reveal a zealous endeavour to withstand circumstances of drastic change with which, there is every indication, its authors and those whom they addressed were confronted. Are not such leading features of Deuteronomy, features which make Deuteronomy Deuteronomy, so to speak, more plausibly accounted for by the conditions of exile, which were corrosive of social and cultural identity and inheritance and threatened a creeping assimilation?

This goes also for the 'depoliticizing' of Israel which Assmann identifies, in my opinion rightly, as a leading feature of Deuteronomy, an 'internal culture' with its own distinctive designation of Israel as 'the people of YHWH' and, adopting a familial description, a community of 'brothers' through 'adherence to "the law and the prophets"'. As noted above, he views this feature of the book as a development within the larger framework of the Persian empire, and attributes it to the Jewish community of Persian Transeuphratene who were 'concerned with purity of life, teaching, and interpretation, whilst delegating the management of worldly affairs to the Persian occupying power'. But why would such an 'internal culture', with its distinctive nomenclature, not have emerged much earlier and among the Judaean exiles under the impact of 'the hegemony of Babylonian culture' on which Assmann places due emphasis? In the matter of the rule and governance of an imperial power, to which 'the management of worldly affairs' could be delegated, there could scarcely have been any distinction between the Jewish community of fifth-century Persian Transeuphratene and the Judaean exiles marched away from their homeland by the imperial might of Babylonia. Does it not seem likely that the calamitous end of the Judaean state in the wake of its reckless involvement in the international power-struggles of the time, and the ruinous outcome of this in the events of the early sixth century, would have generated an 'internal culture' that identified itself theologically as 'the people of YHWH' and socially as a community of 'brothers', and resigned 'the management of worldly affairs' to the ruling imperial regime? Why would an endeavour to create a new self-awareness salvaging national identity not have asserted itself from an early stage among those who were now stateless, landless, deprived of their ancient citizenship, and for many of whom the temptingly easy possibility would have suggested itself of 'ridding themselves of all their burdensome problems at a stroke by turning their backs on the muddled history of their own people and immersing themselves in the ethnic mosaic of the Babylonian Empire'?[62] Similarly, why should an appeal to national 'brotherhood' offering a means to cohesion as a way of fortifying and sustaining societal structures and communal bonds that had been violently fractured not have suggested itself to the generations of exiles during the long years of Babylonian hegemony? And if the conception of Israel as a 'depoliticized' 'internal culture' was a development of the homeland community in the post-exilic satrapy of Transeuphratene, in what way did an earlier, and as Assmann himself suggests, significant exilic stage in the book's development characterize the exiled Israelite society to whom its authors addressed themselves?

A further observation suggests itself concerning the recon-ceptualizing of Israel as an 'internal culture' with its distinctive terms of communal identity. Arising from the book's conspicuous concern with encroachment, such terms amount to an expression not only of a 'depoliticized' Israel, but also reflect the sharp dissonance between Deuteronomy's 'vision' of Israel and the social reality of its authors' time, which was evidently characterized by trends inimical to national survival that were fostered, not by foreigners and 'outsiders', but within the Israelite community itself, that is, by 'indigenous out-siders' whose evident influence in the community, if left unchecked, would result in cultural eclipse. It is against such a background of mounting cultural mutation that a further prominent feature of Deuteronomy is most plausibly understood—the *choice* that it ardently lays before Israel. The rationale of the covenant, so central a feature of Deuteronomy, is choice, YHWH's choice of Israel but also Israel's choice of YHWH:[63] 'You have declared this day concerning the Lord that he is your God . . . and the Lord has declared this day concerning you that you are a people for his own possession' (Deut. 26: 17–18). It finds expression in the insistent, pleading style of the book, and is reinforced by the admonitions 'remember', 'do

---

[62] Albertz, *Israel in Exile*, 105.

[63] For this see Ernest Nicholson, *God and His People: Covenant and Theology in the Old Testament* (Oxford, 1986), ch. 10 and esp. pp. 215–17. See also Chapter 4, 'The Legacy of the Prophets in the Deuteronomic Corpus', pp. 97–8.

not forget', 'do not forsake', which contribute significantly to the character of the book, as well as by the elaborate 'memory technique' and procedures, to which Assmann draws special attention. The urgency of the choice that Israel is solemnly summoned to make is memorably captured in the following passage, whether or not it belongs to an earlier or later stage in the composition of the book:

If your heart turns away, and you will not hear, but are drawn away to worship other gods and serve them, I declare to you this day that you shall perish; you shall not live long in the land which you are going over the Jordan to enter and possess. I call heaven and earth to witness against you this day, that I have set before you life and death, blessing and curse; therefore choose life, that you and your descendants may live, loving the Lord your God, obeying his voice, and cleaving to him; that means life to you and length of days, that you may dwell in the land which the Lord swore to your fathers, to Abraham, to Isaac, and to Jacob, to give them. (Deut. 30: 17–20)

Such blessing-or-curse, life-or-death 'choosing' suggests a society whose members are no longer identified solely by genealogical descent, or tribal or clan affiliation, but also by commitment to and the fulfilling of prescribed norms and goals, which are enshrined in 'the book of the *torah*'.[64] Here indeed is a striking departure from state and nationhood, with their attendant institutions, and from a close identity between deity and nation, viewed as self-evident, built into national identity. Choice and commitment to God, individual and communal life given identity and shaped by 'the book of the *torah*', which daily life is commanded to internalize—these signal a newly envisaged society constructed 'as a community of learning and remembering', an aspect of Jewish identity 'that has been absolutely central to the present day'[65] and that emerged and took shape in the community of the Judaean exiles in Babylonia in the sixth century BCE.

---

[64] For social status that is 'achieved' rather than 'ascribed', see H. Eilberg-Schwartz, *The Savage in Judaism: An Anthropology of Israelite Religion in Ancient Judaism* (Bloomington, IN, 1990), who employs it to characterize the essential difference between the priestly community and the early Christian community. For their applicability to Deuteronomy, see Mayes, 'Deuteronomy 14 and the Deuteronomic World View', in F. García Martínez *et al.* (eds.), *Studies in Deuteronomy in Honour of C. J. Labuschagne on the Occasion of his 65th Birthday* (Leiden, New York, and Cologne, 1994), 165–81.

[65] Assmann, *Religion and Cultural Memory*, 19.

Nothing makes it clearer that Deuteronomy did not emerge merely in response to an interim situation, as the compositional deposit, so to speak, of 'survival strategies' in an alien environment pending a return home to reconstitute society, nationhood, and statehood. For many among the waves of Judaean exiles of the early sixth century, among whom were the political, religious, and intellectual elite of the nation, the notion of an interim sojourn in Babylonia would have worn thin and faded with the passing of the years—all too humanly so—and for their children and grandchildren would not have been a realistic option on which to plan their future. In contrast to those whose focus was upon a restored Judaean community re-established in the land and centring upon a rebuilt temple, those to whom we owe the book of Deuteronomy confronted the reality that there was now emerging a permanent Judaean Diaspora for whom life and livelihood in Babylonia had taken, or was taking, root, whose stateless existence and status as a social underclass was corrosive of cultural identity and innovative of a hybrid ethos that, left unchallenged and unchecked, was a significant stride towards assimilation, with all that this entailed. The leading features of the book reflect a determined resistance to such threatened loss. It is of course history that, as prophets foretold and as many kept on hoping and believing, there was indeed eventually a return to the homeland, in more than one wave, from the late sixth century into the fifth. It is also history, however, that many remained where several generations of their forebears had lived and thrived, constituting a community of Judaeans, secure and confident enough to remain as a distinctive ethnic and cultural entity in Babylonian society and subsequently under Persian imperial rule and governance.[66]

A rethinking of the provenance of Deuteronomy should therefore include in its agenda a consideration of ways in which the book reflects other long-term theological and social norms and institutions born of, and indicative of, the religious, spiritual, and moral needs of the many Judaeans who regarded themselves as a permanent Diaspora community. Such is, for example, and as many have agreed, the commandment for the observance of the Sabbath day (vv. 12–15), upon which Deuteronomy's presentation of the

---

[66] See the discussion of this by Becking, ' "We All Returned as One!" ', 3–18.

Decalogue places special emphasis,[67] and which, as suggested above, has every appearance of having been conceived among the exiles as a distinctive way of expressing and conserving the community's cultural and social identity. Such also is the so-called 'name theology' so distinctive of Deuteronomy. It represents an advance from an older symbolism of divine dwelling, and was probably a theological development in the wake of the destruction of the temple in 587 BCE.[68] It finds classic expression in the prayer of Solomon (1 Kgs 8: 29, 30, 35, etc.), where the prayers of the exiles made in the direction of the ruined temple are heard by YHWH whose presence transcends the temple (cf. 1 Kgs 8: 27). To these should be added the significance attached to prophecy in Deut. 18: 9–22, which narrates the promise by God at Sinai of a succession of prophets like Moses, here declared as the first of the prophets. Such a succession prompts the question whether this short pericope already presupposes a corpus of prophetic literature taking shape as 'scripture' alongside the emergent *torah*.[69] Understood in such a way, Deut. 18: 9–22 would provide further evidence of a decisive step towards a religion that is 'scripture centred', quite in line with Assmann's suggestion that in Deuteronomy Israel is 'constructed as a community of learning and remembering'.

In such ways, and responding to historical events and circumstances that had overtaken inherited religious practice and symbolism, the thinking and teaching of the authors of Deuteronomy reflect a shift from Israelite religion and institutions of the pre-exilic period to the antecedents of post-exilic Judaism. The book thus sheds light not only upon the travail for cultural and national survival in the wake of the calamitous upheavals of the early sixth

---

[67] See N. Lohfink, 'Zur Dekalogfassung von Dt 5', who argues that the structure of the Decalogue in Deut. 5 has the effect of presenting the Sabbath command as central to the Decalogue and not simply as its fourth commandment. Cf. also Mayes, *Deuteronomy*, 164–5.

[68] See T. N. D. Mettinger, *The Dethronement of Sabaoth: Studies in the Shem and Kabod Theologies*, ConBOT 18 (Lund, 1982). See also R. E. Clements, *God and Temple* (Oxford, 1965), and his more recent 'A Dialogue with Gordon McConville on Deuteronomy: l. The Origins of Deuteronomy: What Are the Clues?', *SJT* 56 (2003), 508–16, and 'The Deuteronomic Law of the Centralisation and the Catastrophe of 587 B.C.E.', in J. Barton and D. J. Reimer (eds.), *After the Exile: Essays in Honour of Rex Mason* (Macon, GA, 1996), 5–25, esp. 14–20. For a more recent discussion see M. Hundley, 'To Be or Not to Be: A Reexamination of the Name Language in Deuteronomy and the Deuteronomistic History', *VT* 59 (2009), 533–55.

[69] For a consideration of such a possibility, see the Chapter 4.

century, but also upon the gap in our knowledge of the period between Deutero-Isaiah and Nehemiah.[70]

A number of issues have arisen in this and the foregoing chapter that require further consideration, especially the significance of kingship in Deut. 17: 14–20; what light its contents may shed upon other features of the book, such as its 'depoliticizing' of Israel; and whether it may offer any evidence of a Josianic background for the first stage of its composition, that is, as some have argued, an Assyrian background to the book's earliest formulation. I begin, however, with the pericope on prophecy in 18: 9–22, and specifically with the question whether this pericope offers evidence of the emergence of a corpus of prophetic literature as scripture alongside 'the book of the *torah*'.

---

[70] See L. Perlitt, 'Hebraismus—Deuteronomismus—Judaismus', in *Deuteronomium-Studien*, FAT 8, (Tübingen, 1994), 245–60. Cf. also T. Veijola, 'Die Deuteronomisten als Vorgänger der Schriftgelehrten. Ein Beitrag zur Entstehung des Judentums', in id., *Moses Erben. Studien zum Dekalog, zum Deuteronomismus und zum Schriftgelehrtentum*, BWANT 149 (Stuttgart, 2000), 192–240.

4

Deuteronomy, the Prophets, and Scripture

Deuteronomy's instruction (Deut. 6: 6–9; 11: 18–20), so fervently expressed, concerning learning and meditating upon the words of the *torah*, which are to be 'upon the heart' of every Israelite, persistently talked about, taught in the family, personally and publically displayed—in a phrase, permeating daily life[1]—is itself indicative of the authority which these authors claimed and commanded for 'the book of the law'. Deuteronomy has thus been recognized as a first step in the emergence of a growing corpus of writings which during the centuries that followed, though with variation in content from one Jewish community to another, constituted for each a body of scripture.[2] It is widely agreed among scholars, however, that other books in the Old Testament display a greater or lesser involvement of Deuteronomic authors and redactors in their composition and

---

[1] See R. D. Nelson, *Deuteronomy: A Commentary*, OTL (London, 2002), 91–2, who writes of a 'double merismus of place and time' in v. 7 adding up 'to "always and everywhere"'.

[2] Though they carried authority for the communities that inherited them or in which they originated, the description 'canon/canonical' is incorrect as a description of such collections. The notion of a 'canon' was a development of the early Christian centuries, and in so far as it was known in Judaism of this period it was employed for the Pentateuch alone, to which, the evidence suggests, no one felt free to add. On the distinction between 'scripture' and 'canon' see A. C. Sundberg Jr, 'The Bible Canon and the Christian Doctrine of Inspiration', *Interpretation*, 29 (1975), 352–71, who writes (p. 356) that 'scripture' designates 'writings that are regarded as in some sense authoritative', whilst 'canon' designates 'a closed collection of scripture to which nothing can be added, nothing subtracted'. On the issues involved in the 'canon v. scripture' debate, see esp. J. Barton, '"The Law and the Prophets": Who Were the Prophets?', *OtSt* 23 (1984), 1–18, now repr. in his *The Old Testament: Canon, Literature, and Theology* (Aldershot, 2007), 5–18; *Oracles of God: Perceptions of Ancient Prophecy in Israel after the Exile*, 2nd revised edn. (Oxford, 2007), esp. chs. 1 and 2; and his 'The Old Testament Canons', forthcoming in Joachim Schaper and James Carleton Paget (eds.), *The Cambridge History of the Bible*.

literary growth. The Deuteronomistic corpus, for which the leading theological themes and features of Deuteronomy provide the purpose and thrust, is the most substantial, but it is well known that a number of prophetic books bear the stamp of Deuteronomistic redaction and *Fortschreibung*, among them, and most extensively, Jeremiah. Such interest in what we refer to as the 'classical prophets' is of a piece with the significance attached to prophets and prophecy in the Deuteronomistic corpus itself, and it raises the question of whether these authors may be attributed with conjoining an assemblage of these prophetic writings as a body of scripture alongside of 'the book of the *torah*'.

A further reason for considering such a possibility is suggested by comments of Jan Assmann on the cultural crisis that the Babylonian exile brought about. As noted earlier,[3] he writes of the upheaval of deportation, the breach in social bonds that exile inflicts, and the threat of a disintegration of tradition understood as 'lived knowledge . . . that is passed on in active association with others . . . a form of knowledge that is largely self-evident and that has become unconscious and implicit'.[4] In such a situation, he suggests, in which 'the contact with living models is broken, people turn to the texts in their search for guidance', adding that in such circumstances 'we find not only that new texts emerge, but also that already existing texts are given an enhanced normative value' (p. 69). In these comments Assmann has in mind the emerging 'book of the *torah*', with its concern for the revival and assertion of a normative Israelite tradition as constitutive of its very identity and thus of its survival, so threatened by the circumstances of exile. The question is prompted, however: does it not seem likely that among the 'already existing texts' which in these perilous circumstances were 'given an enhanced normative value' the writings of some of the so-called 'classical prophets' were included?

In what follows[5] I shall argue that a consideration of the references in the Deuteronomistic corpus to God's 'servants the prophets', and the warnings of judgement they are described as having announced, together with evidence adduced from some of the prophetic books

---

[3] See Chapter 3, 'The Provenance of Deuteronomy', p. 67.

[4] J. Assmann, *Religion and Cultural Memory* (Stanford, CA, 2006), 69.

[5] With some revision and supplementation, what follows was first published in J. Day (ed.), *Prophecy and the Prophets in Ancient Israel: Proceedings of the Oxford Old Testament Seminar* (London, 2010), 151–71.

proper offers persuasive reasons for believing that such a body of prophetic scripture did indeed begin to emerge alongside of, and complementary to, 'the book of the *torah*'.

GOD'S 'SERVANTS THE PROPHETS': WHOM HAD THE DEUTERONOMISTIC AUTHORS IN MIND?

Deuteronomy devotes more attention to prophecy—its foundation at Horeb/Sinai (18: 9–22), its purpose, and its potential for abuse— than to any other national institution or office, including even kingship (17: 14–20). The authors of the Deuteronomistic corpus also assign a distinct role to prophets and prophecy. It was YHWH's 'servants the prophets' who were commissioned to summon Israel to repentance and obedience to the *torah*, and who are said to have announced the judgement upon Israel and Judah which came in the cataclysmic events of 722 and 587 BCE:

> The Lord had warned Israel and Judah by every prophet and seer: Turn from your evil ways and keep my commandments and statutes according to the whole law which I commanded your fathers and which I have sent to you by my servants the prophets. (2 Kgs 17: 13–14; cf. 17: 23; 21: 10; 24: 2)

Such a text reminds us immediately of the promise in Deut. 18: 15–18 of the prophets[6] whom YHWH would appoint in

---

[6] Later Jewish tradition interpreted the promise in Deut. 18:15 eschatologically as referring to 'that prophet who should come', and, differently, Sirach 46: 1 describes Joshua as 'the successor of Moses in the prophetic office', an interpretation that has its modern advocates (e.g. H. M. Barstad 'The Understanding of the Prophets in Deuteronomy', *SJOT* 8 (1994), 236–51; G. M. H. Ratheiser, *Mitzvoth Ethics and the Jewish Bible: The End of Old Testament Theology*, LHBOTS 460 (New York and London, 2007), 275–91; B. Štrba, *Take Off Your Sandals From Your Feet! An Exegetical Study of Josh 5, 13–15*, Österreichische Biblische Studien, 32 (Frankfurt a.M., 2008), 197–8, 261–4 *et passim*). The majority of modern commentators, however, understand that the promise in this text is to meet a continuous and permanent need of the people to know the will of God when they settle in the land of Canaan (v. 9), and that the singular 'prophet' here thus refers to a series of prophets (just as, for example, the singular 'king' in 17: 14 refers to a succession of kings). The context is one in which these promised prophets and not practitioners of the various mantic practices listed in vv. 9–14 are the mediators of YHWH's will; the distributive understanding of the word is also confirmed by the warning against the danger of the (false) 'prophet who speaks presumptuously' in YHWH's name, which can scarcely refer to a single occurrence of this phenomenon but to any and all such prophets.

succession to Moses, and the inference is warranted that the author or editor who penned these texts intended by 'my servants the prophets' the sequence of prophets promised in that text. But who were these prophets referred to in 2 Kgs 17: 13–14? Similarly, when a few verses later 2 Kgs 17: 23 refers to the judgement that had been announced by YHWH 'through all his servants the prophets' (cf. also 2 Kgs 21: 10–12; 24: 1–3), which prophets might this general description 'my servants the prophets' have had in mind?

Elsewhere the phrase 'my/his servants the prophets' occurs in texts that can be generally described as 'distanced reflections' on past prophecy epitomized as having announced judgement upon Israel/Judah, judgement that has since struck (Amos 3: 7; Ezek. 38: 17).[7] Sharing the same character are several texts in prose passages in the book of Jeremiah (7: 25; 25: 4; 26: 5; 29: 19; 35: 15; 44: 4). Here too there is a degree of 'distanced reflection' on an ostensibly long history of the announcement of judgement by 'my/his servants the prophets', who according to Jer. 7: 25 were active 'since the day that your fathers came out of the land of Egypt unto this day', as though they constituted an unbroken succession.

The similarity between these texts in Amos, Jeremiah, and Ezekiel and the Deuteronomistic texts recounting the testimony of YHWH's 'servants the prophets' against Israel/Judah (2 Kgs 17: 13–14; 17: 23; 21: 10; 24: 2) is evident. Here too in Kings the history of prophecy in Israel and Judah is précised and invoked in an almost stereotypical manner in explaining the disaster that overtook, first the Northern Kingdom of Israel, and subsequently Judah: 'The Lord banished Israel out of his sight, as he had threatened by his servants the prophets. So Israel was carried into exile from their own land to Assyria, and are there to this day' (2 Kgs 17: 23; cf. 24: 1–4). It is generally agreed that the texts in Amos, Jeremiah, and Ezekiel show Deuteronomistic influence, whether direct or indirect,[8] and it might therefore be deduced from this that the referent of the phrase

---

[7] On Zech. 1: 2–6 see Chapter 4, 'The Background to the Composition of Deuteronomy 18: 9–22', p. 92.

[8] On Amos 3: 7 see H. W. Wolff, *Joel and Amos* (Philadelphia, 1977), 181, 187–8. For Ezek. 38: 17, which alone in the book employs the phrase 'my servants the prophets', see W. Zimmerli *Ezekiel 2: A Commentary on the Book of Ezekiel Chapters 25–48* (Philadelphia, 1983), 312, who regards the verse as a secondary addition to the basic material of this chapter. P. M. Joyce, *Ezekiel: A Commentary*, LHBOTS 482 (New York, 2008), 10–11 (cf. 213–15) attributes it to Deuteronomistic influence upon Ezekiel himself.

YHWH's 'servants the prophets' is so-called 'old prophecy' represented by such figures as Samuel, Ahijah, and others who are
prominent in the narratives of Samuel–Kings. That, with the
exception of Isaiah, none of the 'canonical' prophets is mentioned
in the books of Kings lends prima facie support to such an inference.
But such a limitation of the connotation of the phrase strains
credulity.

First, it is difficult to imagine that the authors/editors responsible
for the texts in Amos, Jeremiah, and Ezekiel excluded these prophets
themselves from the company of YHWH's 'servants the prophets'
to which they refer. Secondly, and more importantly, it does not
seem at all likely that 'old prophecy' was a source of the notion of a
cataclysmic judgement by the national God upon Israel/Judah such
as these various texts presuppose. Among the prophetic figures who
are representative of 'old prophecy', only Ahijah at the foundation of
the northern state of Israel announces judgement on such a scale
upon this newly founded kingdom: 'For the Lord will strike Israel, till
it trembles like a reed in the water; he will uproot its people from this
good land which he gave to their forefathers and scatter them beyond
the Euphrates . . . because of the sins of Jeroboam' (1 Kgs 14: 15–16).
There cannot be any doubt, however, that this is to be attributed to
the Deuteronomistic editor of these narratives, who already here at
this earliest of stages in the history of the two kingdoms registers
inexorable doom upon the northern state on account of the 'sins
of Jeroboam'. In only two other texts in Kings is judgement on this
scale announced—Isaiah's prophecy in 2 Kgs 20: 17 of the sacking
of Jerusalem and the exile of Hezekiah's descendants by the
Babylonians in 'days to come', and Huldah's oracle announcing
the 'unquenchable anger' of YHWH against Judah following the
discovery of 'the book of the *torah*' (2 Kgs 22: 15–20).

Such a record of the declaration of judgement scarcely furnishes
the testimony of prophetic preaching against Israel/Judah that 2 Kgs
17: 23 and 24: 2–4 reflect. These texts give the impression that for
their author(s) a more substantive message of judgement lay behind
the catastrophes that overwhelmed Israel and Judah and brought the
exile than these three texts in the Deuteronomistic corpus convey.
We make sense of the Deuteronomistic epitome of the prophetic
announcement of judgement against Israel and Judah, as also of the
similar texts cited above, only if we understand the referent of the
phrase 'my/his servants the prophets' to embrace some at least of

the line of prophets from the eighth century onwards beginning with Amos, whose radical message of judgement announced doom upon Israel. The oracle editorially placed on the lips of Ahijah, the prophecy of Isaiah in 2 Kgs 20: 17, which cannot have been composed earlier than 598 BCE,[9] and Huldah's oracle, which bears the imprint of Deuteronomistic redaction, do not by themselves offer a credible alternative.

THE CALL OF JEREMIAH AND THE PROPHETS OF DEUTERONOMY 18: 9–22

These considerations prompt the question of whether the author of Deut. 18: 9–22 had in mind some of the 'canonical' prophets as being among the prophets whom YHWH here promises to raise up. Among features of the text that might lend support to such a suggestion is the clause 'I will put my words in his mouth and he shall speak to them all that I command him' (v. 8), which immediately reminds us of the commissioning of Jeremiah as narrated in the account of his call: 'Then the Lord put forth his hand and touched my mouth; and the Lord said to me, "I have put my words in your mouth"' (Jer. 1: 9). This in turn raises the further question, however, of which text influenced the other, since commentators generally have attributed priority to Deuteronomy and in more recent research have found evidence of extensive Deuteronomistic redaction in the book of Jeremiah, which prima facie supports dependency of the call narrative in its present form upon the text in Deuteronomy.[10]

The narrative of the call of Jeremiah (Jer 1: 4–19) is a compilation comprising an account of the call and commissioning of Jeremiah

---

[9] M. Cogan and H. Tadmor, *II Kings: A New Translation with Introduction and Commentary*, Anchor Bible 11 (Garden City, NY, 1988), 262–3 date vv. 17–19 to the period of Babylonian hegemony over Judah 598–587, and point out (p. 259) that the language of the criticism of Hezekiah here is strikingly akin to the book of Jeremiah.

[10] This is the view I argued in my monograph *Preaching to the Exiles: A Study of the Prose Tradition in the Book of Jeremiah* (Oxford, 1970), 113–15. Research since then has shown, however, that the redaction of Deuteronomy, including its central law section, is more complex and expansive than hitherto perceived. One result of this is that it can no longer be assumed that a passage in Jeremiah bearing a resemblance to one in Deuteronomy is necessarily dependent upon the latter.

in vv. 4–10 to which other originally independent units have been attached (vv. 11–12, 13–16, 17–19).[11] W. McKane considers the narrative, including the account of the call proper in vv. 4–10, to be among of the latest in the book and, indeed, 'built out of a book of Jeremiah already in existence' (p. 25), and providing a sort of résumé of Jeremiah's prophetic ministry, an estimate of Jeremiah after he has 'run his course' (p. 14). We shall have to return later to this estimate of the narrative. Important for our present purposes is McKane's suggestion that if 'we are searching for a prototype for הנה נתתי דברי בפיך ['I have now put my words in your mouth'] the poetry of 5.14 הנה נתתי דברי בפיך לאש ['I shall make my words like fire in your mouth'] is a likely candidate' (p. 13). That is, the assumption that the phrase 'I have now put my words in your mouth' is derived from Deut. 18: 18 is unnecessary. Independently of McKane, Werner H. Schmidt sees in Jer. 5: 14 evidence that the phrase 'I have now put my words in your mouth' is firmly anchored in imagery original to the book of Jeremiah.[12] This is further evidenced by the testimony of some of the 'confessions' (15: 16; 17: 15; 20: 8–9); in this latter text (v. 9) the imagery of YHWH's word being 'like fire' is found again, as also in the polemic against false prophecy in 23: 29: 'Is not my word like fire, says the Lord, and like a hammer which breaks the rock in pieces?'

All this suggests that the phrase in Deut. 18: 18, 'I will put my words in his mouth', is more probably derived from the narrative of Jeremiah's call rather than being the source of it. Commenting upon the immediately following phrase in Deut. 18: 18—'and he shall speak to them all that I command him'—Schmidt further plausibly suggests that this phrase too is more likely to be derivative of the similar parallel construction in Jer. 1: 7—'to all to whom I send you, you shall go, and whatever I command you, you shall speak'—than vice versa.[13]

There is still further evidence of the influence of the book of Jeremiah upon the composition of Deut 18: 9–22, in this instance

[11] For details see W. McKane, *A Critical and Exegetical Commentary on Jeremiah*, Vol. I, ICC (Edinburgh, 1986), 1–25.

[12] W. H. Schmidt, 'Das Prophetengessetz Dtn 18:9–22 im Kontext erzählender Literatur', in M. Vervenne and J. Lust (eds.), *Deuteronomy and Deuteronomic Literature. Festschrift C. H. W. Brekelmans*, BETL 133 (Leuven, 1997), 61–2.

[13] See W. H. Schmidt, *Das Buch Jeremia: Kapitel 1–20*, ATD 20 (Göttingen, 2008), 47–8.

the warning in v. 20 against false prophecy: 'the prophet who speaks a word presumptuously in my name which I have not commanded him to speak . . . that same prophet shall die.' Though we know of false prophecy in the pre-exilic period from such texts as Mic. 3, Hos. 4: 5(?), Isa. 28: 7–13, there is no recorded incident of inner-prophetic conflict centring upon this issue in the Deuteronomistic corpus,[14] and no narrative of anyone either being accused and condemned to death or dying by direct divine intervention as a *poseur* 'arrogantly presuming' to speak in YHWH's name what he has not been called and commissioned to speak.

The evidence strongly suggests that it was in the closing years of the kingdom of Judah that an inner-prophetic struggle on the issue of true and false prophecy erupted on a new and, as far as we know, unprecedented scale of intensity. Lam. 2: 14 tersely condemns those prophets who 'have seen false and deceptive visions . . . who have not exposed your iniquity to restore your fortunes, but have seen for you oracles false and misleading'. Ezek. 13 announces judgement against the prophets 'who prophesy out of their own hearts and according to what they have not seen' (v. 3). But at once the most extensive and also the most intensive coverage of this issue is found in the book of Jeremiah (5: 30–1; 6: 9–15; 14: 11–16; 23: 9–32; chs. 27, 28, 29). Both the concern and the gravity with which Deut. 18: 20 views the problem of false prophecy are here amply represented.[15]

The issue came to a head in the confrontation between Jeremiah and his prophetic opponents in the politically highly charged years that led up to the Babylonian onslaught upon Jerusalem in 587 BCE and the end of the Judaean state, and those to whom we owe the extant book of Jeremiah dwelt upon this theme, which has even been worked into narratives where it originally did not belong (chs. 27,

---

[14] The episode narrated in 1 Kgs 22 is not such an example, since the source of the falsehood here is not 'presumption' on the part of Zedekiah ben Chenaanah and the prophets with him but rather a 'lying spirit' from among the 'host of heaven' who is commissioned by YHWH to go and 'entice' Ahab to a disastrous strategy through the words of the unwitting Zedekiah ben Chenaanah.

[15] For detailed analyses of these texts and discussion of the theme of false prophecy in Jeremiah see McKane, *A Critical and Exegetical Commentary on Jeremiah*, Vol. II (Edinburgh, 1996), pp. cxxxiv–cxl, and Vols. I and II ad loc.; F. L. Hossfeld and I. Meyer, *Prophet gegen Prophet. Eine Analyse der alttestamentlichen Texte zum Thema: Wahre und Falsche Propheten*, Biblische Beiträge 9, Schweizerisches Katholisches Bibelwerk (Freiburg, 1977); I. Meyer, *Jeremia und die falschen Propheten*, OBO 13 (Fribourg and Göttingen, 1977).

28, 29).[16] For our immediate purposes the proposal is justified that the concern with false prophecy in Deuteronomy 18 is more plausibly understood as presupposing and reflecting the expansive treatment of this issue and theme in the book of Jeremiah rather than being the source or stimulus of what amounts to one of the preoccupations of those to whom we owe the book of Jeremiah.

The fate of the self-styled prophet in Deut. 18: 20 is itself evidence of this, for though death is declared for false prophets, there is no prescription of execution, whether by the state or the local community. It seems rather that the decreed penalty is overseen by YHWH directly, so to speak, just as in the case of anyone who does not obey the words of the prophets sent by YHWH it is written that YHWH himself will 'require it of him' (v. 19). We are immediately reminded of the fate of the prophet Hananiah, whose imminent death is announced in an oracle by Jeremiah (Jer. 28: 16) and who, we are told, 'died the same year in the seventh month'.[17] Others too are similarly condemned as false prophets by Jeremiah, and their fate likewise decreed through the prophet and overseen by YHWH— Shemaiah the Nehelamite, the civic leader of the exiles, who is to be without descendants among future generations (29: 31–2), and Ahab and Zedekiah who, we are told, were delivered by YHWH into the hands of Nebuchadrezzar for execution on account both of their acts of adultery and also because 'they spoke words falsely in my name, which I did not command them' (vv. 21–3).

From the evidence outlined in the foregoing paragraphs of the dependence of Deut. 18: 9–22 upon the book of Jeremiah the inference is warranted that for its author Jeremiah was among the prophets promised at Horeb. Such a conclusion is consonant with texts in the book of Jeremiah, again especially sayings and narratives of a Deuteronomistic stamp, in which Jeremiah belongs to the company and succession of YHWH's 'servants the prophets' whom he had been sending to his people 'since the day that your fathers came out of the land of Egypt unto this day'. The referent of the promise of prophets in Deut. 18: 9–22 is accordingly this much broader at least than the impression given by the Deuteronomistic corpus, where the story of so-called 'old prophecy' predominates, almost exclusively so.

---

[16] On the secondary nature of the theme of false prophecy in these chapters, see McKane, *Jeremiah*, Vol. I. ad loc.

[17] See Schmidt, 'Das Prophetengessetz Dtn 18:9–22', 62–3.

THE EIGHTH-CENTURY PROPHETS

Such a conclusion in turn suggests the possibility that the author of this passage had still other prophets in view, and here the eighth-century predecessors of Jeremiah come immediately to mind. Not least in favour of this is the evidence of the influence of the preaching of these prophets in a number of ways upon Jeremiah and upon those to whom we owe the book of Jeremiah.[18] There can be little doubt that Jeremiah saw himself as standing in the tradition of these prophets of doom, whether or not the well-known saying to Hananiah in 28: 8 can be attributed to him: 'The prophets who preceded you and me from ancient times prophesied war, famine, and pestilence against many countries and great kingdoms.'

Accordingly, since Isaiah alone among the canonical prophets is accorded a place in the Deuteronomist's narrative of Kings (2 Kgs 18: 13–20: 19), and since the collection of oracles bearing his name has undergone a certain amount of Deuteronomistic editing, we can include him alongside Jeremiah among the prophets whom the author of the pericope in Deut. 18: 9–22 had in mind, and with Isaiah also Micah, who is mentioned and quoted in Jer. 26: 17–19, which, citing his words of judgement against Jerusalem (Mic. 3: 12), depicts him as a forerunner of Jeremiah. We can with confidence also allow that Amos too would have been included by the author of Deut. 18: 9–22, since a Deuteronomistic editor has placed him among the company of YHWH's 'servants the prophets' (Amos 3: 7), and the same hand has placed on Amos's lips the accusation in Amos 2: 11–12: 'I raised up (ואקים) some of your sons for prophets . . . but you commanded the prophets "do not prophesy"'—which, since Amos was expelled by Amaziah from Bethel, reinforces the inclusion of Amos among these prophets whom YHWH 'raised up', the same verb 'I raised up' (ואקים) being employed as in Deut. 18: 15, 18.[19] Hosea too can plausibly be included: the book that bears his name shares with Amos, Micah, and Isaiah a Deuteronomistic superscription. More importantly are the many and often-cited

---

[18] For this evidence see Schmidt's helpful summary *Das Buch Jeremia*, 9–12, where also additional bibliography relating to this is provided (see esp. p. xiii).

[19] On Amos 2: 10–12 see Wolff, *Joel and Amos*, 169–70.

connections between traditions and themes in Hosea's preaching
and the traditions and theological teaching of Deuteronomy.[20]
If such an analysis is justified—I shall return to it later—and these
prophets are among the promised prophets of Deut. 18: 18, it raises
the further question of whether this pericope already presupposes
an emergent scripture embracing not only 'the book of the *torah*',
which already has such a standing in the Deuteronomistic corpus
(cf. Deut. 17: 18–20; Josh. 1: 8), but also a core collection of prophetic
books.[21] A consideration of this calls first, however, for some further
comments upon the character of Deut. 18: 9–22.

From our examination of this pericope it seems clear that it does
not belong to the 'statutes and ordinances' of Deuteronomy;[22] it is
not *sensu stricto* legislation or customary law, since it prescribes no
penalties to be imposed, whether by the state or the local community.
Instead, as we have seen, punishment appears to be directly visited
upon offenders by YHWH. This is the case also with the peroration
about the various 'repugnant' ritual and mantic practices listed in
vv. 9–13. Here too no civic penalty is prescribed, whether for those
skilled in such techniques and rites or for those who resort to them to
unlock mysteries.[23] Rather, as in the case of false prophets or those
who disobey the words of YHWH's prophets, punishment, in this
case dispossession of the land, comes from YHWH (v. 12), just as
the former occupants of the land were driven out on account of
their practice of these 'abominations'. In the historical situation in

---

[20] See e.g. H. W. Wolff, *Hosea*, Eng. trans. G. Stansell, Hermeneia (Philadelphia, 1974), pp. xxxi–xxxii.

[21] For recent discussions of a possible contribution of a Deuteronomistic 'school' to the beginnings of a corpus of scripture see T. Römer, 'L'École deutéronomiste et la formation de la Bible hébraïque', in T. Römer (ed.), *The Future of the Deuteronomistic History*, BETL 147 (Leuven, 2000), 179–93; J. Vermeylen 'L'École deutéronomiste aurait-elle imaginé un premier canon des Écritures?', in ibid. 223–40. Neither essay discusses Deut. 18: 9–22 in any detail. See also S. Tengström 'Moses and the Prophets in the Deuteronomistic History', *SJOT* 8 (1994), 257–66, esp. 265–6.

[22] Against the widely held view that the passage is part of a written 'polity' comprising 16: 18–18: 22 focusing upon the primary state offices—judge, king, priest, prophet—see Chapter 5, 'Context: A Deuteronomic "Polity" For Israel (Deut. 16: 18–18: 22)?', pp. 103–6.

[23] It is doubtful whether this list was derived from a legal source, since, from the point of view of genre, the passage has neither the form nor the character of a statute outlawing these rituals and practices and prescribing an appropriate penalty. Rather, it has the appearance of an attempt to compile a comprehensive list of these rituals and practices, and may thus have been composed for its present context where it acts as a foil setting off the prophets promised by YHWH as the means of mediating his will to his people.

which the passage was composed, however, this of course was what had happened (cf. 2 Kgs 17: 17; 21: 6), and Judah had been dispossessed of its land and was in exile; similarly, the nation that had not obeyed the prophets whom YHWH had 'raised up' had suffered judgement (Deut. 18: 19), and likewise, delusion had been laid bare and the false prophets who fostered it with their easy words of well-being and security (שׁלום) exposed for what they were.

For the author of this pericope, therefore, who wrote against the background of the catastrophic events of the early sixth century and the exile, the significant voices now were the prophets whom he believed to have been raised up by YHWH, the prophets of doom. He employed the title prophet for Moses,[24] and in so doing placed these prophets apparently on a par with Moses as channels of the divine will to Israel after Moses: as Moses exercised the prophetic role of mediating YHWH's will to Israel, so the promised prophets are to mediate YHWH's word after Moses when Israel is in the land. Put conversely, in conferring the title of prophet upon Moses, the author has apparently bestowed the authority of Moses, the mediator of the *torah*, upon the prophets. The law and the prophets were thus apparently conjoined.

Two issues have emerged that now call for further comment and consideration: first, the claim made immediately above that Deut. 18: 9–22 places 'the *torah*' on a par with 'the prophets'; secondly, and related to this, how credible the suggestion is that this pericope reflects an emerging corpus of prophetic scripture.

THE SCROLL OF THE *TORAH* AND THE SCROLL OF JEREMIAH'S ORACLES

On the first of these issues, I draw attention to the well-known narrative in Jeremiah 36 of the writing down of the prophet's oracles as a

---

[24] The depiction of Moses' role here as a prophet arises from the circumstances at Horeb as described in Deut. 5 (cf. 18: 16), and owes nothing to the allusion to Moses as a prophet in Hos. 12: 14, where the reference is to the exodus rather than to Horeb/ Sinai. The glorifying of Moses at the end of his life (Deut. 34: 10–12) by stressing his incomparability as prophet has the ring of a panegyric death account common in folkloristic literature, and derives from the desire to portray him as a heroic figure; it is not a comment upon Deut. 18: 15, 18 (see R. R. Wilson, *Prophecy and Society in Ancient Israel* (Philadelphia, 1980), 162, n. 52).

dramatic fresh announcement of YHWH's judgement upon Judah, and its subsequent supplementation with other words of Jeremiah as enduring testimony to later generations, that is, its launch as what we would term scripture. What is also striking about this narrative, however, is the close equivalence it draws between this scroll of the prophet's oracles and 'the scroll of the *torah*' in the narrative in 2 Kgs 22.

It is well known that Jeremiah 36 bears significant resemblances to the narrative in 2 Kgs 22 recounting Josiah's reaction to the discovery and reading of 'the scroll of the law': the two scrolls make their public appearance, so to speak, in the temple (2 Kgs 22: 8; Jer. 36: 10), royal officials are involved (2 Kgs 22: 8–10; Jer. 36: 11–13), the reaction of the two kings is narrated (2 Kgs 22: 11–13.; Jer. 36: 23–6), followed by a prophetic oracle (2 Kgs 22: 15–20; Jer. 36: 27–31). That these similarities between the two narratives are not simply coincidental is clear from the pointed contrast drawn between Josiah's penitence on hearing the scroll of the law and Jehoiakim's reaction to the scroll of the prophet's oracles:

And when the king heard the words of the book of the law, *he rent his garments.* (2Kgs 22: 11; cf. v. 19)	But neither the king nor any of his aides who heard all these words was afraid, *nor did they rend their garments.* (Jer. 36: 24)

The impression created is that the behaviour of Jehoiakim and his royal officials is an antitype to that of Josiah and his state officials (שרים).

The LXX preserves elements of an earlier form of the narrative, however, which looks much less like a replication of the narrative in 2 Kgs 22.[25] Thus, instead of the MT's reading פחדו 'they feared' at v. 16 expressing the dread of the officials who read the scroll of Jeremiah's oracles, LXX reads συνεβουλεύσαντο, 'they took counsel with one another', suggesting a Hebrew *Vorlage* ויועצו. That is, the LXX suggests that the assembled royal officials upon hearing the scroll went into session on what advice to give to the king. Again, whilst MT at v. 25 describes Elnathan, Delaiah, and Gemariah as pleading with Jehoiakim not to burn the scroll, in LXX it is narrated that these officials (it reads Gedaliah instead of Delaiah) urged the king to do so. 'This is a case', as McKane concludes, 'where, according

---

[25] For a detailed discussion of the chapter and the relevance of LXX see McKane *Jeremiah*, Vol. II, pp. cxliii–cxlv, 899–921.

to Sept., chapter 36 is better understood as a historical narrative which reports the conflict between Jeremiah and the king's advisers rather than a Deuteronomic narrative which makes the שרים [śārīm] his disciples.'[26]

Conversely, the MT represents a revision of this earlier version of the narrative to yield an account which heightens the depiction of Jehoiakim as the antitype to Josiah. Thus in MT the LXX reading 'they took counsel together' has been replaced by פחדו 'they feared' at v. 16, which is difficult to construe with the phrase that follows איש אל רעהו 'one to another'. The same hand has also added the comment in v. 24 on the lack of piety on the part of Jehoiakim and 'all his aides', whilst this latter phrase 'all his aides (כל עבדיו)', instead of the usual 'all the royal officials (שרים)' (cf. vv. 12, 14, 19), has likewise been introduced to suggest that two groups were involved in the events described, the one in support of Jehoiakim, the other a group of 'closet' sympathizers with Jeremiah who bear names apparently relating them to some of Josiah's pious officials—Micaiah ben Gemariah ben *Shaphan* and Elnathan ben *Achbor* (Jer. 36: 11–12; 2 Kgs 22: 12). The same hand has also edited v. 25 to state that the three officials referred to urged the king not to burn the scroll.

Thus a narrative (LXX) of the measures taken by Jehoiakim on the advice of his 'cabinet' for the avoidance of possible serious unrest as a result of Jeremiah's action, or to counter what they viewed as the defeatism of the contents of the prophet's scroll, has been transformed into one (MT) contrasting the penitence of Josiah upon reading the 'scroll of the law' with Jehoiakim's contemptuous rejection of the scroll of Jeremiah's oracles. The focus of each narrative is the scroll and the fear it evokes or should evoke, and this carries with it the implication that the prophet's scroll has the same divine sanction as the 'scroll of the law' in the narrative of 2 Kgs 22, which the narrative in Jeremiah 36, as reshaped from its earlier content as represented by LXX, replicates so as to depict Jehoiakim as the antitype to Josiah.

Following Jehoiakim's burning of the scroll of Jeremiah's oracles, it was rewritten by Baruch at the dictation of the prophet (v. 32). Perhaps Jehoiakim's action in cutting off two or three columns of writing at a time for destruction in the fire was motivated by a belief that the written form of the oracles of the prophet effects an

---

[26] McKane *Jeremiah*, Vol. II, pp. cxlv, 919.

intensification of the threat they proclaim.[27] By the rewriting of them their special threat is reactivated. Though this may have been the immediate reason for the rewriting of the scroll, however, the phrase at the conclusion of the narrative (36: 32), 'and many like words were added', suggests something further, since it refers to the expansion of the scroll in the years following the events here narrated.[28] The rewriting of the scroll and its supplementation represented also its permanence and endurance as testimony to the word of YHWH spoken by the prophet Jeremiah. That is, the scroll has become scripture to be read and so to instruct, convict, exhort, threaten, and promise in future generations.

A CORPUS OF PROPHETIC SCRIPTURES?

These observations lend further substance to the conclusion argued earlier that the prophet Jeremiah and the book bearing his name were in the mind of the author of Deut. 18: 15–18. They also return us to the suggestion that other prophetic collections familiar to us in the Hebrew Bible were also in the mind of this author, among which those bearing the names of the eighth-century prophets have a good claim prima facie to be included. The question now is: did the scrolls bearing the names of these prophets share the authority and standing of scripture which the narrative in Jeremiah 36 appears to associate with the book of Jeremiah?

Modern research has yielded evidence that renders this altogether likely. This lies in the manner in which the collected oracles and sayings of these prophets were subject to a process of ongoing reinterpretation and reapplication involving insertions and redaction to address changing historical circumstances. Redactors, including Deuteronomistic editors but also others, whom we can rightly describe as prophets, or 'traditionists' with a prophetic

---

[27] See McKane *Jeremiah*, Vol. II 919.

[28] McKane, *Jeremiah*, Vol. II 920 suggests that the scroll was expanded upon its rewriting by Baruch: 'The special threat embodied in a written collection of doom-laden oracles is reconstituted and enlarged by a supplement.' Since it is already narrated (v. 2) that the scroll contained all that the prophet had spoken since his call, however, perhaps the phrase in v. 32, 'many like words were added', more likely refers to the expansion of the scroll in subsequent years to include a record of the prophet's activity during the reign of Zedekiah and up to his abduction to Egypt.

bent, have editorially focused sayings of these figures upon new situations in the changing world of their own day, and have not hesitated to supplement them anonymously with additional sayings or insertions, in this way casting the mantle of the authority of these prophets over their own new message. Evidence of additions and insertions reflecting an exilic background in the books of Amos, Hosea, Micah, and Isaiah offers confirmation of this,[29] and there is further evidence to suggest still earlier, pre-exilic stages of supplementation and redaction.[30]

Such redaction and *Fortschreibung* of the inherited sayings of these prophets was self-evidently not a private matter carried out by bands of disciples, of whom, in any event, we hear nothing, but was in the public domain, as we might put it, in which these prophetic collections evidently carried authority as being revelatory, and were read and heard as scripture—as theodicy, as call to repentance, as exhortation to trust, as warning and threat, as promise. We must presume that the initial impetus for such authority and also for the survival and transmission of their oracles over such a protracted period derived from the historical vindication of what they declared, not least of all in the case of Amos and Hosea whose announcement of judgement upon northern Israel was fulfilled with shocking immediacy. The reinterpretation and application of the oracles of these four prophets in the wake of the events of 587 BCE in terms of judgement and of hope beyond judgement offered both an explanation of these events and also declared the sovereignty of YHWH against any despairing surrender to what seemed to be aimless chance and mere historical contingency. As noted above, Jeremiah is described in Jer. 28: 8 as having identified himself with

---

[29] On Amos see Wolff, *Joel and Amos*, 106–13; on Hosea see Wolff, *Hosea*, 29–31; G. I. Davies, *Hosea*, NCB (London 1992), 34–7; on Isaiah see R. E. Clements, 'The Prophet Isaiah and the Fall of Jerusalem', *VT* 30 (1980), 421–36; id., *Isaiah 1–39*, NCB (London, 1980), 6–8; on Micah see Wolff, *Micha*, BKAT 14:4 (Neukirchen-Vluyn, 1982), pp. xxvii–xxxvi, followed, with some differences, by W. McKane, *The Book of Micah: Introduction and Commentary* (Edinburgh, 1998), 17–21.

[30] For example, sayings have been identified in Isaiah and Amos reflecting the buoyant and confident age of Josiah when the power of Assyria was on the wane. On such material in Isaiah, see H. Barth, *Die Jesaja-Worte in der Josiazeit: Israel und Asssur als Thema einer produktiven Neuinterpretation der Jesaja Überlieferung*, WMANT 48 (Neukirchen-Vluyn, 1977); id., *Isaiah 1–39*: 5–6; J. Vermeylen *Du prophète Isaïe à l'apocalyptique. Isaïe I–XXXV, miroir d'un demi-millénaire d'expérience religieuse en Israël*, Vol. II, Études Bibliques (Paris, 1978), 688–92; for Amos, see Wolff, *Joel and Amos*, 111–12.

the prophets of doom that preceded him, and, on the evidence we have from the Hebrew Bible, these can scarcely have been other than this quartet of eighth-century prophets.

THE BACKGROUND TO THE COMPOSITION OF DEUTERONOMY 18: 9–22

We are led by these observations to the question of the background to the inclusion of this pericope on prophecy and to some further considerations to which this gives rise. The superscriptions to the books of the four eighth-century prophets are usually regarded as Deuteronomistic and need not therefore be later than the exilic period.[31] Since the passage that is the focus of our attention is likewise from a Deuteronomistic hand an exilic background again suggests itself, at least as a *terminus a quo*.

The period in which the author of Deut. 18: 9–22 wrote depends more precisely, however, upon the composition of the call narrative in Jeremiah 1 upon which, as we have seen, it draws. This is a more complex and controversial issue, since the composition of the book of Jeremiah was a protracted process lasting well into the post-exilic period. In particular, McKane has argued that this narrative is among the latest chapters in the book, and is not the work of the prophet himself but was 'built out of a book of Jeremiah already in existence' by editors in the exilic period or more probably, he suggests, the post-exilic period.[32] The allusion in Jer. 1: 5, 10 to the oracles against the nations, which he regards as post-Jeremiah and late, is the main basis for his conclusion.

There is not sufficient space here to discuss this problem in any detail. A counter to it, finding much more of the prophet's hand in vv. 4–10, is offered in Werner Schmidt's first volume of his commentary on Jeremiah.[33] Schmidt's analysis[34] confirms my own conviction that the core call account in vv. 4–9 derives from Jeremiah himself. At each stage of this short passage there are echoes and overtones of the invasion and takeover of the prophet's life by his call, his sense

---

[31] On these superscriptions as the theological terms for revelation, see Chapter 4, 'God's "Servants the Prophets"', p. 94.

[32] McKane, *Jeremiah*, Vol. I 25.

[33] See Schmidt, *Das Buch Jeremia*, 44–50, 52–6.

[34] Schmidt, *Das Buch Jeremia*, esp. 48–9.

of which was so overwhelming that he seemed to have been born with it, its hold on him so obsessive from an early age that he denied himself marriage and the begetting of a family; the motif of being already designated a prophet in the womb, and the divine reiteration of his commission in the face of his protestation of inadequacy (v. 6)—'to whomever I send you, you shall go; and you shall speak to them whatever I command you' (v. 7)—are expressive of the compulsion he experienced in his calling, however much he recoiled from it and took up a lament against the adversity it inflicted upon him; his cry, 'Ah! My Lord YHWH' (v. 6), together with the divine oracle of assurance and protection—'Do not be afraid ... I am with you to keep you safe; you have my word' (v. 8), which reads like the *Heilsorakel* in response to a lament—are redolent of his confessions and laments. The genre (*Gattung*) employed is well attested, but this does not rule out individual, personal content—anymore than the employment of the genre of the lament inhibits an outpouring of an individual's personal plight—and the content of these verses is unmistakably singular. If it is the work of editors and thus composed at second hand, as it were, it is a remarkably true-to-life summation. This cannot simply be ruled out as impossible, but it is a less compelling explanation of the conception and writing of such a text than the text itself narrates, and the comment offers itself that if it were not for the allusion to Jeremiah as 'a prophet to *or* for the nations' (v. 4) and as 'a prophet responsible for nations and kingdoms' (v. 10), no one would seriously question that the passage derives from the prophet himself.

This, indeed, is what Schmidt has urged, emphasizing the distinction between 'to *or* for the nations' (לגוים) in v. 5 and 'responsible for nations and kingdoms' (על הגוים ועל הממלכות) in v. 10, the latter manifestly a late redactional addition to the original call account, the former, however, cohering with a distinct theme of the book represented by texts reflecting a broader political horizon that Jeremiah had in mind in fulfilling his prophetic calling, not least of all the theme of the 'foe from the north' who is described as 'the destroyer of nations (גוים)' (Jer. 4: 7).[35] There is no reason why, in an earlier form, the core call account may not have been located in another context in the emerging book—as part of the scroll of the prophet's oracles narrated in Jeremiah 36?[36]—but has been

---

[35] Schmidt, *Das Buch Jeremia*, 49–50, 52–3.   [36] Schmidt, *Das Buch Jeremia*, 49.

secondarily adapted to a new context in this introductory chapter, just as the following two visions in vv. 11–14 (the almond branch and the seething cauldron), neither of which can be disengaged from the historical Jeremiah, originally had a different context or contexts. It would have been at such a stage in its transmission that v. 10, with its (probably late) content, was appended as part of the redactor's intention to provide a résumé of Jeremiah's prophetic ministry, 'an estimate of him after he has run his course'.

On such an assessment of the origin of this call narrative, a Deuteronomistic redactor of the exilic period could have known and had access to it in composing the pericope on prophecy in Deuteronomy 18. Some texts from the early post-exilic period provide a further possible indicator, however. These are Zech. 1: 1–6; 7: 7, 8–14 which refer to 'the earlier prophets', that is, most probably the pre-exilic prophets,[37] and show the influence of some of these prophetic texts.[38] These texts in Zechariah already show familiarity with an emerging corpus of prophetic literature as well as a knowledge of Pentateuchal materials in the early post-exilic community to which they were addressed, and the allusion to YHWH's 'words' as having been sent to the people by the 'spirit' of YHWH through 'the earlier prophets' (7.12) confirms the impression that the books of these prophets had attained the standing of scripture alongside some part or parts of the Pentateuch, including Deuteronomy.[39] Thus, in Zech. 7: 11–14 Judah's 'stubborn resistance was to the "Torah" and to the words of Yahweh proclaimed "through the earlier prophets"',[40] and the combination in 1: 6 of the 'words' of the prophets with 'statutes' reflects the same conjunction of 'the law and the prophets' that is found in Deut. 18: 15–20 and Jer. 36.[41]

---

[37] See C. L. Meyers and E. M. Meyers, *Haggai, Zechariah 1–8: A New Translation with Introduction and Commentary*, Anchor Bible (Garden City, NY, 1987), who suggest (p. 94) that the phrase 'earlier prophets' may be 'a designation for the Yahwistic prophets of the pre-exilic period' and that 'Jeremiah in particular was no doubt one of those prophets included in the term'.

[38] See J. D. Tollington, *Tradition and Innovation in Haggai and Zechariah 1–8*, JSOTSup, 150 (Sheffield, 1993), 26 and n. 1.

[39] See Meyers and Meyers, *Haggai, Zechariah 1–8*, 405–7.

[40] *Haggai, Zechariah 1–8*, 407.

[41] Cf. R. A. Mason, *Preaching the Tradition: Homily and Hermeneutics after the Exile* (Cambridge, 1990), 201, 203, suggests that the paralleling of the legal term 'statutes' with 'my words' in 1: 6 implies 'that the prophetic word is now becoming regarded as authoritative teaching on a par with Torah'. Meyers and Meyers suggest that the combination 'words' and 'my statutes' in 1: 6 may be a hendiadys, with 'statutes' constituting the specific aspect of the divine revelation indicated by 'words'.

Such evidence as we have, therefore, suggests an exilic or early post-exilic setting for the composition of the pericope on prophecy in Deut. 18. In favour of such a background to this passage are the following observations.

The end of the state of Judah and the devastation of Jerusalem and its temple and the exile would have been a landmark in the emergence and establishing of a corpus of prophetic scriptures. There would have been two main impulses for this, the first a desire amidst the destruction of the state and the collapse of national institutions, as well as the exile of elites and leaders, to preserve and conserve tradition, which would assuredly have included the extant prophetic literature. Secondly, prophecy was newly stirred by the events of 597–587 BCE and their aftermath, yielding not only further redaction and *Fortschreibung* of earlier prophetic collections, as we have seen, but also the ongoing development of the book of Jeremiah, and the labours of the two major prophetic figures of this period, Ezekiel, who was among the first exiles of Jerusalem in 597 BCE, and later the anonymous prophet of the return whom we refer to as Deutero-Isaiah, at whose hands, as Hugh Williamson has persuasively argued,[42] the book of Isaiah entered a major new stage of the history of its composition. Thus, a new age in the history of prophecy sprang to life in the aftershock of the events of 587 BCE that was as creative and foundational as that of the eighth-century prophets, and without which who can say what might have been the outcome for the future of the Jewish people and their worship of YHWH?

It is in this context, in my opinion—that is, the exilic and early post-exilic period—that we can best understand the purpose of the Deuteronomistic author of Deut. 18: 9–22 who writes of the prophets as a promise of YHWH to Israel at the very moment of its foundation as his people at Horeb, and summons the people of his own day to the witness of the prophets.

---

[42] H. G. M. Williamson, *The Book Called Isaiah: Deutero-Isaiah's Role in Composition and Redaction* (Oxford, 1994).

GOD'S 'SERVANTS THE PROPHETS'

Who, then, were these prophets? That in addition to Jeremiah this author included the eighth-century prophets among the promised prophets of Horeb is surely likely, as suggested above. The superscriptions to the books bearing the names of these prophets themselves suggest that they belonged to an emerging corpus of scripture. These various brief descriptions of the content of such books—'the words of Amos', 'the vision of Isaiah', and so on—are properly understood as theological terms for *revelation*, no longer referring, however, to individual oracles originally given orally but to the words of the prophet now written down, which have become scripture to be copied and read in future generations.[43] That some at least of the book of Isaiah of Jerusalem was included is of course suggested by the narrative in 2 Kgs 18: 13–20: 19, the only reference to any of the 'canonical' prophets in this corpus. The Deuteronomistic author of Deut. 4: 1–40 was evidently familiar with Deutero-Isaiah,[44] an indication that the oracles of this prophet were already in circulation and, if we follow Williamson, that their anonymous author himself incorporated them as a continuation of 'Proto-Isaiah'. The presence of Deuteronomistic elements in Ezekiel has been more disputed. Whilst some have found evidence of extensive Deuteronomistic redaction, others argue that much of the influence of Deuteronomstic style and theology in the book may derive from the prophet himself. Thus Joyce has argued that there 'is no reason to believe that Ezekiel himself would have been untouched by the influence of Deuteronomistic theology and style either in his native Jerusalem or in the Babylonian exile', whilst conceding, however, that '[r]edactors may well be responsible for a proportion of the deuteronomistic features in the book'.[45] Further support can be found in the texts from the book of Zechariah cited above, in which such a corpus of prophetic literature seems taken for granted.

---

[43] See G. M. Tucker, 'Prophetic Superscriptions and the Growth of a Canon', in G. W. Coats and B. O. Long (eds.), *Canon and Authority: Essays in Old Testament Religion and Theology* (Philadelphia, 1977), 56–70.

[44] See Chapter 3, 'Deuteronomy as Counterfactual Literature', pp. 57–9.

[45] Joyce, *Ezekiel*, 39. See his discussion on pp. 37–41, where further bibliography is provided.

Since we cannot determine precisely when Deut. 18: 9–22 was composed, suggestions as to other prophetic books which this author may have had in mind must remain only tentative. It is scarcely throwing caution to the wind, however, to suggest that such a corpus would have included a scroll of the oracles of Zephaniah, whose activity is generally agreed to have been in Jerusalem during the reign of Josiah, and the superscription to which—'the word of YHWH that came to Zephaniah . . . in the days of Josiah'—is similar to those of Hosea, Amos, and Micah and, like them, portrays the words of the prophet here written down as revelation. There is also evidence suggesting that several themes and motifs of the book reveal the influence of Isaiah, Amos, and Micah.[46] Given a so-called 'Assyrian' redaction of the book of Isaiah during reign of Josiah, Nahum's oracles prophesying the fall of Nineveh, which must have pre-dated 612 BCE, might also have gained a place among a growing corpus of prophetic literature. If the current majority opinion is correct that the background of the book of Habakkuk is the late Neo-Assyrian or early Neo-Babylonian period, this prophet too may have been included in the emerging corpus of prophetic scripture in the exilic period. Obadiah's invective against Edom (vv. 1–14, 15b), which may derive from the early exilic period,[47] would have established itself in a community, whether in exile or in the homeland, that was to hand on an enduring bitter memory of the treachery of the Edomites in 'the day of Jerusalem' (Ps. 137: 7; cf. Lam. 4: 21–2; Amos 1: 11–12). Whilst caution is duly required, therefore, and some of these suggestions remain more tentative than others, the evidence of an exilic/early post-exilic stage of redaction exhibited in a number of these books suggests an emergent of a corpus of prophetic scripture.

Alongside such a developing corpus must be included the Deuteronomists' long narrative with its record of the series of prophetic figures whose exploits and prophetic activity characterize this corpus, beginning with Deborah in Judges and ending with Huldah at the end of Kings. It cannot be seriously doubted that the redactor responsible for Deut. 18: 9–22 included them among the

---

[46] See M. A. Sweeney, *Zephaniah: A Commentary* (Minneapolis, 2003), 14–18.

[47] On this division of the book and its dating see J. Barton, *Joel and Obadiah: A Commentary*, OTL (London, 2001), 118–23.

promised prophets of this text.[48] That is, the author of Deut. 18: 9–20 was familiar with a corpus of scripture that included Deuteronomy and its related literary corpus—whether or not either had assumed the dimensions of its extant form can be left open—as well as a series of prophetic books such as those suggested above, several of which, not least of all Isaiah and Jeremiah, were undergoing or would later undergo further compositional growth.

THE LEGACY OF THE PROPHETS IN THE DEUTERONOMIC CORPUS

Some additional observations and considerations, which there is space here to outline only briefly, suggest themselves in support of the case argued in the foregoing pages, specifically that the authors and redactors of Deuteronomy–2 Kings were indebted to and, indeed, developed leading aspects and features of the preaching of the prophets who preceded them, and not least of all those with whom the series had its beginnings in the eighth century BCE.

One thinks immediately of theodicy, which in its usage as an explanation for the national disasters that befell, first the northern state of Israel and its citizens and later Judah and Jerusalem, entered Israel's theological thought in the preaching of the eighth-century prophets. Thus Amos,[49] foreseeing and announcing approaching and irreversible national catastrophe upon the northern state of Israel and its people—starkly encapsulated in 8: 2, 'The end has come upon my people Israel'—declared this to be a judgement visited by God upon the moral offences of Israel, which the prophet's oracles

---

[48] There is, however, little if anything in Deut. 18: 9–22 that draws specifically upon the tradition of 'old prophecy'. A possible exception is the criterion of non-fulfilment for recognizing 'the word that the Lord has not spoken' (vv. 21–2), which may reflect the prophecy-fulfilment motif which is a prominent feature of the Deuteronomistic corpus. However, these verses are clearly a secondary addition to the pericope (see Hossfeld and Meyer, *Prophet gegen Prophet*, 151). The verb 'to raise up' can be employed for any prophet commissioned by YHWH or believed to be so commissioned (cf. Amos 2: 11–12; Jer. 29: 15).

[49] For the comments that follow I am indebted to John Barton's recent study *The Theology of the Book of Amos* (Cambridge, 2012), 99, ch. 3, 'The Theology of Amos and his Circle', and especially the subsection 'Repentance and Salvation'. See also R. Smend, 'Das Nein des Amos', *EvT* 23 (1963), 404–23, repr. in id., *Die Mitte des Alten Testaments* (Tübingen, 2002), 219–37.

trenchantly highlight. In such a way, his declaration of YHWH's action against Israel provides not only the *why* of the coming devastation, but also and simultaneously hope on the other side of national calamity for those who will seize it, since YHWH's sovereign will and not some divine caprice is at work in the events that are to enfold. Thus Amos's apparently 'totally unhopeful message still contains within itself the seeds of hope!'[50] The same proclamation of coming disaster lies at the heart of the call of Hosea, Micah, and Isaiah, a disaster understood as an outworking of YHWH's judgement upon his people, a judgement that portends an end of the nation that has been and yet summons trust in YHWH for a future beyond this.

Theodicy would have been among the leading features that rendered these prophetic collections enduringly relevant following the catastrophe that overtook northern Israel at the hands of the Assyrians, and no less in the generations that followed the destruction of the Judaean state by the Babylonians and the ensuing exile. Theodicy is likewise a preoccupation of the authors of Deuteronomy and its related corpus, providing a theological explanation of the fall of the two kingdoms, and since the proclamation and theological rationale of these catastrophes is placed throughout this corpus on the lips of YHWH's 'servants the prophets'—including Isaiah (2 Kgs 20: 12–19)—the inference is warranted that these prophetic collections, which in any event display evidence of Deuteronomistic *Fortschreibung*, lie behind the manner of presentation of this preponderant theme by these authors.

Further, at the hands of the Deuteronomic authors the fearful guilt of which the prophets indicted Israel/Judah, and the retribution which they proclaimed and which swept away both kingdoms, yielded a new and highly distinctive way of understanding the relationship between YHWH and Israel, that is, the theological coinage of a *covenant*, the formulation proper of which we owe to these authors.[51] In this too they were indebted to the preaching of the

---

[50] Barton, *The Theology of the Book of Amos*, 99.

[51] The book of Hosea alone among the eighth-century prophets refers to such a covenant (6: 7; 8: 1), but it seems likely that its usage derives from the remarkable range of imagery that he employs, rather than from a developed theology of covenant, and that it is to the Deuteronomic authors that we owe its formulation and deployment. For a discussion of these texts, see Ernest Nicholson, *God and his People: Covenant and Theology in the Old Testament* (Oxford, 1986), ch. 9.

eighth-century prophets, central to whose thinking was a radical break with the belief, intrinsic to national self-awareness and identity, that the relationship between God and Israel was an unalterably fixed natural bond, a 'given' in God's ordering of the world that rendered the nation's institutions sacral and guaranteed its well-being.[52] The eighth-century prophets broke the mould of this traditional 'creation theology' and gave rise to a new style of religious thought that challenged and *de*-legitimated the apparently stable and divinely ordained social structures.[53] For them, YHWH had indeed chosen Israel, but this called for a reciprocal choosing on Israel's part, a blessing-or-curse, life-or-death 'choosing'. What is thus implicit in the preaching of these prophets was conceived of by the Deuteronomic authors as grounded in a covenant between God and Israel, a concept that decisively shaped their people's identity and self-awareness through the disasters that befell them and threatened to engulf them, and that developed into a rich hope for their future.

Inherent in the radical reconceptualization of the relationship between Israel and YHWH which the preaching of these prophets generated was a 'de-mystification' of kingship and its supporting ideology according to which the king is viewed as being virtually God's 'plenipotentiary'. Among the eighth-century prophets,[54] however, Isaiah denounced the notion that 'the king and the power elite of Judah can commandeer Yahweh for their military and political aims', and it was he who 'broke apart the identification of royal military policy and the divine rule of the world which kingship theology had made'; YHWH 'does not allow himself to be tied to the power interests of the Davidic king; the chance of salvation which he accords the king can be seized only if political and military safe-guards to power are dispensed with'.[55] The special target of Isaiah's condemnation were the political and military alliances that featured so much in the affairs of Judah under both Ahaz and Hezekiah, and which he denounced as a betrayal of trust in YHWH. Thus, 'for the first time in the history of Israel's religion, in the prophecy of Isaiah

---

[52] For a fuller treatment of role of religion in ancient Near Eastern societies, see Nicholson, *God and his People*, esp. ch. 10.

[53] I have written at greater length about this development in *God and his People*.

[54] For the prophetic criticism of military power and alliances in Isaiah and Hosea, see R. Albertz, *A History of Israelite Religion in the Old Testament Period* (Göttingen, 1992), Vol. I 167–71, esp. 168.

[55] Albertz, *A History of Israelite Religion*, Vol. I 168.

Yahweh emerges at a fundamental distance from state and military power' (p. 168).

Striking and significant, therefore, is the Deuteronomist's narrative of Isaiah's denunciation of Hezekiah's reception of emissaries of the Chaldean prince Merodach-baladan (2 Kgs 20: 12–19), who was bent on recruiting Judah's support, and that of others, in a coalition against Assyria,[56] and whose emissaries Hezekiah is said to have been 'pleased'[57] to welcome and whom he allowed to survey his wealth and his military resources. Isaiah's response and prophecy, which reads like a brief 'prologue' to the final act of a tragedy that enfolds in the ensuing scenes of the descent of the Judaean state to its end, is of course from the hand of a Deuteronomistic author, but it authentically reflects Isaiah's denunciation of Judah's engagement in the international politicking of the time, and his condemnation of Ahaz's and Hezekiah's misplaced confidence in inter-state military alliances as a lack of trust in YHWH. That nothing of this is anticipated in the preceding Deuteronomistic narrative of the reign of Hezekiah and his dealings with Isaiah (2 Kgs 18–20: 11) is testimony that the author who here penned Isaiah's fearful prophecy was familiar with a larger collection of Isaiah's oracles than is suggested by this narrative, including the prophet's decisive distancing of YHWH from state and military power.

The question that immediately arises, however, is whether Deuteronomy and its related corpus offers any further indication of a 'delegitimation' of what Isaiah viewed as the pretensions of state ideology, especially the role of kingship. The so-called 'law of the king' in Deut. 17: 14–20, which has already been the subject of comment in Chapters 2 and 3, here calls for further and more expansive consideration. The two chapters here following focus attention upon this passage. The first (Chapter 5) offers a critique of recent assessments of the role and significance that Deuteronomy assigns to kingship in the life of the Israel envisaged. The second (Chapter 6) focuses upon what scholars agree to be the most enigmatic clause of the passage (v. 15b): 'do not dare to set a foreigner over you,

---

[56] On Merodach-baladan (Marduk-apal-iddina) and his encounter with Hezekiah, see H. W. F. Saggs, 'The Assyrians', in D. J. Wiseman (ed.), *Peoples of Old Testament Times* (Oxford, 1973), 156–78; and W. G. Lambert, 'The Babylonians and Chaldaeans', in ibid. 179–96.

[57] With LXX, which suggests a Hebrew Vorlage וישמח 'and he rejoiced (at their coming)' instead of MT וישמע 'and he listened'.

one who is not a brother Israelite.' In considering this clause we shall encounter again the view that Josiah's reformation came on a tide of liberation as Assyrian imperial power waned during the final decades of the seventh century, and that the reformation's root-and-branch purging of non-Yahwistic cults was itself an expression of a buoyant nationalistic revival. This is a view that has wide acceptance among scholars. More recently, Josiah's purging of non-Yahwistic cults and the fervent 'mono-Yahwism' that characterizes the reform measures has been additionally and directly attributed to rebellion against Assyrian hegemony, which, it is argued, imposed the cult of Assyrian gods upon their vassals alongside that rendered to the local deities.[58] How secure is this claim? What light might Assyrian imperial suzerainty shed upon the forcefully expressed interdiction of v. 15b?

---

[58] See the expansive study by H.Spieckermann, *Juda unter Assur in der Sargonidenzeit*, FRLANT 129 (Göttingen, 1982).

5

The 'Law' of the King in Deuteronomy 17: 14–20

In each of Chapters 2 and 3 I have referred to kingship as having no 'rootage', so to speak, in Deuteronomy where, apart from chapter 17: 14–20, kingship and kingly rule are unmentioned and play no part in the ordering of the society to which the book is evidently addressed. Contrast this absence of reference to the diverse roles of the king in the governance of the state—in legislation, the ordering of the national cult, and in defence—with, for example, the requirement for centralization of the cult, which is statutorily formulated in the opening chapter of the central legal section of the book, and its consequences and ramifications for various customary rites and festivals then followed through and provided for in this and succeeding chapters—the offering of tithes at 'the place which YHWH shall choose' (12: 17–18; 14: 22–7), profane slaughter of animals for food (12: 15–16, 20–5), the centralized celebration of the Passover and of other festivals (ch. 16). In short, kingship, though provided for in Deut. 17: 14–20, leaves no discernible 'footprint' elsewhere in the book. This is all the more striking a feature of Deuteronomy since this text stands alone among the 'law codes' of the Pentateuch in providing for the institution of kingship in Israel. How, then, is it to be understood, and what did its authors intend by its inclusion in the book?[1]

As a matter of fact, no passage in Deuteronomy contains more problems or has attracted more controversy than these seven

[1] With some revision what follows is based upon an earlier essay '*Traditum and traditio*: The Case of Deuteronomy 17: 14–20', published in D. A. Green and L. S. Lieber (eds.), *Scriptural Exegesis: The Shapes of Culture and the Religious Imagination. Essays in Honour of Michael Fishbane* (Oxford, 2009), 46–61.

verses. Is the passage a unity or, as some argue, has an original Deuteronomic core been edited by a secondary Deuteronomistic hand? Did the passage or a core of it belong to the original book of Deuteronomy? How is its portrayal of the nature and role of kingship in Israel to be related to texts elsewhere in the Old Testament concerning kingship? How does it cohere with what is narrated concerning the Davidic dynasty elsewhere in the Deuteronomistic corpus? Is it rightly described as part of a 'polity' or 'constitution' that the authors of Deuteronomy sought to establish for their nation? Was it an attempt to redefine and revamp the role of the king at a time of disillusion with the institution of kingship, or perhaps to restore an idealized but limited monarchy after the exile? Alternatively, was it intended as a measure whereby the history of the monarchy in Israel and Judah was found irremediably wanting, permitted by God at the outset only because of the hubris of the people, but which had proved a disaster for Israel, as the Deuteronomistic history of the monarchy both in northern Israel and in Judah narrates?

Each verse of the passage has itself been the subject of controversy. Is the very phrasing of the people's request for a king in v. 14, 'like the nations round about', anti-monarchical (cf. 1 Sam. 8: 5), thus registering at the outset a attitude of censure towards kingship, and signalling a negative view of the institution that is continued in the instructions concerning the conduct of, and the conditions placed upon, the monarchy in vv. 16–17? Most enigmatic of all in these verses, what historical event or circumstances could have necessitated the remarkable and strong prohibition in v. 15b, 'do not dare to set a foreigner over you, one who is not a brother Israelite', since it is difficult to imagine why, in any normal circumstances, the rule of a foreigner rather than a native Israelite would have appealed to Israelites? Verses 16–17 similarly pose well-known problems: what lies behind the proscription in v. 16 of the king's acquisition of horses, which can only have been for the quite normal purpose of military defence of the state? How are we to understand the phrase warning against 'causing the people to return to Egypt', and its accompanying motivating clause, 'since the Lord has said to you "You shall never return that way"'? To what extent does this verse have in mind the behaviour of Solomon, who is narrated as having purchased horses and chariots from Egypt (1 Kgs 10: 26, 28–9)? Similarly, does v. 17 allude to Solomon's legendary acquisition of silver and gold (1 Kgs 10: 21, 27) and to his celebrated multinational harem, said to have consisted of seven hundred wives and princesses, as well as three hundred concubines (1 Kgs 11: 1–3)?

CONTEXT: A DEUTERONOMIC 'POLITY' FOR ISRAEL (DEUT. 16:18–18: 22)?

Most commentators regard Deut. 17: 14–20 as part of the original book of Deuteronomy,[2] and in more recent scholarship it has been associated with the remainder of 16:18–18: 22, which as a whole is viewed as a self-contained pericope providing an outline 'constitution' or 'polity' focusing upon the primary national offices of judge, king, priest, and prophet.[3] Lothar Perlitt's incisive observations on such a reading of this pericope reveal how very tenuous it is.[4] Chapter 16: 18 begins with the general command to provide 'judges' and 'officers' for the maintenance of justice, but this is soon interrupted (16: 21–17: 1) by exclusively cultic matters relating to 'asherah', stone pillars, and blemished sacrifices, none of which can be considered pertinent to a 'Constitutional Proposal'[5] or series

---

[2] Some have attempted to isolate an original Deuteronomic core which has been subsequently expanded, recently e.g. F. García López, 'Le roi d'Israel: Dt 17,14–20', in N. Lohfink (ed.), *Das Deuteronomium: Entstehung, Gestalt und Botschaft*, BETL 68 (Leuven, 1985), 277–97; B. Gosse, 'Deutéronome 17, 18–19 et la restauration de la royauté au retour de l'exile', *Bibbia e oriente*, 181 (1994), 129–38.

[3] N. Lohfink, 'Die Sicherung der Wirksamkeit des Gotteswortes durch das Prinzip der Gewaltenteilung nach den Ämtergesetzen des Buches Deuteronomium (Dt 16, 18–18, 22)', in H. Wolter (ed.), *Testimonium Veritati* (Festschrift Wilhelm Kempf), Frankfurter theologische Studien, 7 (Frankfurt a.M., 1971), 144–55, repr. in N. Lohfink, *Studien zum Deuteronomium und zur deuteronomistischen Literatur I*, SBAB 8 (Stuttgart, 1990), 305–23, Eng. trans. 'Distribution of the Functions of Power: The Laws Concerning Public Offices in Deuteronomy 16:18–18:22', in D. L. Christensen (ed.), *A Song of Power and the Power of Song* (Winona Lake, IN, 1993), 336–52; B. Halpern, *The Constitution of the Monarchy in Israel*, HSM 25 (Chico, CA, 1981); S. Dean McBride, 'Polity of the Covenant People: The Book of Deuteronomy', *Interpretation*, 41 (1987), 229–44; U. Rüterswörden, *Von der politischen Gemeinschaft zur Gemeinde: Studien zu Dt 16,18–18,22*, BBB, 65 (Frankfurt a.M., 1987); B. M. Levinson, 'The Reconceptualization of Kingship in Deuteronomy and the Deuteronomistic History's Transformation of Torah', *VT* 51 (2001), 511–34; R. D. Nelson, *Deuteronomy: A Commentary*, OTL (Louisville and London, 2002), 210–36.

[4] L. Perlitt, 'Der Staatsgedanke im Deuteronomium', in S. E. Ballentine and J. Barton (eds.), *Language, Theology, and The Bible: Essays in Honour of James Barr* (Oxford, 1994), 182–98.

[5] For this description of Deut. 16: 18–18: 22 see Nelson, *Deuteronomy*, 213.

of ordinances for the appointment of state officers. Chapter 17: 2–7 provides for the 'stoning to death' of anyone found guilty of worshipping of other gods, with provision for how such cases are to be judged, none of which, again, is immediately pertinent to the provision of state officers and a description of their functions. Chapter 17: 8–13 provides for a central court to adjudicate difficult cases, but is vague about its officers—the priests and 'the judge who shall be in those days'—and seems to presuppose such a court rather than providing for its institution. Indeed, as a general comment, the 'offices' here supposedly being instituted are left virtually undefined as to the duties and responsibilities they entail and the authority with which their bearers are invested, all of which one would normally expect in a 'Constitutional Proposal'. Thus 18: 1–8 is concerned with regulating the emoluments of the priests rather than with their installation and their official duties. And how can 'the prophet' whom YHWH promises 'to raise up' (18: 9–22) be classified as a 'state official', since neither prophets in general nor 'the prophet' here promised can be said to be 'installed'? This text has nothing to say of the 'investiture' of an official required by the constitutional needs of the state.[6] Rather, it is through these promised prophets that God's will and words will be mediated, and not through recourse to the assorted methods of soothsaying, sorcery, divinization rituals, and other similar 'abominations' native to the nations of Canaan.[7]

A major difficulty for understanding Deut. 17: 14–20 as part of a 'Constitutional Proposal' is that outside these verses the authors of the book have nothing to say of kingship in Israel. They prescribe no role for the king that bears any resemblance to how this office operated in the ancient Near East, including Israel and Judah. Neither within the passage nor elsewhere in the book is there any mention of the king's leadership in war and in the defence of his kingdom and people, or of his responsibility for the maintenance and administration of justice, or for the ordering of the national cult. Nothing of the quintessential functions of kingship is here prescribed. Put differently, given what is well known from elsewhere in the Old Testament concerning kingship in Israel, it is a strange 'constitution' indeed that evidently prescribes for the king the sole duty of meditating upon the book of the *torah*, whilst authority for

---

[6] Perlitt, 'Der Staatsgedanke im Deuteronomium', 187.
[7] Perlitt, 'Der Staatsgedanke im Deuteronomium', 187.

traditionally royal core functions—the conduct of war, the national cult, the maintenance of justice[8]—is exercised by others who are nowhere in the book said to be royal officers or in any way answerable to the king. In sum, there is no realistic provision in Deut. 17: 14–20 for the institution or 'office' of kingship as normally understood in ancient Israel. A further indication of this is the prohibition imposed by v. 16 denying the king the option of providing and sustaining a standing army with a chariot force, since, as Perlitt has aptly commented,[9] although a king might perhaps negotiate about the extent of his harem, he could scarcely accept the restraint here imposed upon equipping and maintaining a chariot force for the defence of the state. Such a restraint is but a further indication that Deut. 17: 14–20 is not a statute, much less part of a state 'constitution', providing for the institution of monarchy for which, as Perlitt again aptly observes (p. 187), it would indeed be 'ein wunderliches Gesetz'!

Deut. 17: 14–20 cannot have had Josiah in mind, for whom 'the book of the *torah*' is not described as a basis for a reform of the state but of the cult and religion.[10] Indeed, Josiah's conduct as king in exercising the normal powers of a head of state, making policies and seeking to implement them, including the reform of the cult and the conduct of war, does not resemble the rather 'unkinged' figure of Deut. 17: 14–20.[11] There is, as Perlitt remarks, an absence in Deuteronomy of the nature and essence of 'kingship' (מלוכה) or

---

[8] Cf. Nelson, *Deuteronomy*, 221, who, commenting upon the 'judge who shall be in those days' (Deut. 17: 8–13), speculates: 'Perhaps this judge was intended to be a substitute for the king, whose appellate role in the judicial system has been eliminated.'

[9] Perlitt, 'Der Staatsgedanke im Deuteronomium', 189.

[10] Perlitt, 'Der Staatsgedanke im Deuteronomium', 192.

[11] Levinson, 'The Reconceptualization of Kingship in Deuteronomy and the Deuteronomistic History's Transformation of Torah', describes Deut. 17: 14–20 as a 'utopian manifesto for a constitutional monarchy that sharply delimits the power of the king', a 'redefinition of royal authority' whereby the authors of Deuteronomy 'redefine the jurisdiction of each branch of public office' in Deut. 16: 18–18: 22. If this was the intention of its author, however, the outcome is scarcely a statute for a 'constitutional monarch', since this king is ascribed no state functions, has no evident authority, and is in effect 'redefined' out of public life, quite 'unkinged', as we may put it. The note of censure upon monarchy struck at the outset of the passage and the stress upon what the king must not do rather than upon what public and state roles he is to exercise invite an alternative attempt to understand the rationale behind the text (see below).

'kingdom', 'sovereignty', 'dominion' (ממלכה),[12] whilst the verb משל 'to rule', 'reign', 'have dominion over' occurs only in Deut. 15: 6, where it refers to Israel's dominion over 'many nations'; he correctly observes that 'the people envisaged in Deuteronomy is not constituted as a state; it has no king, nor any other secular head'.[13]

A STATUTE FOR A RECONSTITUTED MONARCHY?

Does Deut. 17: 14–20 then reflect an exilic or post-exilic move to restore an *idealized* but limited monarchy after the exile? Among recent attempts to argue this, Anselm Hagedorn suggests[14] that in formulating this legislation the authors of Deuteronomy, which he dates to the post-exilic period, provided for a new and 'democratic' kind of monarchy, the intention being to protect 'the community of brothers'—Israel as conceived of in Deuteronomy—'which has the desire to place a king over them, but at the same time wants to remain free from despotic rule' (p. 156). But what 'desire'? Deut. 17: 14b bears an unmistakable resemblance to 1 Sam. 8:5b, which belongs to a narrative censuring the people's demand for kingship 'like all the nations' (see below). It does not read as though those who penned it 'desired' the institution of kingship (that is, on Hagedorn's hypothesis, the reintroduction of kingship in the post-exilic period). Though he makes no reference to it, might the programme of restoration beyond exile envisaged in Ezek. 40–8, with its role for a downgraded royal figure referred to as 'the prince' (הנשיא), offer support for Hagedorn's understanding of a similar post-exilic 'democratization' of kingship by the authors of Deuteronomy?[15] For the same reason mentioned above, however,

---

[12] Perlitt, 'Der Staatsgedanke im Deuteronomium', 192–3. For the absence of other usual trappings of state and of state management with requisite officers in Deuteronomy, see ibid. 192–5.

[13] Perlitt, 'Der Staatsgedanke im Deuteronomium', 193: 'Das hier vorgestellte Volk hat keine staatliche Verfasstheit, weder einen König noch auch sonst eine weltliche Spitze.'

[14] A. Hagedorn, *Between Moses and Plato: Individual and Society in Deuteronomy and Ancient Greek Law*, FRLANT 204 (Göttingen, 2004), 144–6.

[15] Paul Joyce, 'King and Messiah in Ezekiel', in J. Day (ed.), *King and Messiah in Israel and the Ancient Near East*, JSOTSup 270 (Sheffield, 1998), 336 suggests that

such an analogy does not hold, for whereas the authors of Ezek. 40–8, whilst demoting the role of kingship, apparently had no objection in principle to a place for a royal figure in their envisaged restored community,[16] the passage on kingship in Deuteronomy censures at its outset the people's demand for the institution, and what follows in vv. 16–17, which are manifestly an encapsulation *ex eventu* of excesses, transgressions, and offences of the historical monarchy as narrated in Samuel–Kings (see below), strikes the same chord of reproach. The suggestion that authors with such a critical stance towards kingship were intent upon reinstating monarchy in the post-exilic period, when the future of the institution had long been in crisis, lacks persuasion. In short, either the authors of Deut. 17: 14–20 wrote in a context in which the monarchy was in place and a historical fact which they had to accommodate, that is, the pre-exilic period, as most commentators suggest, or the passage has a different rationale and was composed for a different purpose.

DEUTERONOMY 17: 14–20 AS A CRITIQUE OF KINGSHIP

Though ostensibly providing for the establishment of a monarchy, was the intention of the author of Deut. 17: 14–20 rather a critique of kingship? Has the passage perhaps more to do with the verdict of the Deuteronomistic history upon kingship in Israel/Judah than with sanctioning, however circumspectly, the institution? [17]

both texts share the same critique of monarchy but also a desire to give kingship a place, though a strictly limited one, 'in the community of the people of God', without, however, suggesting that Deuteronomy is as late a composition as Hagedorn proposes.

[16] For a recent discussion of this, see Joyce 'King and Messiah in Ezekiel'.

[17] Gary N. Knoppers, 'The Deuteronomist and the Deuteronomic Law of the King: A Reexamination of a Relationship', *ZAW* 108 (1996), claims that the Deuteronomistic history, especially in its presentation of Solomon, 'explicitly endorses substantial royal powers' and thus 'revises the quasi-antimonarchical stance of Deuteronomy' and in this way, whilst subjecting the king to the law, advances a competing notion of what this entails. But it remains the case that the ideal by which the kings are relentlessly measured in the history is fulfilment of the *torah*. In this respect it is difficult to discern any substantive difference in outlook between Deut. 17: 14–20 and the Deuteronomist, as though the latter was more of a 'monarchist' than the author of the former. On the question whether the promises to David (2 Sam. 7: 11b–16) mitigated for the Deuteronomistic authors the threat of judgement implicit in Deut 17: 18–20, see below.

(1) As noted above, the opening statement of the passage already strikes a negative attitude to the monarchy, and finds an echo later in the Deuteronomistic history when Samuel resists the people's move to institute a monarchy in Israel (1 Sam. 8). Against Hagedorn's claim (p. 141) that the passage 'does not take a critical stance against the monarchy as is the case in 1 Sam 8', the phrase 'I will appoint (אשימה) a king over me like all the nations (ככל הגוים) that are round about me' in Deut. 17: 14b is so closely similar to 1 Sam. 8: 5b (cf. v. 20)—'now appoint (שימה) for us a king to govern us like all the nations (ככל הגוים)'—that there can scarcely be serious doubt that, like the latter, it is intended as polemical. It looks, indeed, as though the scribe who penned the text in Deuteronomy and the author of the story in 1 Sam. 8, if they were not one and the same, intended the very words of the people to Samuel to bear out virtually verbatim Moses' 'forecast' of the people's clamour for a king 'when you come into the land which the Lord your God is giving you'. This beginning itself does not suggest that the 'instructions' that follow represent an initiative of Moses to provide for the institution of kingship 'when you come into the land'.[18] Rather, kingship is a concession to a people bent on aping 'the nations round about'. And on this negative note the passage continues (the historical reality that kingship had been instituted having been acknowledged)—'you may indeed set a king over you' (v. 15a).[19]

(2) There are grounds for believing that this opening censure upon the demand for kingship is reflected also in what immediately follows, that is, v. 15b with its extraordinarily striking and forcefully drafted prohibition, 'do not dare to set a foreigner over you, one who is not a brother Israelite'. Since it is highly unlikely that in any normal circumstances a choice between a native Israelite and a foreigner as king of the nation would have suggested itself to the people, what conditions or events inimical to national well-being might have necessitated such a forcefully drafted prohibition? A more expansive consideration of this, the most enigmatic clause in this series, will be provided in the Chapter 6. There I shall argue that the long period of Assyrian hegemony over Syria–Palestine, which endured for upwards of a century from the mid-eighth century,

---

[18] See Perlitt, 'Der Staatsgedanke im Deuteronomium', 189.

[19] That v. 15 cannot be separated from v. 14 and regarded as a once independent Deuteronomic command, see Perlitt, 'Der Staatsgedanke im Deuteronomium', 188–9.

offers the most likely explanation of this strongly phrased interdiction, which most likely reflects the memory of northern Israel's and Judah's participation in the power politics of their time and the catastrophic consequences which this occasioned at the hands of the superpowers of the day. More specifically, its author viewed entry into a client-state relationship with Assyria as effectively 'setting a foreigner' over the nation in the person of 'the Great King', the king of Assyria. Thus understood, this interdict offers further evidence that Deut. 17: 14–20, though ostensibly providing for a monarchy in Israel, is in reality critical of the institution of kingship, and might indeed be regarded as a founding text, so to speak, of the theme of the failure of the monarchy so prominent in the Deuteronomistic corpus (see below).

(3) That the trio of prohibitions that follow in vv. 16–17 are also critical of the institution of kingship is self-evident, and their resonance with and echoes of the narrative of the reign of Solomon suggests strongly that the author of Deut. 17: 14–20 probably had such texts in mind. Thus Moshe Weinfeld, for example, sees Solomon's 'sins' reflected in these two verses. He finds in the interdict against the acquisition of horses (v. 16a) an allusion to Solomon's intensive horse trade with Egypt as narrated in 1 Kgs 10: 26, 28–9.[20] Caution is, of course, required here, for Solomon was not the only king of Israel to maintain an effective army including a strong chariot force,[21] and for this reason some have argued that this verse has no individual king in mind.[22] The suggestion remains persuasive, however, that the narrative of Solomon's grand army-building enterprises was primarily in the mind of the author of Deut. 17: 16, even if not necessarily to the exclusion of allusions to other kings, and certainly a reader of the narrative of Solomon's massive chariot force is immediately reminded of Moses' interdict precisely against such an enterprise.[23]

[20] Moshe Weinfeld, *Deuteronomy and the Deuteronomic School* (Oxford, 1972), 168.

[21] According to the annals of Shalmaneser III, 'Ahab the Israelite' had 2,000 chariots at the battle of Karkar. See *ANET* 278–9.

[22] See e.g. A. D. H. Mayes, *Deuteronomy*, NCB (London, 1979), 272.

[23] Not every feature of this verse, however, is to be explained by reference to the narrative of Solomon's reign in 1 Kgs. In particular, it is unlikely that 'the people' in the phrase 'he shall not ... cause the people to return to Egypt' has in mind the Israelite merchants dispatched by Solomon to purchase horses from the Egyptians, and no criticism of these commercial transactions is made in the narrative in Kings. The command in Deut. 17: 16a may have in mind the trading of Israelites as mercenaries in exchange for horses.

The conduct of inter-state diplomacy by means of royal marriages between dynasties lies behind the prohibition in v. 17a: 'Neither shall he acquire numerous wives for himself, lest his heart be turned aside', 'turned aside', that is, to worship foreign deities or to make provision for their cults. Harems were the privilege of kings and were commonplace in the courts of the kings of Israel and Judah, and the influence of a foreign consort to foster an alien cult in Israel is also exemplified in the narrative of the assertive figure of the Tyrian princess Jezebel, whose marriage to Ahab may have been for the purpose of sealing a treaty between Israel and Tyre, and whose vigorous patronage of the worship of Baal was evidently memorably notorious. In the case of the injunction in v. 17a, however, the suggestion remains compelling that this verse has in mind the narrative of the fabled and fabulous harem of Solomon (1 Kgs 11: 1–10), whose numerous foreign wives 'turned away his heart',[24] and whose patronage of foreign cults is said to have embraced the gods of all his foreign wives and included Astarte, Milcom, Chemosh, and Molech (1 Kgs 11: 6–8).

The coincidence of the three prohibitions in vv. 16–17 with what the narrative in 1 Kgs 10: 1–11.8 describes as achievements and attainments, whether celebrated or infamous, of Solomon's reign— the formation of a formidable chariot force, the acquisition of immense opulence (1 Kgs 10: 14–23, 27), and an incomparable and multinational harem with resulting religious and cultic 'pluralism'— surely renders it all the more likely that it was primarily Solomon's notorious excesses as here narrated that the writer of this threesome of prohibitions had in mind. And this too signals an unmistakably negative judgment of kingship in Israel/Judah.

(4) The question arises whether, on the analogy of probable allusions in vv. 16–17 to the narratives of Solomon's reign, the enigmatic prohibition in v. 15b, 'do not dare to set a foreigner over you', might similarly find an echo elsewhere in the Deuteronomistic corpus, specifically in the narrative of the reign of Ahaz in 2 Kgs 16, since the Deuteronomistic editor here wrote of Ahaz as having brought Judah under thraldom to Assyria under Tiglath-pileser.

---

[24] Since harems were normal in Israelite and Judaean courts, the ellipsis 'that his heart be not turned away' (v. 17) is perhaps a further indication that this verse has in mind such a narrative as 1 Kgs 11: 1–10.

In 2 Kgs 16: 7 Ahaz, in appealing to Tiglath-pileser, describes himself as the Assyrian king's 'servant' and his 'son'. Though 'servant' is a term familiarly used for the relation of a vassal to a suzerain, the term 'son' is not.[25] The combination does not therefore reflect diplomatic usage, and it is more likely that it is a coinage of the author of the account of the story of Ahaz's reign.[26] The combination is all the more unusual for being unique to this narrative in the Hebrew Bible, and the use of the term 'son' in addition to the conventional 'servant' is striking, since no vassal 'would have dared to use the term "son," which expressed familial dependency'.[27] It has been suggested that since 'servant' expresses a relationship of subservience and dependence, the accompanying term 'son' is used 'to moderate the inferior status by arousing fatherly feelings toward the "servant"'.[28] It is surely doubtful, however, that the author of this narrative was concerned to uphold the pride or dignity of King Ahaz, who, he narrates, pillaged the temple to pay what is described as a 'bribe' (שֹׁחַד) to the king of Assyria (v. 8). An alternative suggestion is that the combination is intended to underscore Ahaz's unfaithfulness to YHWH, whose 'servant' and 'son' he was according to the theology of the Davidic dynasty.[29] The promises to the House of David and Ahaz's lack of faith in them during the Syro-Ephraimite crisis are the substance of the oracles of Isaiah in Isa. 7: 1–8: 8, oracles which were subsequently reshaped in the wake of the ruinous outcome of Ahaz's appeal to Assyria.[30] But the narrative of Ahaz's reign in 2 Kgs 16 makes no mention of the promises to David, and it seems more likely that the combination of 'servant' and 'son' is expressive of subservience and dependency, though in this way also reflecting the same humiliation and submission to Assyria as the Isaiah pericope.

---

[25] The combination is rarely attested in extra-biblical documents, evidently only twice in two Amarna letters, the addressees of which are a high Egyptian official and an Egyptian royal scribe respectively. See M. Cogan and H. Tadmor, *II Kings: A New Translation with Introduction and Commentary*, Anchor Bible 11 (Garden City, NY, 1988), 187.

[26] Cogan and Tadmor, *II Kings*, 187.

[27] Cogan and Tadmor, *II Kings*, 187.

[28] Cogan and Tadmor, *II Kings*, 187.

[29] See S. A. Irvine, *Isaiah, Ahaz and the Syro-Ephraimite Crisis*, SBL Dissertation Series 123 (Atlanta, GA, 1990), 88.

[30] See R. E. Clements, 'The Davidic Covenant and the Isaiah Tradition', in A. D. H. Mayes and R. B. Salters (eds.), *Covenant as Context: Essays in Honour of E. W. Nicholson* (Oxford, 2003), 44–8.

The narrative of Ahaz's reign, which was so fateful for Judah, does not lend itself as transparently as the account of Solomon's reign as a text that the author of Deut. 17: 14–20 may have had in mind. Nevertheless, though the suggestion must remain tentative, the portrayal of Ahaz's description of himself as in a 'father–son' relation with the king of Assyria can readily be read as placing himself and his kingdom not only under the protection of Tiglath-pileser as a client state but in abject subservience to the Assyrian suzerain whom, in effect, he had 'set over' both his kingdom and his people.

(5) The solitary constructive instruction concerning the king in Deut. 17: 14–20 is delayed until its final two verses (vv. 18–20). It adds nothing, however, that transforms the content or tone of the passage into a realistic provision for kingship 'when you come into the land'. No king in the usual sense of the word is here in mind, no head of state with the normal functions pertaining to this office— indeed, no state, properly understood. The only leadership with which the bearer of the 'office' is here charged is to be an exemplary Israelite in meditating upon and fulfilling the requirements of 'the book of the *torah*', upon which conduct also depends the future of his dynasty. More than any other among the instructions concerning kingship in Deut. 17: 14–20, this solemn requirement will resound throughout the history of the kingdoms in the Deuteronomistic corpus, for it is against the standard declared by this injunction, which binds closely the fate of the monarchy with 'the book of the *torah*', that the history of the kingship is measured—and found wanting. In such a way also this injunction pre-empts, so to speak, any reading of the promises to the House of David as unconditional (2 Sam. 7: 11b–16).

DEUTERONOMY 17: 14–20 AND THE PROMISE TO DAVID

Such a reading of Deut. 17: 14–20 runs counter to the view that, notwithstanding the outcome of history in the destruction of Jerusalem and the exile and the plight of the surviving members of the royal family now in exile, the promises to David were by no means consigned to history by the Deuteronomists, and that the closing record in 2 Kgs 25: 27–30 of the release of Jehoiachin from prison in exile leaves open the possibility that YHWH's promises to David endure and can resume. This view was famously expressed by Gerhard von Rad,[31] who wrote of the Deuteronomist that he

could never concede that the saying about the lamp which was always to remain for David had now in fact 'failed.' As to any goal to which this saving word was coming he had nothing to say: the one thing he could do was just, in this direction, not to close the door of history, but to leave it open. This he did in the reflective conclusion of his work (2 Kgs 25. 27 ff.).[32]

The contrary view had earlier been concluded by Martin Noth.[33] Noth acknowledged that it is probable that all kinds of hopes of revival were connected with the person of Jehoiachin, both among those remaining in the homeland and among the scattered exiles, but 'in the end Jehoiachin died, as the deuteronomist reports at the end of his work . . . without any of the hopes that had been placed in him having been fulfilled'.[34]

These opposing views have attracted much debate, but more recently von Rad's reading of the text has found less favour,[35] even with those who, like him, urge that the prominence given in the Deuteronomistic history to the dynastic promise to David can only mean that that it remained in this corpus a source of hope and

---

[31] Gerhard von Rad, *Deuteronomium-Studien*, FRLANT 58 (Göttingen, 1947), 52–64; Eng trans. D. M. G. Stalker, 'The Deuteronomistic Theology of History in the Book of Kings', in *Studies in Deuteronomy* (London, 1953), 74–91; id., 'Die deuteronomistische Geschichtstheologie in den Königsbüchern', in *Gesammelte Studien zum Alten Testament* (Munich, 1958), 189–204; Eng. trans. E. Trueman Dicken 'The Deuteronomistic Theology of History in I and II Kings', in *The Problem of the Hexateuch and Other Essays* (Edinburgh, 1966), 205–21; id., *Theologie des Alten Testaments*, Bd. I, *Die Theologie der geschichtliche Überlieferungen Israels* (Munich, 1957); Eng. trans. D. M. G. Stalker, *Old Testament Theology*, Vol. I, *The Theology of Israel's Historical Traditions* (Edinburgh, 1962).

[32] Von Rad *The Theology of Israel's Historical Traditions*, 343, n. 22. Cf. id., 'The Deuteronomistic Theology of History in I and II Kings', 219–20.

[33] M. Noth, *Überlieferungsgeschichtliche Studien* (first published 1943; 2nd edn. Tübingen, 1957), 108; Eng. trans. by H. G. M. Williamson, *The Deuteronomistic History*, JSOTSup 15 (Sheffield, 1981), 98. Cf. id., *Geschichte Israels* (2nd edn. Göttingen, 1954), 262, Eng. trans. by P. R. Ackroyd, *The History of Israel* (London, 1960), 290.

[34] Noth, *The History of Israel*, 290.

[35] e.g. F. M. Cross, *Canaanite Myth and Hebrew Epic* (Cambridge, MA, 1973); W. McKane, *Jeremiah*, Vol. II, ICC (Edinburgh, 1996), 1388; J. G. McConville, 'King and Messiah in Deuteronomy and the Deuteronomistic History', in J. Day (ed.), *King and Messiah in Israel and the Ancient Near East*, JSOTSup 270 (Sheffield, 1998), 271–95; Cogan and Tadmor, *II Kings*.

expectation even in the shadow of the catastrophe of the early sixth century. An inauspicious view on the future of the Davidic monarchy in 2 Kgs 25: 27–30 as against the prominence given to the promise to the House of David in 2 Sam. 7 is readily explained, it is argued, by the recent trend towards reading the books of the Deuteronomistic history as separate works, each with its own *Tendenz* and theology.[36] Others, whilst sharing von Rad's view that the promises to David are a dominant theme of the Deuteronomistic corpus, argue that this was so only of a first edition of this history, and that an exilic editor added material, including 2 Kgs 25: 27–30, contradicting this theme in the belief that the promises to David had finally been aborted by the gross apostasy of Manasseh (cf. 2 Kgs 21: 2–15).[37]

My own further thoughts about 2 Kgs 25: 27–30 and its parallel account in Jer. 52: 31–4[38] are that the case for the so-called 'pessimistic' reading of the text is the more persuasive. Jehoiachin, described as being released from prison and permitted to discard his prison clothes after thirty-seven years in exile, is a figure of some pathos in this text, and since, as the text implies, he is now dead and cannot himself therefore be the centre of hopes for a new dawn for the promises to David, the absence of any reference to his sons renders it all the more unlikely that this text is motioning that these events are a sign that the 'lamp' of David has not failed and that YHWH has turned the tide in the fortunes of his people. In short, what is reported is too meagre a basis from which to infer that the text is to be understood as *kerygma*, even a muted one.[39]

The same assessment of this brief narrative is strengthened by other evidence. The doom-laden prophecy concerning Coniah in Jer. 22: 24–7 and the further decree of doom in vv. 28–30 are evidence that whilst some held hopes for the future centring upon Jehoiachin (cf. Jer. 28: 1–4),[40] which are here dubbed 'false

---

[36] See e.g. McConville, 'King and Messiah in Deuteronomy and the Deuteronomistic History', 294–5.

[37] See esp. the discussion of this by Cross, *Canaanite Myth and Hebrew Epic*, ch. 10.

[38] Cf. E. W. Nicholson, *Preaching to the Exiles:A Study of the Prose Tradition in the Book of Jeremiah* (Oxford, 1970), 78–80.

[39] Von Rad uses the word 'nachdenklichen' ('reflective', 'pensive') of 2 Kgs 25: 27–30, but such a description is imported to the text rather than necessarily arising from it.

[40] Beginning at ch. 1: 2, the book of Ezekiel (1: 2; 33: 21; 40: 1) suggests that the exiles dated their years from the deportation of Jehoiachin, who was regarded by at least some of the exiles as still king of Judah.

hopes'[41] (22: 27), others wrote off any such hope that the line of David would continue through Jehoiachin and his sons: 'I will cast you [Coniah] out, with the mother who bore you, into a land where you were not born, and there you shall die' (v. 26); 'These are the words of Yahweh: Record that this man is stripped of rank, one ill-fated in his lifetime. None of his children will achieve custody of the throne of David, or become a king again in Judah' (v. 30).[42] 2 Kgs 25: 27–30 does not toll the same grim knell as the texts in Jeremiah, but its matter-of-fact narration suggests that it was primarily written to record the final fate of Jehoiachin rather than announce a future for the promises to his ancestor David. Von Rad commented on the work of the Deuteronomists that 'it was not often that Israel expressed her realisation of the law's judging and destroying power in such a radical way'.[43] Whatever stages the Deuteronomistic corpus underwent in acquiring its present literary form, its exilic authors/redactors do not seem to have believed that the tradition of the promises to David could moderate this; no plea came from them resembling that of the author of Psalm 89, who asks in the midst of national tragedy—probably the exile—'Lord, where is your steadfast love of old, which by your faithfulness you swore to David?' (v. 50), and prays expectantly. For these authors or editors Israel's future lay in 'turning again' to YHWH, whom Solomon petitions to hear and forgive when the people 'repent with all their mind and with all their heart in the land of their enemies, who carried them captive', pleading for such forgiveness on the basis of the election tradition grounded in the exodus: 'they are your people, and your heritage, whom you brought out of Egypt ... whom you separated from among all the peoples of the earth to be your heritage' (1 Kgs 8: 46–53).[44] This text, which is unquestionably a Deuteronomistic composition, here places no suggestion on the lips of David's son that a future for the people in exile is assured on the grounds of YHWH's promises to his father David.

---

[41] For this translation see W. McKane, *Jeremiah*, Vol. I, ICC (Edinburgh, 1986), 545.

[42] The translation of both verses is McKane's, *Jeremiah*, Vol. I 540, 547.

[43] Von Rad, *The Theology of Israel's Historical Traditions*, 343.

[44] Cogan and Tadmor, *II Kings*, 330 suggest that 2 Kgs 25: 27–30 is 'merely an epilogue by an exilic writer who brought the narrative of Jehoiachin's life up to date. Exilic readers might have found some measure of consolation in the preferred treatment of their aged king; from this point of view the book of Kings does end on positive note. But the restoration of Israel, in Deuteronomic terms, required a return to YHWH.'

This returns us to our main text in Deut. 17: 14–20, for here, in advance of the history of the monarchy in Israel/Judah, the (anticipated) request for a king 'like all the nations round about' is presaged as a failure on the part of the people, and what follows is expressive of a deep mistrust of kingship, if not, indeed, thinly disguised hostility towards the institution, and culminates in a statement of conditions which render kings and dynasties subject to 'the law's judging and destroying power'. In the wake of the destruction of Jerusalem and the exile, it implicitly views the promises to David no longer as though they were *sub specie aeternitatis*, so to speak, but 'demystifies' them of any mythic dimension and renders them conditional upon obedience to 'the book of the *torah*'. In such a way this text casts a long shadow ahead of itself. The passage is the work of a Deuteronomistic editor who has placed on the lips of Moses in 'the book of the *torah*' an ominously foreboding statement, though ostensibly presented as statutes alongside other 'statutes and ordinances', about kingship in the nation. It represents an editorial 'key note' that resonates throughout the history of the kingdoms of both Judah and Israel narrated in the second half of the Deuteronomistic corpus.

6

'Do not dare to set a foreigner over you':
The King in Deuteronomy and
'The Great King'

In the foregoing chapter I considered briefly the enigmatic clause in
v. 15b in the short pericope concerning kingship in Deut. 17: 14–20.
The clause reads לא תוכל לתת עליך איש נכרי אשר לא אחיך הוא
and is usually translated in English Versions in some such way as:
'you may not *or* you shall not set a foreigner over you, one who is not
a brother Israelite.' In what follows I offer a fuller discussion of this
enigmatic prohibition,[1] a solution to which might shed light on some
of the other issues that arise in the study of this passage.

I

Commentators have remarked on the strangeness of the clause, since,
as S. R. Driver put it, 'it is difficult to imagine what attractions the
rule of a foreigner can have possessed for Israel, and there are no
traces in the history of either kingdom of a desire to establish it'.[2] A
number of well-known solutions to the circumstances that gave rise
to this prohibition have been suggested: that behind it lies the plot of
the Syro-Ephraimite conspirators against Judah in the reign of Ahaz

---

[1] This chapter, with some necessary revision in the light of further reflection on
the provenance of Deuteronomy, is based upon an earlier article '"Do not dare to set
a foreigner over you": The King in Deuteronomy and "The Great King"', *ZAW* 118
(2006), 46–61.

[2] S. R. Driver, *Deuteronomy*, ICC (3rd edn., Edinburgh, 1902), 210.

to usurp the throne of Judah in favour of one Tab'el (Isa. 7: 6), who was probably an Aramaean, or alternatively Omri, king of Israel, whose name may suggest that he was of foreign (Arabic) descent, or the memory of the infamous Tyrian princess Jezebel, wife of Ahab, or perhaps the story of Abimelech's kingship (Judg. 8: 29–9, 57), whose mother was a Canaanite and who might thus be regarded as a 'foreigner'. But the notion that the Syro-Ephraimite conflict with Judah lies behind the clause is an uncertain inference from Isa. 8: 6;[3] nothing is made of Omri's supposed foreignness in the narratives concerning his dynasty; Jezebel, whatever her influence, was not monarch of Israel, and could have not have been considered as grounds for a fear that the nation might choose a foreigner as king; and the suggestion that the (probably ancient) story of Abimelech might have inspired Moses' pre-emptive prohibition is surely strained.

A more recent and, as far as I am aware, novel suggestion has been made by Anselm Hagedorn, who argues that since in Isa. 45: 1 Cyrus is addressed as someone anointed by YHWH,

> if one reads Deut 17.15b with the eyes of an author who is familiar with the work of Deutero-Isaiah, the additional restriction on the ethnic origin of the king becomes understandable ... Maybe the author of Deut 17.14–20 reacts against the circle around Deutero-Isaiah where one could actually imagine having a foreign king appointed by YHWH over Israel. The mentioning of the איש נכרי in the same verse suggests that we are dealing with a problem of the 5th century.[4]

But how and why would a sixth-century proclamation concerning Cyrus have been considered in the fifth century to pose a threat prompting such a forcefully formulated prohibition placed on the lips of Moses in Deut. 17: 15b? Why should anyone in the fifth century have seen in Deutero-Isaiah's words about Cyrus, long since dead, a possible basis on which some group might wish, in the name of YHWH, to make a foreigner king over an envisaged or newly established Jewish state? And what foreigner might have been thought of as a possible candidate?

---

[3] Driver, *Deuteronomy*, 210.
[4] A. Hagedorn, *Between Moses and Plato: Individual and Society in Deuteronomy and Ancient Greek Law*, FRLANT 204 (Göttingen, 2004), 141.

II

The main difficulty with the various suggestions offered is that none of the incidents or historical figures cited indicates any tendency or movement in either northern Israel or in Judah to usurp the indigenous monarchy in favour of a foreigner such as would call for a 'pre-emptive' prohibition placed by the authors of Deuteronomy upon the lips of Moses in Deut 17: 15b, which is more strongly expressed than is usually perceived (see below). Against these various suggestions, it seems more likely that there lies behind this injunction more than a passing incident.

What has been lacking in the discussion of this prohibition is an adequate consideration of the Hebrew construction employed.[5] This is the use of the verb יכל with the negative particle לא employed in various contexts to express injunctions and interdicts of special importance and consequence, morally or otherwise, as, for example, in the observance of cultic requirements, ritual taboos, or the protection of family and social rights (e.g. Gen. 43: 32; Judg. 21: 18). The construction is mostly attested in Deuteronomy itself. Thus, for example, within the context of the law of the centralization of cultic worship, so significant a feature of Deuteronomy, 12: 17 reads, 'you may not eat (לא תוכל לאכל) within your towns the tithe of your grain or of your wine . . . but you shall eat them before the Lord your God in the place which the Lord your God will choose'. The sense is captured by, for example, 'do not dare *or* you are forbidden[6] to eat within your towns the tithe . . .'. Similarly, the Passover law in chapter 16 stipulates, 'do not dare *or* you are forbidden to offer (לא תוכל לזבח) the Passover sacrifice within any of your towns which the Lord your God gives you, but at the place which the Lord your God will choose' (vv. 5–6). The same emphasis is employed in various instructions protecting family rights and in prescribing communal duties (cf. 21: 15–17; 22: 13–21; 22: 9; 24: 1–4; 22: 3).

---

[5] An exception is D. Daube, 'The Culture of Deuteronomy', in *Orita: Ibadan Journal of Religious Studies*, 3: 1 (1969), 27–52, who argues that the use of this construction in Deuteronomy pertains to what he describes as 'the shame cultural bias of the book'. However, a desire or attempt to appoint a foreigner as king over Israel is scarcely adequately described merely or only in terms of 'shame' or 'impossible behaviour'.

[6] See M. Weinfeld, *Deuteronomy and the Deuteronomic School* (Oxford, 1972), 2–3.

In the light of these usages of this construction there can be no mistaking the emphasis of the formulation in Deut 17: 15b, which can aptly be translated in some such way as: 'Do not dare *or* you are forbidden to set over you a foreigner, one who is not a brother Israelite.' Such a solemnly expressed injunction suggests that the prohibition against setting a foreigner over Israel was based not upon some isolated, passing incident, of which in any event we have no sound evidence, but upon circumstances in which Israel was indeed, or had been, subject to the rule and authority of a foreign king. When and how might this have come about and been so?

III

The mid-eighth century BCE saw the beginning of a new period in the history of the ancient Near East that almost immediately brought disaster upon the northern kingdom of Israel and in due course an end also of the Judaean state. Under a series of able rulers, beginning with Tiglath-pileser III, the Assyrians established themselves as a revived international superpower, which for more than a century was to exercise hegemony not only over Mesopotamia but also over the minor states of Syria–Palestine and for a time even Egypt also.

According to 2 Kgs 16, Rezin of Damascus and Pekah of northern Israel made an alliance to attack Judah. Ahaz of Judah appealed to Tiglath-pileser, paying tribute. The Assyrians moved against the coalition of Damascus and northern Israel. Rezin was killed and his people exiled to Kir. Pekah too was killed, but the kingdom of Israel survived under Hoshea, who became a vassal of Assyria. Subsequently, however, Hoshea rebelled against Assyria (2 Kgs 17: 1–6). The Assyrians, now under Shalmaneser V, invaded and the kingdom of northern Israel suffered the same fate as Damascus, including exile. We know from Assyrian sources that Samaria now became the centre of a new Assyrian province, bearing the name Samerina. Galilee and the Israelite territory east of the Jordan had earlier been organized as provinces of the empire.

There is uncertainty about why Rezin and Pekah invaded Judah, and it is also unclear whether Ahaz's appeal to Tiglath-pileser recorded in 2 Kgs 16 was his initial act of submission or whether he had earlier become a vassal and was now appealing to his overlord for protection. Whatever the historical facts, however, it is clear that the author of 2 Kgs 16 presupposes the former of these alternatives, and that his narrative views Ahaz's appeal as the beginning of the vassalage of Judah to Assyria. For this author it is Ahaz's politics rather than his cultic arrangements in the temple that are the focus of condemnation. The description of the construction and innovation of the new altar contains no suggestion that Ahaz's intention was the introduction of an Assyrian or other new cult; the account in vv. 10–18 lacks the sort of denunciation we would expect from the Deuteronomist author(s) if the installation of a foreign cult was Ahaz's purpose in this matter. By contrast, the tribute paid by Ahaz to Tiglath-pileser is described as a 'bribe' which was raised in part by seizing silver and gold from the temple treasury and pillaging other items in the temple (v. 17). The report that Ahaz, when appealing to the Assyrian king, described himself as his 'son' as well as his 'servant' is expressive of subservience and dependency and is thus also polemical. For the Deuteronomistic authors, therefore, Ahaz's appeal to Tiglath-pileser, though it rescued him from the immediate threat from the Syro-Ephraimite coalition, was fateful, for it brought subjugation to Assyria and the virtual thraldom that being a vassal entailed (see below).

Put differently, what Ahaz did was—to employ the phraseology of Deut 17: 15b—'to set a foreigner (לתת איש נכרי) over (על)' the people—and himself. And so it continued: for a century Judah remained subject to the successive 'Great Kings' of the Assyrian empire. Hezekiah became involved in attempts by western states to throw off the Assyrian yoke and openly rebelled in 701 BCE, having made a pact with Egypt. The rebellion was short-lived, however, and Hezekiah for the remainder of his reign conformed to his treaty with the Assyrians.[7] There followed the long reign of Manasseh, who remained a loyal vassal to Assyria. When, in the latter part of the seventh century, Assyria's power waned and Judah under Josiah made an attempt to regain its independence, international politics once again proved fateful. Josiah died at Megiddo (2 Kgs 23: 29) in an attempt to thwart an Egyptian army on its way to assist the Assyrians

---

[7] For Sennacherib's account of the siege of Jerusalem see *ANET* 287–8, including Judah's loss of territory and the increased tribute exacted of Hezekiah who, it is narrated, 'in order to deliver the tribute and to do obeisance as a slave sent his (personal) messenger' to Sennacherib.

against the rising power of Babylon. There followed a period of political turmoil, marked by the making and breaking of treaties, until finally, at the hands of the now ascendant Babylonians under Nebuchadrezzar, Judah suffered the same fate as the northern state in the late eighth century.

IV

Isaiah declared the Syro-Ephraimite coalition to be doomed to failure and counselled Ahaz not to fear Rezin and Pekah (Isa. 7: 1–10), but to no avail. Later he inveighed against Hezekiah's league with Egypt against Assyria (30: 1–7; 31: 1–3). Earlier, Hosea also poured scorn upon northern Israel's international negotiations and treaty-making (5: 13–14; 7: 11; 8: 7–10), and upon its dealings with 'the Great King'.[8] *Realpolitik* rather than faith in YHWH and his promises, however, governed Ahaz's decision for vassalage to Assyria.

What did vassalage involve at the hands of the Assyrians?[9] There were degrees of severity in what 'the Great King' imposed upon his vassals, ranging from payment of annual tribute to complete loss of statehood and incorporation as a province of the empire under a governor appointed by the imperial authorities. The arrangements varied to some extent, depending upon how submissive and loyal a vassal was. Networks of garrisons were strategically positioned to counter any sign of rebellion in vassal nations. Agents (*qēpu*) were deployed in the courts of the subject monarchs to report to the Assyrian king anything that might affect security of the empire or the terms imposed by the suzerain. Secret agents were employed to collect intelligence, and, as ever, local collaborators were recruited for the same purpose. The annual tribute was the main tax upon a vassal, and was never less than heavy. Failure to pay the tribute was regarded as an act of rebellion and invoked appropriate reprisal. Vassals were also required to support the imperial garrisons in their territory, and

---

[8] Most modern commentators understand the clause מלך ירב in Hos. 5: 13 (cf. 10: 6) to refer to 'the Great King'. See G. I. Davies, *Hosea*, NCB (London, 1992), *in loc.*; A. A. Macintosh, *Hosea*, ICC (Edinburgh, 1997), *in loc.*

[9] See H. Spieckermann, *Juda unter Assur in der Sargonidenzeit*, FRLANT 129 (Göttingen, 1982), 307–18.

could be required to supply troops for the imperial armies.[10] They could also be asked to contribute to the suzerain's building operations in the imperial homeland. The suzerain held the power of veto over the succession to a vassal's throne after the death of the vassal. In these ways—administratively, militarily, and economically—becoming subject to Assyria meant that the vassal in effect did indeed set 'a foreigner' over him and his nation. The vassal retained sovereignty up to a point over his own state, but in all matters concerning the suzerain there was no mistaking who held the reins of power.

What this means is that although Ahaz, Hezekiah, Manasseh, and Amon were each king of Judah, they were subject to the will, demands, and impositions of 'the Great King'.

V

It is an obvious question, and by no means a new one, whether these kings' subjection to successive Assyrian suzerains also entailed the imposition of Assyrian religious obligations upon Judah's religion and cult over which they presided. There has been upwards of a century of debate about this, but no consensus has emerged. Two main and opposing views have been argued: on the one side, that the Assyrians imposed the worship of Assyrian gods upon their vassals, though alongside and not replacing the cult of the vassal's own gods; and, on the other, that no such practice was part of Assyrian imperial polity. In more recent research the first of these views has been freshly argued by Hermann Spieckermann,[11] whilst the second is represented by John McKay's well-known monograph.[12] An alternative analysis of the evidence, which offers something of a compromise between these two views, has been argued by Morton (Mordechai) Cogan,[13] who draws a distinction between vassal

---

[10] Ashurbanipal lists Manasseh amongst twenty-two kings who were vassals and who, when he marched against Tirhakah, came to him and 'kissed my feet' and were made to march with him against Tirhakah. See *ANET* 294.

[11] Spieckermann, *Juda unter Assur in der Sargonidenzeit.*

[12] J. W. McKay, *Religion in Judah under the Assyrians 732–609 B.C.* (London, 1973).

[13] M. Cogan, *Imperialism and Religion: Assyria, Judah and Israel in the Eighth and Seventh Centuries B.C.E.*, SBLMS 19 (Missoula, MS, 1974).

states proper and former independent states fully incorporated as provinces into the Assyrian empire and under direct Assyrian governance. In the latter the Assyrians did impose religious and cultic obligations, but no such policy was carried out in the case of vassals or, as they are now usually termed, client states.

Steven Holloway's more recently published work is an extensive reassessment of the evidence, and in significant ways advances our knowledge of the role of religion in Neo-Asssyrian imperial polity.[14] He finds that in regard to subjugated states and territories such polity was much more flexible and nuanced than earlier scholars have perceived, and ranged from the despoliation of national gods to substantial patronage of the ancestral cults of conquered nations. There was no 'one size fits all' policy; rather, polity varied with circumstances—local, geopolitical, the strategic position of a subjugated state, whether militarily or for the purposes of trade—over the several centuries of the Neo-Assyrian empire and in the dealings of the imperial authorities with hundreds of kings and across the thousands of square miles encompassed by 'Greater Assyria'. He points up the peril of extrapolating general conclusions from limited testimony or evidence from one period of this expansive imperial history.[15]

According to Cogan (p. 49): 'Only the populations of those lands permanently annexed to Assyria as provinces experienced partial religious dictation; residents of vassal states were free of any religious obligations toward their Assyrian master.' In the former, the annexed provinces, the citizens were treated in every way as Assyrian citizens and were required to 'revere god and king', paying taxes to both palace and temple, whilst in the case of vassals 'wholly political demands were their lot' (p. 56), that is, tribute, military support, and the like. The treatment of the northern kingdom of Israel after 722 BCE (2 Kgs 17: 1–6) evidences the procedure when a state was reconstituted as a province of the empire under a governor. Thus Sargon records the deportation of a large number of the people to other parts of the empire, and the resettlement in northern Israel of subjugated people from elsewhere.[16] An

---

[14] S. W. Holloway, *Aššur is King! Aššur is King! Religion in the Exercise of Power in the Neo-Assyrian Empire* (Leiden, 2002).

[15] For Holloway's general critique of the work of McKay, Cogan, and Spieckermann, see *Aššur is King!*, 53–64.

[16] See *ANET* 284–7.

official (*šaknu*)[17] was placed over them by Assyria, and henceforth the people were treated in every way as citizens of Assyria, with the obligations that this carried with it, including religious obligations, whilst allowing the continuance of the customary local cult. Thus Sargon records that he imposed obligations upon them 'just as if they were Assyrians'—a phrase, or one similar to it, reproduced or echoed elsewhere[18]—and arranged for the northern Israelites to be 'trained in proper conduct',[19] that is, 'to revere god and king'.[20] By contrast, however, Neo-Assyrian sources make no mention of religious impositions made upon client states, whether of sacrificial dues or the setting up of religious symbols, for example, 'the weapon of Aššur' erected in provincial territories where, he suggests, it was probably a focal point for cultic observances of the Assyrian gods (see below).[21]

Spieckermann rejects such a conclusion, arguing that the cultic requirements imposed by Esarhaddon upon Egypt know of no such distinction in the treatment of provinces and client states. The Assyrian arrangements for their Egyptian territories, he argues, were more varied and complex, some areas organized as provinces whilst others were treated or organized as client states. The different titles employed by the Assyrians for the officials whom they appointed for the oversight of different individual states within the Egyptian territories conquered by Esarhaddon (*šarrāni, pāḫāti, šaknūti, šāpiri*) evidence this.[22] The cultic imposition was, however, uniform and thus applied to vassals no less than to the rulers of newly constituted provinces within Assyria's Egyptian territories: 'I established regular sacrificial offerings for all times for Aššur and the great gods, my lords.'[23]

Spieckermann further argues that Tiglath-pileser's record of the rebellion of Gaza casts similar doubt upon the distinction drawn by Cogan between client states and provinces. This record narrates the rebellion, its suppression, the subsequent reprieve of Gaza, the

---

[17] The precise meaning of the title is unknown. See Cogan, *Imperialism and Religion*, 50, n. 43.

[18] See Cogan, *Imperialism and Religion*, 50.

[19] For this translation see *Imperialism and Religion*, 50 and n. 43.

[20] *Imperialism and Religion*, 50–1.

[21] *Imperialism and Religion*, 56. Cf. p. 112.

[22] See Spieckermann, *Juda unter Assur in der Sargonidenzeit*, 338–9. Cf. ANET 293.

[23] Spieckermann, *Juda unter Assur in der Sargonidenzeit*, 338. Cf. Cogan, *Imperialism and Religion*, 52. See ANET, 293.

transfer of (images of) the local deities to Assyria, and the installation of 'images of the great gods' and of himself in the royal palace, and the reinstatement of its ruler Hānūnu.[24] Since the placing in the palace of 'images of the great gods' and thus a possible object of worship is mentioned, Cogan suggests that Gaza may have been a province.[25] But the reinstatement of Hānūnu, who after his rebellion against Assyria fled to Egypt but subsequently returned and submitted to Tiglath-pileser, was as a vassal and not as governor of a (newly created) province.[26] It seems, in fact, that Gaza never was a province of the empire.[27]

Against Spieckermann, Holloway counsels caution in drawing conclusions from Esarhaddon's supposed arrangements for cultic dues exacted from Egypt, and raises doubts also about his conclusion from the (badly mutilated) record of the case of Hānūnu and Gaza. Thus, only one of the accounts of Esarhaddon's conquest of Egypt— the Zinjirli stele—narrates the imposition of cultic dues upon Egypt, whilst the Nahr el-Kelb author and other accounts of Esarhaddon's Egyptian triumphs make no mention of this. Holloway makes the point that the

iconography of the Zinjirli stele is strikingly aggressive and threatening even by Assyrian standards, and control over the western provinces was chronically at risk. A customized piece of imperial theatre like the greater-than-life gateway Zinjirli stele might incorporate a fictive action such as a pan-Egyptian requirement to furnish the larder of the temple of Aššur in the Assyrian heartland in order to impress upon the provincial elites the omnipotence of the Assyrian Wehrmacht.[28]

In the case of Gaza, Holloway argues, advantageous ad hoc arrangements rather than the execution of a preordained religious polity were more likely the reason for the lenient treatment of Hānūnu, which 'may have come with a variety of unsubtle "reminders" of Assyrian sovereignty. An image of Tiglath-pileser III . . . prominently displayed in [Hānūnu's] palace, was probably intended to remind the wayward ruler that a sizable cut of his annual

---

[24] See Spieckermann, *Juda unter Assur in der Sargonidenzeit*, 325–30.

[25] Cogan, *Imperialism and Religion*, 55, n. 79.

[26] See H. Donner, 'The Separate States of Israel and Judah', in J. H. Hayes and J. M. Miller (eds.), *Israelite and Judaean History* (London, 1977), 425.

[27] See Spieckermann, *Juda unter Assur in der Sargonidenzeit*, 328.

[28] Holloway, *Aššur is King!*, 63–4.

profits was earmarked for the Great King.'[29] Hānūnu was thus left on his throne because the economic network he dominated rendered him 'more useful alive than flayed'. Holloway cautions, against both Cogan and Spieckermann, that 'either the Assyrian sources do not reveal enough information to reconstruct their foreign religious policy in reliable detail, or their foreign religious policy was sufficiently flexible that we cannot with any certainty extrapolate its behavior where our sources are silent'.[30]

Both Cogan and Spieckermann draw special attention to the treatment of the local deities by the Assyrians—as, for example, at Gaza—as a significant aspect of Assyrian strategy in dealing with conquered states.[31] The transport of the images of local gods to Assyria constituted a claim that the victory of the Assyrians over subjugated states was by the will of the gods of these states who, angered by their people, had abandoned them and yielded them to defeat by the Assyrian victors. In such a way the native gods of conquered states were claimed by the Assyrian victors to have been on their side. This strategy is famously illustrated by the narrative in 2 Kgs 18 and its parallel in Isa, 36, in which the Assyrian royal envoy, the *rab shakeh*, is described as making just such a claim to the state representatives of Judah on the walls of Jerusalem and to the people there (see 2 Kgs 18: 25; Isa. 36: 10), much to the discomfort of the these representatives.[32] Thus Cogan concludes that '"Ashur and the great gods" were not the only authors of Assyria's victories; the Assyrian conqueror claimed that local foreign gods, in control of the destinies of their adherents, were also active in Assyria's behalf' (p. 111). The 'transport' of the images of local deities was likewise an unmistakable statement of the superiority of the imperial gods. The planting of the 'weapon of Aššur' in a conquered nation's or state centre, he suggests, was a further potent reminder of this superiority (see below).

But were such enactments—the transportation of the local gods, the claim that the local gods were on the side of the Assyrians, the planting of 'the weapon of Aššur' in conquered territories or, as is

---

[29] *Aššur is King!*, 193.
[30] *Aššur is King!*, 58.
[31] See Cogan, *Imperialism and Religion*, chs. 1 and 2; Spieckermann, *Juda unter Assur in der Sargonidenzeit*, 344–62.
[32] See Spieckermann, *Juda unter Assur in der Sargonidenzeit*, 346–7.

recorded in the case of Gaza, the placing of 'images of the great gods' in the palace—also associated with cultic observances required by Assyria throughout its conquered territories and states?

Spieckermann considers the record concerning Gaza as evidence that Tiglath-pileser imposed the cult of the Assyrian gods upon his vassal Hānūnu, and that the placing of an image of 'the great gods' in his palace signals this. Against this, however, from the location chosen for the image—the royal palace, not the state temple—it does not seem that the Assyrians were imposing the cult of Aššur upon the official cult at Gaza. Further, it is not clear whether there was one image—that of Tiglath-pileser with accompanying typical iconography of the Assyrian pantheon—or two, one of Tiglath-pileser and one of Aššur. That religious obligations were intended by the installation of this image (or images) in the state palace is likely, but, as Holloway suggests (p. 193), these would have consisted of a requirement to supply annual dues for the cult of Aššur in the Assyrian heartland.

Spieckermann also cites evidence from the so-called 'treaties of Esarhaddon'. Shortly before the long curse list in these texts,[33] the requirement of reverence towards the Assyrian gods on the part of the vassals is stated and is extended to succeeding generations of the vassal's line; they are placed under oath to 'revere as your own god Aššur, king of the gods, and the great gods, my lords . . .'.[34] In the light of more recent research, however, the evidence adduced from these texts is no longer admissible, since M. Liverani has shown that these texts are not treaties imposed upon client states in far-flung parts of the Assyrian empire; rather, they concern loyalty oaths (*adū*) imposed upon royal bodyguards, who were Medes, charged with the personal protection of the crown prince Ashurbanipal.[35] It is natural that guards living in Assyrian royal palace(s) and responsible for the protection of the crown prince, who was under the protection of Aššur and the great gods, would have been charged to 'revere as your own god Aššur, king of the gods, and the great gods, my lords . . .'. But such a demand cannot be used as evidence of what the Assyrians required of other vassals; as Liverani comments, 'the fact that we

---

[33] See *ANET* 534–41.

[34] For the text see *ANET* 538. See Spieckermann *Juda unter Assur in der Sargonidenzeit*, 332–5.

[35] Mario Liverani, 'The Medes at Esarhaddon's Court', *JCS* 47 (1995), 57–62.

have recovered only the Mede oaths can now be explained in the simplest terms: there were no similar oaths with other "vassals"' (p. 62).

Cogan draws attention to three texts, the only texts out 'of the entire corpus of N[eo-] A[ssyrian] historical inscriptions' that 'explicitly tell of cultic imposts' (p. 52): one from Sennacherib recording that, having captured H̱irimmu on the Assyro-Babylonian border, he 'established one ox, ten sheep, ten homers of wine, twenty homers of its choicest dates as regular offerings for the gods of Assyria, my lords, for all times'; another from Ashurbanipal follow- ing the defeat of Shamash-shum-ukin imposing 'the finest regular sacrificial offerings for Ashur, Ninlil, and the gods of Assyria'; and the third from Esarhaddon, referred to above, imposing upon Egypt 'regular sacrificial offerings for all times for Ashur and the great gods, my lords' (p. 62). Cogan suggests, however, that what is entailed by these arrangements is inconclusive beyond the rendering of taxes to palace and temple, since 'we cannot tell whether all or part of the cultic dues were transferred to established Assyrian sanctuaries or if they were rendered at new cult places founded in the provinces' (pp. 52–3). That is, perhaps these prescribed offerings were sent as tribute to the Assyrians rather than for cultic rituals in the centres of vassal states themselves.

Holloway's conclusion from his own extensive re-examination of administrative and royal correspondence as well as records of royal prophecies shifts the balance of probability to this latter suggestion, since these sources nowhere 'suggest that a cult of Aššur was established on foreign soil'; nor do they 'provide evidence that Assyrian temples were constructed for Assyrian deities outside Mesopotamia'.[36]

Cogan finds evidence that the 'weapon of Aššur' (*kakki ša Aššur*) as well as other such emblems ('the dagger of Aššur', 'the spear of Aššur') played a part in the legal and cultic life of the Neo-Assyrian period, as they had in the Old Assyrian period, that the display of these emblems in new provinces probably served as more than just a reminder of reverence due to Assyrian gods, and that a cult in their honour was probably instituted. 'Once again, however', he concludes, 'the role demanded of provincials in such cult remains unknown.'

---

[36] Holloway, *Aššur is King!*, 200.

However, Holloway's re-examination of the evidence again casts doubt upon any suggestion that such emblems were objects of cultic worship: 'Based on the limited number of references to the "symbol of Aššur" in royal inscriptions, the absolute dearth of epistolary allusions to this "cult," and zero evidence for the existence of Aššur temples outside the Neo-Assyrian heartland, I am inclined to believe that these images were used in the administration of oaths to peoples of both client and provincial status—and little else.'[37]

Holloway's work thus shifts the balance of probability to the view that the Assyrians did not impose their national cult upon subjugated territories, whether client states or provinces. Indeed, Cogan himself, finding the Assyrian sources inconclusive on whether worship of the imperial gods was required of citizens of provinces, already acknowledged that the view of Landsberger and others 'may prove correct: Assyria "never forced conquered peoples to revere Ashur", but remained content to show Ashur's superiority to their own gods' (p. 61).[38]

Spieckermann is more confident and argues that the narrative of Ahaz's sojourn in Damascus offers evidence of the imposition of Assyrian cultic obligations upon Judah and of how the king managed this (pp. 362–9). At Damascus Ahaz saw an altar and sent instructions to Uriah in Jerusalem to have an altar on this model constructed and installed in the temple. Upon this new altar Uriah was to offer the usual offerings of the people and perform the rituals associated with this, but is also directed that the old bronze altar is to be reserved for Ahaz for a purpose described as לבקר (2 Kgs 16: 15b, see below). Spieckermann suggests that, though the meaning of לבקר is obscure, what may here be indicated was Ahaz's strategy to take upon himself his cultic obligations to the Assyrian suzerain as discreetly and inoffensively as possible in the political circumstances of the day. If this is so, Spieckermann argues (pp. 368, 371–2), Ahaz succeeded in a compromise that maintained his responsibility as king for the national cult, here manifest in his construction of the new altar, whilst at the same time fulfilling his treaty obligations to

---

[37] *Aššur is King!*, 160–78, 198–200. The quotation is from p. 177.

[38] The reference is to B. Landsberger's observations in a symposium on 'The Development of Culture in the Great Empires', in C. H. Kraeling and R. M. Adams (eds.), *City Invincible* (Chicago, 1960), 177.

the Assyrian suzerain, though the precise nature of the cultic actions he carried out remains unknown.

Such an understanding of what Ahaz intended by the construction of a new altar and the new use for the replaced bronze altar must remain conjecture, however, and other interpretations are possible. Perhaps, for example, Ahaz's new altar was motivated by the spirit of assimilation to the current international fashions, and his 'voluntary innovation . . . the first wave in the larger movement of acculturation to the practices of the Assyrian empire, which in themselves were heavily Aramaized—a wave which was to reach new heights in the mid-seventh century in the days of King Manasseh'.[39] As for the bronze altar set aside for the king himself, although the meaning of לבקר remains uncertain, it may signal nothing more than that this altar was for the king 'to frequent', 'to resort to',[40] that is, for his private use. There is nothing in the text to suggest that this usage was for Assyrian cultic purposes.[41]

A further assumption of Spieckermann in his consideration of Ahaz's motive in redeploying the older altar is that in such a way the king, presiding over a monolatrous cult, would have been enabled to take upon himself his cultic obligations to the Assyrian suzerain discreetly and inoffensively.[42] Modern assessments of the nature of Israelite religion throughout the monarchical period cast doubt upon such an assumption, however. Though there were groups or parties who were monolatrous Yahwists, the evidence suggests that at both an official and a popular level other deities were worshipped alongside the national God YHWH, and that this was accepted as normal.[43]

---

[39] M. Cogan and H. Tadmor, *II Kings: A New Translation with Introduction and Commentary* (New York, 1988), 193.

[40] Cogan and Tadmor, *II Kings*, 189.

[41] See Chapter 6, 'III', p. 121. Assyrian sources do not report the installation of altars in subject territories (Cf. Cogan and Tadmor, *II Kings*, 192).

[42] Spieckermann, *Juda unter Assur in der Sargonidenzeit*, 362–4, 371–2.

[43] See, most recently, F. Stavrakopoulou, *King Manasseh and Child Sacrifice: Biblical Distortions of Historical Realities*, BZAW 338 (Berlin, 2004). For the sixth century see S. Ackerman, *Under Every Green Tree: Popular Religion in Sixth-Century Judah*, HSM 46 (Atlanta, GA, 1992).

VI

What conclusions may confidently be drawn, then, concerning Assyrian imperial polity in the matter of the religion and cult of subject nations? Subject states and provinces were required to acknowledge the majesty and power of Aššur and the great gods. There is evidence that the Assyrians stipulated offerings to be provided by provincial citizens for Aššur and the great gods. On the other hand, there is no evidence that temples for Aššur and the Assyrian pantheon were erected outside the Assyrian heartland, and there is no archival or inscriptional evidence that the cult of Aššur was established on foreign soil.

In the case of Judah, two conclusions seem warranted. First, like other client states subject to the Assyrians, Judah was required to pay annual tribute to the imperial coffers and was liable to other impositions, such as the supply of troops to aid the imperial armies[44] and contributions to building operations in the Assyrian homeland. Assyrian hegemony also brought with it loss of sovereignty over considerable territory of the Judaean state. Second, however, there is no convincing evidence that the Assyrians sought to regulate the native Judaean cult or interfere with traditional cultic custom. It is fully in line with Holloway's findings, for example, that amidst all the cultic innovations with which the Deuteronomistic authors of 2 Kgs 21 charge Manasseh, there is no mention of the worship of Aššur. A supposed imposition of Assyrian imperial cults upon Judah cannot, therefore, have been the motivation for the interdict of Deut 17: 15b.

Such a prolonged period of Assyrian hegemony was not, however, without effects on Judah. As the generations came and went during the period from the mid-eighth century until the final decades of the seventh, Assyrian suzerainty will more and more have taken on an air of permanence, and imperial influence through a range of activities, including trade, will have induced, as prolonged imperial control of territories across time almost invariably does, a natural process of acculturation.[45] For some in Judah during the long reign of Manasseh there would have been a sense of a *pax Assyriana*, which not only delivered security to Judah from external threat but also

---

[44] See p. 123, n 10.
[45] See Cogan's helpful discussion of this, *Imperialism and Religion*, 91–6.

brought a degree of prosperity through new trading opportunities,[46] even if the yields of this were a monopoly of the few rather than of the many (cf. Zeph. 1: 11).[47] There is some evidence that high-ranking officials and some referred to as 'the sons of the king' wore 'foreign attire', possibly ceremonial clothes signifying some sort of identification with Assyrian hegemony.[48] The case of Ahaz's new altar, as noted above, may provide some evidence of a spirit of assimilation to new international fashions in art and architectural styles.[49] Still others fell willingly into line with the prevailing order, the manifest success of which they took as exhibiting the power of the imperial gods and the powerlessness of YHWH, in whom they abandoned faith: 'YHWH does no good, and he does no evil' (Zeph. 1: 12).[50] And with all this, the various cults mentioned as having been practised in this period may be understood as a manifestation of a popular religious culture that had emerged and was flourishing, comprising elements mediated through Aramaean influence as well as local western Semitic parallels of eastern Semitic cults, including the 'Queen of Heaven' (Jer. 7: 18; 44: 17–19, 25), who may have been a late 'amalgam' of West Semitic Astarte and East Semitic Ishtar, and closely associated with this the cult of Tammuz (Ezek. 8: 14), who in Mesopotamian mythology was the lover of Ishtar who betrayed him;[51] the worship of 'the host of heaven' (2 Kgs 17: 16; 21: 3,5; Zeph. 1: 5; Jer. 8: 2; 19: 3), that is, astral deities, and of the presence in the temple of 'horses dedicated to Shamash' and of 'chariots dedicated to Shamash' (2 Kgs 23: 11), and the reference in Ezek. 8: 16 to the worship of the sun in the inner court of the temple.[52] The settlement

---

[46] For this, see Stavrakopoulou, *King Manasseh*, 108–10.

[47] For this see the comments by M. A. Sweeney, *Zephaniah* (Minneapolis, 2003), 90–2.

[48] Sweeney, *Zephaniah*, 85.

[49] See Cogan and Tadmor, *II Kings*, 193: 'Syrian art and architectural styles are reported even within Assyria proper e.g. "the *bīt-ḫilāni* palace in the manner of the land of Hatti" constructed by Tiglath-pileser III and his successors'.

[50] See Sweeney, *Zephaniah*, 94–5.

[51] For a discussion of the cult of 'the Queen of Heaven' and its possible relationship with the cult of Tammuz see most recently Ackerman, *Under Every Green Tree*, 5–35, 79–92, who argues that 'the Queen of Heaven' is an amalgam of East Semitic Ishtar and West Semitic Astarte.

[52] For a cautious assessment of the provenance of the cult of Shamash see Ackerman, *Under Every Green Tree*, 93–9, who suggests that although there is evidence of a West Semitic cult of the sun, the cult mentioned in Ezekiel and in 2 Kgs 23: 11 probably incorporates elements from both East and West Semitic religion.

in northern Israel of new populations from elsewhere in the empire, bringing with them their own religion and cults and their national culture and customs, will have contributed further to the religious and cultural 'pluralism' of the time.

In various ways the condition of Judah, its society and its national cult, including the temple in Jerusalem, and popular piety, by the last quarter or so of the seventh century reflected the influence of a century of Assyrian hegemony—of the rule of 'the Great King'. The forceful interdict of Deut 17: 15a surely reflects the memory of all that issued from Israel's and Judah's participation in the power-politics of the time and the cataclysmic consequences to which this led, first in 722 BCE and later in 597 and 587. It was, after all, the making of royally agreed treaties with rival superpowers—Egypt and Babylon— and then breach of them during the final years of the seventh century that finally occasioned the catastrophic events of the early sixth century. In such a way, this interdict reinforces the impression that Deut. 17: 14–20, though ostensibly providing for a monarchy in Israel, is in reality critical of the institution of kingship. Viewed thus, Deut. 17: 14–20, as suggested earlier, is a founding text of the prominent Deuteronomistic theme of the failure of the monarchy.[53]

This ardent prohibition in Deut. 17: 15b had yet a further motivation, however. With the remainder of this short pericope it also expresses a significant theme of Deuteronomy to which attention has already been drawn, that is, the 'depoliticizing' of Israel, the striking distancing of the Israel here envisaged from Israel as a historic state, the usual institutions and arrangements of which, not least of all a monarchy, are not apparent in the ordering of the life of the society to which these authors addressed themselves. Here Israel has become an 'internal culture', a society of 'brothers' with a 'non-statelike' identity grounded in a foundation story in the shape of 'the book of the *torah*' that reinforces cultural autonomy and propagates and defends it in a larger political world that surrounds it, encroaches upon it, and threatens it. It is a society that is commanded to disengage from its past history of inter-state politics and from its fateful interventions in the management of worldly affairs, which it is now solemnly enjoined to abandon to the imperial powers that be.

---

[53] On this see Chapter 5, 'The "Law" of the King in Deuteronomy 17: 14–20', pp. 107–12.

Part II

7

Story and History in the Old Testament

The title of this chapter, which was originally contributed to a volume of essays honouring my colleague Professor James Barr upon his seventieth birthday,[1] is partly derived from an essay by Professor Barr,[2] and its contents seek to elaborate some reservations he expressed concerning the description of the long narrative corpus of the Old Testament (notably Genesis–2 Kings) as 'history writing', especially the contrast he briefly drew between the character of this corpus and early Greek historiography.

With a few necessary changes in style for the current publication, I reprint it here for the convenience of the reader, since it is immediately followed (Chapter 8) by my response to a long critique of it by John Van Seters, who, in his well-known and learned work *In Search of History*,[3] argues the claim that the Deuteronomistic corpus bears significant resemblances to early Greek historiography, notably Herodotus' *Histories.*

I

The description 'history' is commonly employed to refer to the prose narrative literature of the Old Testament. We speak of the Former Prophets, for example, as the historical books' or 'the Deuteronomistic history', or of the Pentateuchal 'history' or of the two main sources it contains as 'the Yahwist's history' or 'the Priestly

---

[1] 'Story and History in the Old Testament', in S. E. Ballentine and J. Barton (eds.), *Language, Theology, and The Bible: Essays in Honour of James Barr* (Oxford, 1994), 135–50.

[2] 'Story and History in Biblical Theology', *JR* 56 (1976), 1–17, repr. in James Barr, *The Scope and Authority of the Bible*, Explorations in Theology 7 (London, 1980), 1–17. References here are to the latter.

[3] John Van Seters, *In Search of History: Historiography in the Ancient Near East and the Origins of Biblical History* (New Haven, 1983).

Writer's history'. The justification for such a description seems obvious: the extensive narrative comprising the Pentateuch and the Former Prophets begins with creation and an account of primeval times, and recounts the various periods of Israel's history from the patriarchs to the destruction many centuries later of Judah at the hands of the Babylonians and the ensuing exile. As James Barr has put it (pp. 5–7), the narrative is a unitary story, and cumulative; it is provided with a chronological framework, marking all major events from the creation of the world, and from time to time providing synchronisms against what was understood to be happening in other nations, like the Edomites and Moabites. The narrative is certainly 'history-like'.

Many have gone further, however, claiming that it is more than a matter of appearance and that the description 'history' in a more profound sense can be applied to this corpus. Further, what is claimed for the whole is claimed also of the parts. Thus what is usually regarded as the earliest literary source of the Pentateuch or Hexateuch, the so-called J narrative, has been regarded by many as the work of a historian who collected and assembled diverse materials, both oral and written, and creatively wove them together according to a definite plan to narrate the working out of God's will for his people. Often associated with such a view of the Yahwist's narrative is the further claim that this author's thinking was shaped by a sort of quantum shift from an older and narrower sacral mode of understanding God's self-revelation to the sphere of history, including the dusty terrain of people's dealings with one another and the apparently secular events of everyday life, as the arena of the outworking of the divine will. Since this new way of thinking is believed to have emerged during the reign of Solomon and con-stituted a sort of 'enlightenment', the conclusion is confirmed that history writing originated in Israel long before it emerged in ancient Greece.[4]

It was not seen as detracting from such a view that much that is recounted in the Yahwist's narrative or in the more extensive Deuteronomistic corpus lacks historicity. Thus von Rad, whose

---

[4] See esp. Gerhard von Rad, 'Der Anfang der Geschichtsschreibung im alten Israel', *Archiv für Kulturgeschichte* 32 (1944), 1–42, repr. in *Gesammelte Studien zum Alten Testament* (Munich, 1958), 14–88, Eng. trans. 'The Beginnings of Historical Writing in Ancient Israel', in *The Problem of the Hexateuch and other Essays* (Edinburgh, 1966), 166–204.

studies of the origins of history writing in Israel have been widely influential, held radical views on the pre-literary history and transmission of major Pentateuchal traditions, and attributed the interconnectedness they now have in the narrative to the creativity of the Yahwist. For example, he believed that it was the Yahwist who united the Sinai covenant tradition with the other traditions relating to Israel's deliverance from Egypt and the gift of the land. He argued also that the Yahwist united the originally disparate and separate traditions concerning the patriarchs. When we add to these examples the considerable amount of 'myth' and legendary material, including the account of creation and the garden of Eden and the primeval period, cult-foundation legends, aetiological narratives, folk-tales, and the like, then it seems that the judgement that the Yahwist was a historian is not based upon a belief that he wrote history in the plain man's sense of the word, even though a modern historian might cull some history from some parts of what he wrote.

The situation is not altered in any significant way in the case of those who have taken a more conservative view of the historical reliability of what the Yahwist wrote, for even here at best only a skeletal outline of historical events was gleaned from the narrative, supplemented or supported by archaeological finds and data from other ancient Near Eastern sources, whilst substantial sections of the text were left aside as being of no value for writing a history of the period of Israelite history which they ostensibly record. Once again it seems that the description of the Yahwist's narrative as 'history writing' was meant in a way rather different from what is commonly understood by this phrase.

This was not seen as an embarrassment. The appropriateness of the description 'history writing' was defended on the grounds that we should not judge Israel's history writing by the canons of modern historiography or even by those of ancient Greek historiography, which is usually regarded as the foundation of Western historiography. Israel's concept of history, it was argued, was *sui generis* and totally different from that of ancient Greece. It was Israel's belief in the sovereignty of God in history that led to its historical way of thinking and the historical writings of the Old Testament.[5] The operation of the gods in history is of course recognized by Herodotus and shown here and there in his history,

---

[5] Cf. von Rad, 'The Beginnings of Historical Writing in Ancient Israel', 170.

but is not applied consistently, and is not integrally related to the course of events, whilst Thucydides maintains an 'icy silence' on the subject of divine intervention (p. 171). Both these authors are exclusively concerned in their writings with the history of human beings and their actions. In the Old Testament, by contrast, 'the significance of events is not to be sought in what happens here on earth. The real actors in the drama are neither nations nor kings nor celebrated heroes' (p. 171). Rather, 'History is under God's management. He sets the process in motion by his promise. He sets its limits according to his will, and watches over it . . . All history has its source in God, and takes place for God.'[6]

James Barr has already dealt with this sort of argument in characteristically incisive manner that leaves nothing to be added.[7] For all the debate there is among historians about the nature of history, the proper subjects and methods of historical research and writing, what kind of results it seeks to achieve, and whether they are worth achieving, there is no intellectually serious conception of history that resorts to divine agency as a mode of explanation. The defence outlined above of the appropriateness of the word to describe the narrative of the Pentateuch or its sources or of the Deuteronomistic corpus depended upon a redefinition of what we normally mean by the word history, a redefinition motivated by and grounded in a history-centred understanding of Old Testament theology with all the antinomies this involved and which Professor Barr has so decisively exposed.

II

The matter cannot rest here, however. The claim that the 'historical' literature of the Old Testament may properly be described as history writing has been argued anew more recently but on different grounds and, indeed, in greater detail than hitherto by John Van

---

[6] 'The Beginnings of Historical Writing in Ancient Israel', 170–1, citing L. Köhler, *Old Testament Theology*, Eng. trans. (London, 1957), 93.

[7] 'Story and History in Biblical Theology', 8–9, 12–13 See also his *Old and New in Interpretation* (London, 1966), ch. 3 *passim*. On 'divine intervention' in Herodotus see below, and Chapter 8.

Seters in two substantial studies.[8] More specifically, he seeks to show that the Yahwist[9] and the Deuteronomist, with whose narratives he is primarily concerned, were 'authors' and not merely collectors or transmitters of tradition, and that each can appropriately be described as a 'historian'. He offers an extensive and admirably comprehensive survey of comparative evidence from Mesopotamian, Egyptian, Hittite, and other ancient Near Eastern historiographical texts and inscriptions. He attaches special significance, however, to the comparative evidence of ancient Greek history writings, especially Herodotus, for evaluating the methods and achievement of the authors of ancient Israelite historiography. Often referred to but not hitherto systematically assessed and availed of by Old Testament scholars, the forms and methods of the early Greek historians, he maintains, provide a controlled and adequate means of understanding those of writers of the early prose historiography of the Old Testament.[10]

In narrative style and technique, he argues, the Old Testament historical literature and Herodotus show many similarities. He draws attention to their common use of parataxis and prolepsis as well as of so-called 'ring composition', the use by each of speeches placed on the lips of leading figures in the events narrated, the free composition of appropriate stories and anecdotes where their sources failed them, the insertion of editorial comment to introduce or sum up the theme of a unit or to provide a transition to the next unit, the periodization of history with the dovetailing of eras, themes, and *logoi*, and the association of important themes with major figures.[11] By means of such literary devices these authors skilfully wove together and creatively structured the disparate materials, both written and oral, which they had collected, and gave a sense of unity to the long and complex works they wrote. The use of royal chronologies, genealogies, or genealogical chronologies as a way of ordering separate story units is common in early Greek history writing in general and in Herodotus in particular, and is also prominent in the Old Testament literature.

---

[8] John Van Seters, *In Search of History* and *Prologue to History: The Yahwist as Historian in Genesis* (Louisville, KY, 1992).

[9] Van Seters includes the so-called E material as well as J in the work of this author. See his *Abraham in History and Tradition* (New Haven, 1975).

[10] *In Search of History*, 17.

[11] *In Search of History*, 37–8, 358.

He finds further similarities between Old Testament historical writings and Herodotus in prominent interpretative themes. For example, he claims, both Herodotus and the Deuteronomist show a dominant concern with divine retribution for unlawful acts as a fundamental principle of historical causality; that is, for both 'history is theodicy' (p. 40). Themes of 'divine providence, or retribution or salvation, and the use of the past as a mirror for present and future events in order to deal with the problem of change appear to be basic concerns addressed by both Herodotus and the Old Testament historiographic literature and constitute a major motivation for their existence'.[12] In scope of subject-matter and the themes treated, nothing in the literature of the ancient Near East before the fourth century, he argues, so closely resembles the biblical histories as the Greek histories.

Both deal with recent events, such as the Persian Wars or the Exile, and their causes through successive periods of the past. Both reconstruct the distant past through the technique of genealogy development and with anecdotal or folkloristic digressions. The combination of 'official' sources, such as chronicles, with oral tradition, and of poetic fragments with prose narration in a multigenre product, is not evident in any other body of preserved literature from the Near East in this period.[13]

Thus both the Yahwist and the Deuteronomist can be described as authors and historians in every sense in which these terms apply to Herodotus. The Deuteronomistic corpus, divested of secondary additions, is 'a literary work of superb accomplishment, with a remarkably uniform style and outlook'.[14] In genre it is a work of ancient historiography wholly comparable to that of ancient Greece. Its author's purpose was above all to communicate through his story of the people's past 'a sense of their identity—and that is the *sine qua non* of history writing'.[15] Van Seters argues that the Deuteronomist was Israel's first historian. The Yahwist wrote subsequently in the exilic period and composed his narrative as a supplement to the Deuteronomist's work by extending the history back in time to the beginning of the world.[16]

---

[12] *In Search of History*, 52.   [13] *In Search of History*, 51.
[14] *In Search of History*, 359.   [15] *In Search of History*, 359.
[16] *In Search of History*, 361.

III

In claiming that what the Deuteronomist attempted conforms to the '*sine qua non* of history writing' Van Seters has in mind J. Huizinga's definition of history.[17] What is lacking but surely more to the point, however, is an adequate outline of what the ancient Greek historians understood by 'history', of what it was that essentially characterized their method, purpose, and achievement, since it is in their writings, most notably Herodotus, that Van Seters finds the closest comparisons with the aims and methods of the Old Testament writers with whom he is primarily concerned. It is well known that Herodotus coined the word 'history' to describe the task he set himself:[18] 'Here are set forth the enquiries (*historiēs*) of Herodotus of Halicarnassus that men's actions may not in time be forgotten nor things great and wonderful, accomplished whether by Greeks or barbarians, go without report, nor especially the cause of the wars between one and the other.' By 'enquiry' Herodotus meant primarily travel and the active pursuit of data and a critical assessment of sources, whether written or oral. More frequently he uses the verb (*historein*) 'denoting precisely the activity of questioning, enquiring, researching'.[19] Evidence is examined and facts checked and the result put to the test. It was the development of this critical attitude towards recording events and the development of appropriate methods that characterized Greek historiography.[20] Before this there was an interest in the past, as the writings of Homer show, and in genealogical speculation, as the work of Hesiod illustrates. The art of historical narration in the Greek historians was also indebted to the epic narrative tradition stretching back to Homer.[21] But there is no continuity between either Homer or Hesiod

[17] J. Huizinga 'A Definition of the Concept of History', in R. Klibansky and H. J. Patton (eds.), *Philosophy and History: Essays Presented to Ernst Cassirer* (New York, 1963), 9: 'History is the intellectual form in which a nation renders account of itself to itself.'

[18] For a discussion of the word see John Gould, *Herodotus* (London, 1989), 9–12; S. Hornblower, *Thucydides* (London, 1987), 8–25. I am grateful to my colleague Simon Hornblower for many helpful suggestions in the preparation of this essay.

[19] Gould, *Herodotus*, 9

[20] Cf. A. Momigliano, 'The Herodotean and the Thucyclidean Tradition', in id., *The Classical Foundations of Modern Historiography* (Berkeley, 1990), 30.

[21] For Herodotus' debt to it see the discussion by Gould, *Herodotus*, ch. 3 The Logic of Narrative'.

and what is specific in Greek history writing—the critical attitude towards sources and to the recording of events.

Such an attitude began in the late sixth century and arose from a revolution in thought involving a 'rebellion against tradition, the search for new principles of explanation, the rise of doubt as an intellectual stimulus to new discoveries'.[22] The new attitude was famously expressed by Hecataeus: 'I Hecataeus will say what I think to be the truth; the stories of the Greeks are many and ridiculous.' Hecataeus was not a historian. His famous statement comes at the beginning of his work on heroic myths and genealogies which has been described as a 'false start' to history, 'on the one hand recognizing the need to understand the past in rational terms, but on the other hand using the fundamentally unsuitable material of myth'.[23] But what he discovered marked a decisively new beginning, namely, 'that a systematic criticism of historical tradition is both possible and desirable, and that a comparison between different national traditions helps to establish the truth'.[24]

Herodotus, 'the father of history', and his successors wrote about contemporary or near-contemporary events, Herodotus, for example, about the Persian Wars of the recent past, Thucydides about the contemporary Peloponnesian Wars. Though the choice of subjects was determined by the importance of the events, the reliability of sources was an additional motive, and reliability was determined by enquiry and question and cross-examination of sources and eyewitnesses. 'Herodotus emphasized the importance of reporting what one had seen and heard—and gave definite preference to what he had seen. Thucydides made direct experience the first qualification for proper historiography.'[25]

IV

None of these characteristic features of the method and scope of early Greek historiography is evident in the Yahwist's or the

[22] Momigliano, *Classical Foundations*, 31.
[23] Oswyn Murray, 'Greek Historians', in J. Boardman, J. Griffin, and 0. Murray (eds.), *Greece and the Hellenistic World* (Oxford, 1988), 182.
[24] Momigliano, *Classical Foundations*, 34.
[25] Momigliano, 'Tradition and the Classical Historian', in *Essays in Ancient and Modern Historiography* (Oxford, 1977), 162.

Deuteronomist's narrative. On the contrary, in essentials a wide gulf separates the two literatures:

1. It is misleading, however unintentional, to couple the Deuteronomist with Greek historians as dealing 'with recent events'. It is widely agreed that the Deuteronomist composed his work in the wake of Judah's defeat by the Babylonians and the destruction of the Judaean state, and that these catastrophic events and the deportations that followed were the major reason for his narrative. But he devotes no more space to the recent conflict between Judah and Babylon than to many other events he narrates, and, indeed, less than to many much less significant events. His purpose was not the recording of recent events in the sense in which Herodotus or Thucydides meant this. Certainly Herodotus, in the first four books, gives an expansive description of the build-up of Persian power in the sixth and early fifth centuries, including lengthy excursuses on nations such as the Egyptians, Scythians, and Lydians, and there is much that is only distantly relevant to the conflict proper between the Greeks and Persians which he is primarily concerned to narrate. But it is obvious that one cannot regard such 'prolegomena' as an analogy for the Deuteronomist's expansive narrative from Moses to the early sixth century, as though this narrative was the build-up to the author's real purpose of writing a history of recent events—the destruction of the state of Judah by the Babylonians and the resultant exile. Put differently, no one would seriously suggest that the Deuteronomist's narrative could be given the title or subtitle 'A Narrative of the Conflict between the Judaeans and the Babylonians', in the way in which one may describe Herodotus' history as 'A Narrative of the Conflict between the Greeks and the Persians'.

2. Closely related to this, the scope of the 'history' narrated by the Yahwist and the Deuteronomist would have been unacceptable to Greek historians. The empirical principle that the researcher must report eyewitness accounts and that he should limit himself to what can be established from these sources—in other words, that history writing proper deals only with contemporary or near-contemporary events—would have ruled out any attempt such as that of the Yahwist or the Deuteronomist to write about events so distant from their own times. Herodotus, who emphasized the importance of what one had seen and heard and gave priority to what he had seen,

and Thucydides, for whom direct experience was the first qualification for proper historiography, would have regarded such writings
as the very antithesis of proper historical enquiry. This in itself is
one of the clearest indications that neither the Yahwist nor the
Deuteronomist anticipated and employed the methods of the Greek
historians of the fifth century. In contrast to the latter, the Yahwist
and Deuteronomist writings are devoid of the critical assessment
and evaluation of sources which is such a feature of the writings of
Greek historians from Herodotus onwards. It may be added here
that the nearer in time Old Testament 'history writing' gets to Greek
historians such as Herodotus and Thucydides, the wider the gulf that
separates them, as in the case of the books of Chronicles.

3. Herodotus and the Old Testament writers gave distinctly
different answers to the question why things happen. That is,
causality in the events of history is differently perceived and
described. For the Deuteronomist, the downfall of Israel, first the
Northern Kingdom and subsequently Judah, was brought about
by Yahweh, who rejected his apostate people. The Assyrians and
Babylonians were merely the instruments of his will. The theme of
what apostasy would bring upon the nation at the hand of God is
already struck in the time of Moses (cf. Deut. 3), and subsequently
repeated by other major figures in the narrative such as Joshua
(Josh. 24) and by the prophets (cf. 2 Kgs 17): in spite of all warnings
Israel remained disobedient and so incurred Yahweh's judgement.
What the Deuteronomist was primarily concerned to write was a
theodicy, and for him any idea of contingency in the events that led
to the downfall of Israel and Judah is replaced by the belief in the
outworking of the sovereign will of God. What had happened to
Israel and Judah was not the result of the changes and chances of
history, the outcome of the decisions of men or power-struggles
among nations, that is, a sequence of events caused by many different
subjects which met as chance would have it.

By contrast, Herodotus 'wrote a multi-subjective, contingency-
oriented account' of events and their outcome.[26] 'He wanted to know
how everything had happened, what had followed what, and what
had influenced what. So he showed how the Persian Empire grew up,

---

[26] On the belief in contingency and 'multi-subjectivity' in Herodotus' work, see
C. Meier, 'Historical Answers to Historical Questions: The Origins of History in
Ancient Greece', *Arethusa*, 20 (1987), 41–57; Gould, *Herodotus*, ch. 4, 'Why Things
Happen'.

how Sparta and Athens became powerful, and how it was various chance motives, some of them highly personal, of individual leaders which in a very complicated interaction cause the Ionian conflict with the Persians.'[27] For Herodotus, what happened was not the outworking of a divine will; the claim that for him, as for the Old Testament writers, 'history is theodicy' is wholly unjustified. References to divine intervention in his narrative are for the most part derived from accounts of others which he documents as offering an interpretation of events. But 'whether the gods exert an effective influence or not must remain unrevealed. It goes beyond the bounds of empirical research.'[28] For example, Herodotus himself would not have composed an account of causation such as the Deuteronomist's description of events during Jehoiakim's reign in 2 Kgs 24: 1–3:

In his days Nebuchadnezzar king of Babylon came up, and Jehoiakim became his servant three years: then he turned and rebelled against him. And the LORD sent against him bands of the Chaldaeans, and bands of the Syrians, and bands of the Moabites, and bands of the children of Ammon, and sent them against Judah to destroy it, according to the word of the LORD, which he spake by the hand of his servants the prophets. Surely at the commandment of the LORD came this upon Judah, to remove them out of his sight, for the sins of Manasseh, according to all that he did.

Or to come much closer to events and personalities with which Herodotus was concerned in writing his history of the conflict between the Greeks and Persians, he would not have been satisfied with the Old Testament writer's understanding of what prompted Cyrus the Great to authorize the return of the Jews to their homeland as narrated in Ezra 1: 1–2: 18:[29]

Now in the first year of Cyrus king of Persia, that the word of the LORD by the mouth of Jeremiah might be fulfilled, the LORD stirred up the spirit of Cyrus king of Persia, that he made a proclamation throughout all his kingdom, and also wrote it, saying: 'Thus says Cyrus king of Persia: "All the kingdoms of the earth has the LORD, the God of heaven, given to me; and he has charged me to build him a house in Jerusalem, which is in Judah."'

---

[27] Meier, 'Historical Answers to Historical Questions', 48
[28] 'Historical Answers to Historical Questions', 45. See also Gould, *Herodotus*, 126 f.
[29] See Gould's comment, *Herodotus*, 126–7.

It may be objected that the contingency of events is well in evidence in other narratives in both the Yahwist and Deuteronomist writings. Examples that readily come to mind are the Joseph narrative in Genesis and the so-called 'Succession Narrative' (2 Sam. 9–20 + 1 Kgs 1–2). But the larger picture is not significantly altered by this. What these and other examples suggest is that Israelite writers could acknowledge and describe contingency in the case of shorter sequences of events. When dealing with larger dimensions, however, 'any idea of contingency gets lost in the wholesale assumption that there is some coherence of meaning'.[30] In his essay already referred to James Barr has summed up the matter aptly as follows (p. 7):

The story moves back and forward, quite without embarrassment, between human causation and divine causation, between the statement and description of events in entirely human terms, and the statement of events in a fashion utilizing express and large-scale divine intervention. The ability to mingle these styles is a mark of the genius of the literature, but it is also a sign that history is not a governing factor in the selection and presentation of material.

V

'Historiography' as a genre description is misapplied when used of the Pentateuch or Deuteronomistic literature. It connotes the endeavour to record what really happened. Of course, it is not to be thought of as simply this and nothing more, but the endeavour to discover and record what really happened is of its essence.[31] To quote again from Professor Barr: 'It may not be able to tell us precisely, definitively, or incontrovertibly what really happened; but what really happened is the assumed standard by which it operates.'[32] It was the standard by which the ancient Greek historians operated, whether or not it is believed that they succeeded. But neither the Yahwist nor the Deuteronomist writers worked by such a standard. Their writings are not the result of 'enquiry' (*historia*) in the sense that this term

---

[30] Meier, 'Historical Answers to Historical Questions', 50.

[31] Huizinga, from whom Van Seters derives his definition of history, certainly insisted upon this!

[32] Barr, 'Historical Reading and the Theological Interpretation of Scripture', in id., *The Scope and Authority of the Bible*, 41.

was coined and used by Herodotus. 'Enquiry', questioning and a critical assessment of sources, the active pursuit of dependable historical information, all of which are analytical of writing history in the way that the early Greek historians conceived this, are not in evidence in the work of the Yahwist or Deuteronomist. These authors did not seek to compose an accurate 'record' or reconstruction of past events, and it does not seem that the past was the motivation for their endeavours, even in those narratives which may be regarded as providing historically useful information. One prominent indication of this is the significant extent to which they were evidently con-cerned to provide patterns of God's dealings with his people in promise, fulfilment, and judgement, that is, paradigms intended for thinking about the present and hoping for the future.[33] What they wrote is best described as 'story' rather than 'history', and they brought to their task a highly accomplished artistry, as writers such as Robert Alter have recently shown.[34]

As the brief outline in Section I above indicated, it has been a characteristic of writings proposing the description 'history writing' for such narratives as those of the Yahwist or Deuteronomist that Israelite history writing is nonetheless distinguished from ancient Greek writings such as those of Herodotus or Thucydides and from modern understandings of history writing. Israelite historiography, it is maintained, is not to be judged by the canons employed in these other historiographies. 'History', when applied to the Old Testament, has thus to be redefined. Though the approach and objective of more recent studies such as that of Van Seters, to which may be added Halpern's recent book,[35] are different, the same shift in understanding 'history writing' takes place. Thus, as we have seen, Van Seters, who suggests that the forms and methods of early Greek historians such as Herodotus 'provide a more controlled and more adequate explanation for early prose historiography in ancient

---

[33] R. Smend has drawn special attention to the prominence of aetiology and paradigm as primary motivation of the authors of the Pentateuch and Deuterono-mistic corpus. See his *Elemente alttestamentlichen Geschichtsdenkens*, Theologische Studien 95 (Zürich, 1968). Cf. Barr, 'Story and History in Biblical Theology', 7–8, and 'Historical Reading and the Theological Interpretation of Scripture', 36.

[34] R. Alter, *The Art of Biblical Narrative* (New York, 1981); *The World of Biblical Literature* (London, 1992).

[35] B. Halpern, *The First Historians: The Hebrew Bible and History* (San Francisco, 1988). A detailed discussion of this book has not been possible in the space here available.

Israel',[36] bypasses most of what is distinctive in such writers as Herodotus and Thucydides and redefines historiography, stating in his conclusion that a 'discussion about the "ideas of history", or causation in human affairs, or critical and objective reporting of past events, while not without some value, too often miss[es] the mark'.[37]

Halpern castigates Van Seters for such an approach, upholds the principle that history writing, among other things, should aim at an accurate reconstruction of the past, and argues that the Deuteronomist, by his demonstrable conscientious use of, indeed 'wrestling with', the manifold traditions and sources he inherited and collected shows himself to have been an author with genuine antiquarian interests and curiosity, to have been indeed a historian. But he has to engage in something of a tour de force to show why, notwithstanding a ubiquitous belief in divine intervention and deter-mination of events in the Deuteronomistic corpus,[38] inconsistencies, contradictions between duplicate reports of the same event, attempts to harmonize differing accounts of the same event, the theological beliefs he imposes upon his sources, 'telescoping' of events, and the like, the Deuteronomist nonetheless merits the description historian. Halpern also states: 'The secret of historical method—that one must put the sources to proof—was no mystery in antiquity', but adds: 'Whether [the Deuteronomist] employed the method is moot.'[39] The evidence strongly suggests, however, that the Deuteronomist did not operate with this standard method of historical enquiry. On the contrary, it seems clear that he valued all his sources equally, and that it did not occur to him to examine them critically.[40] In the face

---

[36] *In Search of History*, 17.   [37] *In Search of History*, 354.

[38] For example, the 'prophecy-fulfilment' scheme that is one of the most prominent features of the Deuteronomist's narrative. See G. von Rad, *Studies in Deuteronomy* (London, 1953), ch. 7, Eng. trans. from *Deuteronomium-Studien* (Göttingen, 1947).

[39] *The First Historians*, 235.

[40] See M. Noth, *Überlieferungsgeschichtliche Studien*, 2nd edn. (Tübingen, 1957), 95, n. 3 (cf. p. 96): 'He [the Deuteronomist] ascribed indisputable documentary value to the content of his sources, and he regarded the events reported in them as historical reality which had to be respected as such. One can certainly not expect him to take a critical view of the sources transmitted to him.' Eng. trans. by H. M. G. Williamson, *The Deuteronomistic History* (Sheffield, 1981), 140, n. 2. Cf. p. 86. It is all the more surprising, in view of this, that Halpern can make such a statement as 'the sources for premonarchic times were not all that [the Deuteronomist] (or we) could desire' (*The First Historians*, 235). They are certainly not all that we could wish for, but where is the evidence that the Deuteronomist was anything less than satisfied with what his sources supplied him with for his narration of this period?

of this, as well as of the many other features of his narrative that are alien to any normal concept of history writing and counter to the methods usually regarded as prerequisite for this genre, is it not simply apologetic motives that would nonetheless classify what he composed as history, or at best a failure to distinguish what is 'history-like' from 'history'?

In my opinion the question is warranted whether, contrary to what these two scholars conclude, the comparisons and contrasts each of them draws between the Old Testament writings and other historiographical literature, both ancient and modern, as well as the many valuable insights they themselves provide into the literary artistry of the literature, do not rather confirm the view that the narratives of the Yahwist and the Deuteronomist merit the title 'story' rather than 'history', or as put by Professor Barr in describing the long narrative corpus of the Pentateuch and Former Prophets that now comprises both these sources, 'merit entirely the title story but only in part the title history'.[41] Do these comparisons and contrasts not confirm rather than deny the verdict already given by W. Vatke, one of the founding fathers of modern Old Testament scholarship, in the early nineteenth century?[42]

The Hebrews did not at all raise themselves to the standpoint of properly historical contemplation, and there is no book of the Old Testament, however much it may contain material that is otherwise objectively historical, that deserves the name of true historiography.

[41] 'Story and History in Biblical Theology', 5.

[42] The original quotation is given in Smend, *Elemente alttestamentliehen Geschichtsdenkens*, 33, and the translation is Professor Barr's, 'Story and History in Biblical Theology', 13.

8

The Deuteronomistic Corpus: History or Story?

A Response to John Van Seters

I

Some years after the publication of the foregoing essay, John Van Seters wrote a lengthy critique of it.[1] In response to his essay I offer the following observations, which indicate that, whilst appreciating many insights which his earlier well-known and learned volume *In Search of History* contains into the beginnings and early history of history writing in the ancient world, I remain unpersuaded by the case he has sought to make that the Deuteronomistic corpus, upon which I shall here concentrate, in significant ways anticipates the genre of Herodotus' celebrated *Histories*.

Van Seters criticizes my brief description of what Herodotus intended by the word he employs to describe his work—*historiēs* 'enquiries' and its related verb *historein*—arguing that it is 'misleading because it telescopes a long development that begins before Herodotus and continues after him through Thucydides to a particular historiographic tradition'.[2] What I wrote was:

By 'enquiry' (*historiē*) Herodotus meant primarily travel and the active pursuit of data and a critical assessment of sources, whether written or oral. More frequently he uses the verb (*historein*) 'denoting precisely the activity of questioning, enquiring, researching'. Evidence is examined and facts

---

[1] John Van Seters, 'Is there any Historiography in the Hebrew Bible? A Hebrew–Greek Comparison', *Journal of Northwest Semitic Languages*, 28: 2 (2002), 1–25.
[2] 'Is there any Historiography in the Hebrew Bible?', 4.

checked and the result put to the test.[3] It was the development of this critical attitude towards recording events and the development of appropriate methods that characterized Greek historiography.[4]

As this quotation and the footnotes here and elsewhere in my essay above indicate, my summary is derived from the discussion of it by, among others, such specialists as John Gould in his influential monograph on Herodotus, Simon Hornblower, especially his well-known monograph on Thucydides,[5] and Arnoldo Momigliano in his *The Classical Foundations of Modern Historiography* and *Essays in Ancient and Modern Historiography*, two works that together provide a description of the 'rebellion against tradition, the search for new principles of explanation, the rise of doubt as an intellectual stimulus to new discoveries' which the so-called Ionian Enlightenment of the late sixth century generated.

I could also, however, have cited in support of my summary Van Seters' own major study of ancient historiography, where he writes (emphasis added):[6]

It is generally accepted today that Herodotus did, in fact, *investigate directly and gather firsthand* the largest part of his work, and that he *tested where possible* the views he inherited from other writers. Above all, the way in which he employed *new critical methods* and set his 'researches' down as a unified whole was what made him so superior to all his predecessors and contemporaries.

Among the predecessors Van Seters rightly includes Hecataeus, the only forerunner to whom Herodotus refers directly, and to whom I also referred in my essay, and whose principle of rationalistic deduction, and above all his method of personal investigation (*historiē*), Herodotus emulated (p. 12). Of this method as employed by Hecataeus and adopted subsequently by Herodotus, Van Seters comments (p. 12, emphasis again added by me) that 'it was in the very nature of this method to *scrutinize and correct* previous views as well as *to gather new information firsthand*'.

I find it all the more strange, therefore, that notwithstanding these observations in his earlier, major work, he should ask in his more

---

[3] The quotation here cited is from John Gould, *Herodotus* (London, 1989), 9.
[4] Cf. A. Momigliano, 'The Herodotean and the Thucydidean Tradition', in his *The Classical Foundations of Modern Historiography* (Berkeley, 1990), 30.
[5] *Thucydides* (London, 1987).
[6] *In Search of History* (New Haven, 1983), 9.

recent essay and with my own essay in mind (from which he quotes): 'Does Herodotus in the early stages of this development [of Greek historiography] indeed manifest a "critical attitude towards sources and to the recording of events"?', and, in what appears to be a significant qualification of his earlier assessment of Herodotus' intellectual development and the influence of the new thinking on him,[7] now writes that a 'reading of the history, especially the first half, makes clear that such a statement needs serious qualification', and continues: 'There are many examples of legends and folk-tales that deserve no place in a critical history. No amount of "enquiry"', he contends, 'or travel to foreign lands can test or verify such stories, most of which lie in the distant past.'[8]

Certainly the first four books of the *Histories* are a rather long 'preamble' to Herodotus' main objective—his account of the causes of the wars between the Greeks and the Persians—and, as Simon Hornblower writes, 'such a distribution of attention would alone make it unlikely . . . that the impact and trauma of the Persian Wars can suffice by themselves to explain the invention of history by Herodotus'. Even so, 'the early books', he continues, 'are structured around the growth of the Persian empire and are therefore not wholly discrete. Nor is their content such that they should be seen as a kind of historiographic fossil attached to the living organism of the later more political or "Thucydidean" books.'[9]

As a matter of fact there is a well-argued view, to which Hornblower draws special attention, that in the earlier books of the *Histories* Herodotus' 'investigations', 'enquiries', already display an active critical stance towards the mass of diverse materials which he collected in his travels and interviews. Against the claim of some commentators that Herodotus 'was unconcerned with truth as opposed to myth' and 'did not attach special importance to knowledge as opposed to untested belief', already in the 'long preamble' and immediately following the first four chapters of Book 1 there is evidence of what Hornblower refers to as 'a change of gear', 'an

---

[7] On this new 'critical spirit' and its influence upon Anaximander and through him upon Hecataeus, see Van Seters, *In Search of History*, 10 f., who notes also that 'Hecataeus was recognized in antiquity as a true disciple of Anaximander even though he was too young to have been his student' (p. 10).

[8] 'Is there any Historiography in the Hebrew Bible?' 4.

[9] S. Hornblower, 'Introduction: Summary of the Papers; The Story of Greek Historiography; Intertextuality and the Greek Historians' in id. (ed.), *Greek Historiography* (Oxford, 1994), 18.

important change of approach'.[10] In those early chapters Herodotus writes of the mythical abductions of Io by some Phoenician sailors, of Europa and Medea by some Greeks, and of Helen of Sparta by the Trojan Paris. Herodotus then reports (1.5) what the Persians and Phoenicians say, but declares that *he*, Herodotus, is not going to say whether that is how it was or not, but will 'speak what [he] knows' about the first acts of aggression committed against the Greeks. Hornblower comments: '*This sentence, it has been justly said, marks the creation of a historical work in our sense, in that it limits the historical narrative to historical time*' (emphasis added).[11] It remains the case that the 'mythical' element is not thereby eliminated from Herodotus' narrative, but (1) this does not deny his intention; and in any case (2) the 'mythical' presence fades more and more through the *Histories*.[12]

Some observations by Gould are also significantly pertinent when considering Van Seters' 'serious qualification' of any suggestion that Herodotus in the early stages of the development of Greek historiography displays a 'critical attitude' towards his sources. Gould writes that it 'is vitally important to register that Herodotus is at pains, at every point in the presentation of his narrative, to preserve the traces of his process of enquiry; his narrative, that is to say, incorporates indications of its own limitations as "truth-telling"'.[13] He refers particularly here to an essay by Carolyn Dewald[14] who focuses attention upon the 1,086 examples of Herodotus' authorial intervention as eyewitness, investigator, scrutineer, and writer, intervention which, she suggests, is concerned to 'preserve the record of his struggles with a difficult and problematic medium'.

---

[10] Hornblower, *Thucydides*, 18, 20.

[11] *Thucydides*, 20. Referring to F. Jacoby's celebrated article on Herodotus in Pauly-Wissowa (eds.), *Realencylopädie der klassische Altertumswissenschaft*, supp. Vol. II (1913), reprinted in his *Griechische Historiker* (Stuttgart, 1956), Hornblower (p. 21) further comments: 'Modern philosophers speak of propositions as having "truth-functions"; we might paraphrase and modernise Herodotus here by saying that for him myths lack a truth-function, in that it is not sensible to try to say if they are true or not: you cannot check or "control" them, by sight and hearing.' He concludes this paragraph by underlining his claim in the quotation in the text above: 'Herodotus' announcement that he would "say what he knew" did, I conclude, mark an important change of approach.'

[12] See Hornblower, *Thucydides*, 19.

[13] Gould, *Herodotus*, 110.

[14] Carolyn Dewald, 'Narrative Surface and Authorial Voice in Herodotus' *Histories*', *Arethusa*, 20 (1987), 147–70.

Herodotus' 'contract with the reader', she argues, is constructed so as to 'thwart any tendency we might have had to fall under the spell of his *logoi* and to treat them as straightforward versions of past events'.[15] Gould draws the distinction here with Thucydides, 'who systematically covers the traces of his own investigations and presents the reader instead with narrative as a transparent medium for incorporating the events of the past "as they happened". That was a conscious and deliberate choice: Thucydides the historical investigator presents himself as having conducted his investigations in so rigorous a way as to render his account of them magisterial and definitive: this is the end of investigation.' Thucydidean narrative

claims and enacts authority. Herodotean narrative . . . is a very different thing: it retains the rhythms and forms of oral tradition, familiar to us in folktales and märchen, but at the same time incorporates into the text, as folk narrative never does, its own authorial commentary on the source and truth-value of the narrative. It is of the essence of the traditional tale that it presents its world, however fantastic . . . as unquestionably real, even if timeless: the world of the narrative is 'out there', if we have the eyes of the storyteller to see it.

'On the other hand,' Gould continues (p. 111), 'Herodotean narrative speculates on the reality of the world it presents, not only by authorial interventions and by constant references to its sources, but also by such devices as the tale told in indirect speech and by the presentation of alternative and competing narratives.'

In a subsequent essay, Dewald has further addressed Herodotus' 'interrogation' of his sources.[16] 'Herodotus himself', she writes, 'does not expect us to believe everything we read. For him the word *historiē* continued to carry its Ionian meaning of "research" or "investigation, enquiry", and he often emphasises that what he gives us is provisional information, the best that he has been able in his researches to discover' (pp. xxvii f.). His first-person interruptions as author of the ongoing narration are to remind us not to treat the narrative as definitively true. What Herodotus repeatedly emphasizes is 'that his *logoi* contain real information, but he remains aware, and wants us to be aware too, of the fact that as data they are only as good

---

[15] *Herodotus*, 110 f.

[16] See her Introduction to Robin Waterfield's translation of Herodotus' *The Histories* (Oxford, 1998), pp. ix–xliv, esp. the subsection 'The *Histories* as History' (pp. xxvii–xxxv).

as the quality of his sources' (p. xxix). 'What he claims, at least, to give us is in each case the best version or versions of past events and the distant reaches of the present that he has been able to hear, taken from the most qualified informants he could find' (p. xxviii). Thus he does not 'merely uncritically transcribe on to his pages what he has been told by others and then cover his own doubts with a blanket authorial caveat. The main narrative structure of the *Histories* is built out of the *logoi* that have been told to him, but the active, first-person intervention of Herodotus as narrator also shapes our readerly understanding of the text' (p. xxix). She continues:

Herodotus intervenes in his own voice on almost every page, often expressly as investigator in order to deliver a variety of critical comments on the information he has gathered. Several hundred times he comments on the likelihood of some detail being correct within a particular story. More than fifty times he assures us that he knows something to be so . . . Much more common are various expressions of doubt, ranging from qualified belief to outright disbelief . . . Sometimes he gives two or more variant versions of the same account, or includes particles or adverbs of doubt ('so they say, at any rate'), or suddenly shifts into reported speech when something particularly improbable is being recounted. He sometimes notes when an informant may be speaking from self-interest, or for some other reasons should not be believed . . . In all these ways, although Herodotus' reasoning is not technical and is never encapsulated into a chapter of self-conscious methodology, he often uses his *Histories* not just to tell stories, but also to tell us what kinds of reasoning should be brought to bear on them, if we are to reach an informed judgement on the quality of the information they contain. (pp. xxix, xxx)

These observations and the evidence upon which they draw in the *Histories* provide, in my opinion, a sufficient response to Van Seters' protest against my statement that 'a critical attitude towards sources and to the recording of events' was a feature of Greek historiography from its first representation proper in Herodotus' *Histories*. It seemed to me when I wrote my essay—and it still does, as the discussion below contends—that herein lies a marked distinction between Herodotus' *Histories* and the Deuteronomistic corpus, whose authors[17] cannot seriously be accredited with the same critical or, in Herodotus' terms, 'investigative' stance, whether towards the sources they employed and how their diversity might be handled, or in what

---

[17] There is general agreement that more than one authorial and redactor's hand has contributed to this corpus.

they wrote. There is in this corpus, as I shall argue below, an absence of any sense of *the past as a field of critical study*, no evidence of any endeavour—no Herodotean-like 'authorial' commentary—to discriminate between differing and conflicting accounts of events with a view to establishing *what happened*; *causality* is overwhelmingly attributed to God, who is viewed as the single will, the only will that counts, behind the large-scale unfolding of events;[18] and the theme that unites and pervades the corpus and identifies its genre as *theodicy* is a concern to wrest meaning from circumstances that suggest God's abandonment of his people or his powerlessness to provide them with a future (see below). None of this lends any support to Van Seters' claim in his essay that the work of these authors 'comes very close to what we have in early Greek historiography'.[19]

II

I cite as an example the substantial narrative of the rise and rule of Saul as first king of Israel, the growing rivalry between him and David, and the latter's succession to the throne of Israel (1 Sam. 7–2 Sam. 5), a narrative to which Van Seters himself has devoted close attention.[20]

It is well known that disparate stories and traditions have been incorporated into this narrative, including variant and conflicting versions of the same event or incident. Thus, within the complex of stories narrating the election of Saul as king and the role of Samuel both in his rise to power and in his subsequent rejection, there are two conflicting accounts: the one comprising 1 Sam. 9: 1–10: 16, (23); 11; 13; 14 and often regarded as early and historically reliable, the other a series of stories and speeches reflecting a wary and unfavourable stance towards the institution of monarchy, the request for which by

---

[18] It seems that these authors could acknowledge human causation in shorter sequences of events, but in making sense and constructing coherence out of the catastrophes that struck in the late eighth and early sixth centuries utilised express and large-scale divine intervention. See Barr's comment, cited in the foregoing chapter, p. 148.

[19] 'Is there any Historiography in the Hebrew Bible', 8 (and see below).

[20] *In Search of History*, ch. 8, 'Historiography in the Books of Samuel'. See below.

the people is viewed as an act of rejection of YHWH as their king (7: 1–8: 22; 10: 17–27; 12; 15). Many commentators attribute the latter sequence of stories largely if not entirely to a Deuteronomistic author/editor. Within the former, older narrative there are two accounts of the elevation of Saul as king, the one in 9: 1–10: 16 (23), recounting his secret anointing by Samuel at the command of God, the other in 11: 1–15 narrating the popular acclamation of Saul as king following his defeat of the Ammonites. This story in 9: 1–10: 16 has all the appearance of a popular folktale. Chapter 13: 7b–15 narrates Saul's subsequent rejection by Samuel, a variant account of which is given in chapter 15 without any allusion to this prior narrative. The figure of Samuel in 9: 1–10: 16 as a 'seer' is strikingly different from his appearance elsewhere. Here he is quite unknown to Saul as a 'seer' in a small town not far from his own town, who presides over the local cult, and whose powers as a clairvoyant can be relied upon for dependable information about lost or wandering livestock. In preceding and subsequent narratives in the sequence, however, Samuel is depicted as exercising the role of representative of God among and over the people, who assemble at his summons, and whom he commands and rebukes as and when necessary. In 1 Sam. 7: 15–17 he is depicted as 'judge' of Israel exercising the same judicial role as the so-called 'minor judges' listed in Judg. 10: 1–5; 12: 7–15, whilst in 7: 7–15 he is portrayed as a 'judge-deliverer'—in the mould of the heroic deliverers of Israel in the book of Judges— who miraculously defeated the Philistines. The statement in 7: 13 that 'the Philistines were subdued and did not again enter the territory of Israel' is clearly inconsistent with the subsequent stories about Philistine aggression against Israel in Samuel's lifetime.

The narratives in 1 Sam. 16–2 Sam. 5 recounting the rise of David similarly display duplicate and contradictory accounts of events. There are two accounts of how David entered the service and court of Saul, the one (1 Sam. 16: 14–23) narrating that David was called upon as a gifted lyre-player to relieve Saul's fits of depression, the other (2 Sam. 17) recounting that Saul's first encounter with David was occasioned by the young man's courageous hand-to-hand engagement on the battlefield with Goliath, the giant warrior champion of the Philistines.[21] Samuel's death is reported twice (1 Sam. 25: 1 and

---

[21] Since in 2 Sam. 21: 19 Goliath is said to have been killed by one Elhanan, it is possible that the feat of this warrior was secondarily associated with David. According to the Chronicler (1 Chron. 20: 5), it was Goliath's brother whom Elhanan killed.

28: 3); chapters 24 and 26 are variant versions of a story of how David
spared Saul's life; there are two accounts (21: 10–15; 27: 1–7) of
David's flight to Achish, king of Gath, for refuge from Saul; in 1 Sam.
31 Saul, mortally wounded in battle with the Philistines and fearful
that the Philistines, the 'uncircumcised', would come and dishonour
him in death, commits suicide by falling upon his own sword following his armour-bearer's refusal to despatch him, but in 2 Sam. 1 Saul
is reported to have been killed at his plea by an Amalekite.

From his own analysis of the narrative of the rise, election, and
rejection of Saul as king in 1 Sam. 8–15,[22] which he attributes
to a Deuteronomistic author who inherited and edited the older
stories in 9: 1–10: 16*; 11*; 13*; 14*,[23] Van Seters writes (p. 258)
that it 'would appear that the editor found these stories already in a
fixed written form and *felt under some constraint to retain them as
they were ... even at the expense of creating obvious tensions and
absurdities*' (emphasis added). Such a statement begs the question,
however, of whether this editor was under any such constraint. Van
Seters cannot possibly know this, and the comment is justified that
such a conjecture arises from his theory that the Deuteronomist
corpus is a work of ancient historiography comparable to early
Greek historiography, such as is represented by Herodotus' *Histories*,
in which we do not expect 'such tensions and absurdities' as these,
which therefore have to be explained as due to some postulated
'constraint' upon its author/editor. Herodotus' many authorial
interventions in his narrative, commenting upon the sources he had
collected and asking questions, are evidence that he did not see himself as simply a repository of tradition.[24] There is every appearance,
however, that the Deuteronomistic authors were such a repository,
and that this, rather than some compelled deviation from a
Herodotus-like historiographical agenda, accounts for their adoption
and juxtaposition of variant and conflicting accounts and anomalies
which are such a feature of their lengthy narrative. What these
variant stories and traditions now encompassed in one extensive
narrative suggest is that the authors of the Deuteronomic corpus
manifestly did not subject the sources they collected to the same
investigative questioning and consideration to be found in

---

[22] *In Search of History*, 250–64.
[23] For details see *In Search of History*, 250–8.
[24] See Gould, *Herodotus*, 126.

Herodotus' *Histories* or feel any need to report them with the same authorial commentary as characterizes his work.

III

The Saul–David stories that follow in the remainder of 1 Samuel, offer, as we have seen, further evidence of a similar juxtaposition, in one and the same narrative, of stories that duplicate and conflict with one another, surely reaffirming that the editor/author responsible for bringing them together did not operate with the method of 'enquiry', 'investigation', exemplified in Herodotus' *Histories*. Whatever the objective of the author/editor of the narrative sequence in 1 Sam. 7–2 Sam. 5, it was self-evidently not to provide a historical account of what happened during the period to which they relate. That the editor who here brought together originally discrete and varying or conflicting stories of the same event yet made no attempt to coalesce them into a literary unit providing a coherent account itself evidences this. 'Historiography' as a genre description is misapplied—a 'category error'—when used to describe such a narrative; it belongs to 'story' rather than to 'history writing'.

Van Seters argues a different understanding of the composition of the narrative of David's rise, to whose author[25] he ascribes a 'literary technique' that is characterized by 'repetition of short scenes, motifs, and the like to reinforce the overall theme and unity of the work'.[26] The 'doublets' in this story, he contends, are unlike those in the Pentateuch, which display marked differences in style and purpose. By contrast, the story of David's rise 'has a uniform style and all the episodes appear to be directed to the same purpose' and 'bear the same thematic concern for legitimizing David's role as successor to Saul and for putting Saul in an unfavourable light'. After listing the repetitions, variants, conflicting stories, and anomalies to which commentators have drawn attention, he writes (p. 269) that the 'story [of the rise of David] shows little concern for exact chronology

---

[25] Van Seters writes (*In Search of History*, 268): 'Whatever the nature of the traditional material behind the Story of David's Rise, it has been used with complete freedom by the author, making it virtually impossible to distinguish between the received traditions and the elements of his own composition.'

[26] *In Search of History*, 268 f.

and makes little attempt to overcome inconsistencies and contradictions in the compilation of its scenes and episodes. No amount
of source analysis, tradition criticism, or redaction criticism can
solve what is basically the result of this author's particular literary
techniques.'

What thematic purpose is served, however, and how is the 'unity'
of the narrative advanced, by two conflicting accounts of Saul's
death: what has a twofold account of this incident to do with the
legitimizing of David and how does it place Saul in an 'unfavourable
light'? And in any event, and contrary to Van Seters' analysis,
does not the moving account in 1 Sam. 31 of the death of Saul and
his sons, of his loyal armour-bearer's death beside him, and of the
courageous retrieval of their bodies by the men of Jabesh Gilead and
the grief they express in fasting seven days cast Saul in an noble
rather than an 'unfavourable' light? In what way does the story of
Saul's offer to David of marriage to his daughter Merab (1 Sam. 18:
17–19), who is then given to another bearing the name of Adriel the
Mehlathite, serve to enhance David's choice as successor to Saul? Or
how is the theme of the legitimizing of David as successor to Saul
and its concomitant theme of casting Saul in 'an unfavourable light'
advanced by two accounts of David's flight for refuge to Achish of
Gath, the first (1 Sam. 21: 11–16 (EVV 10–15)), in which David has
to feign madness to escape from Achish's court, where he is hostilely
regarded by the royal officials, who name him 'David the king' and
evidently (cf. v. 12, EVV 11) see in his reputation in warfare a
national threat; the second (1 Sam. 27: 1–4) in which, ostensibly,
David appears a second time at Achish's court, now with a following
of 600 men, and, with no mention of any hostility or threat towards
him, is accepted into service as an ally of the Philistine king? Is Van
Seters' claim credible that one and the same author composed these
two rather uncoordinated stories? And why would this author have
considered that two such stories were necessary for the purpose of
narrating David's flight for safety to Achish, when one would surely
have sufficed? Is it not more likely that an editor inherited them
as variants which have been secondarily used in compiling and composing this narrative? As suggested above, there is sufficient evidence
in the Deuteronomistic corpus that its editors were repositories of
tradition rather than—in the manner of Herodotus—enquiring
and questioning and deliberating upon the reliability of the oral or
written sources they had assembled, or—again in the manner of

Herodotus—upon which among conflicting accounts of events might be the more trustworthy. The Hebrew Bible as a whole provides ample evidence of authors who create and of editors who conflate.

Van Seters offers no comment on why the author of such a sequence of stories showed little interest in the chronology of events and made 'little attempt to overcome the inconsistencies and contradictions' here in evidence; indeed, if, as he claims, one author stands behind the narrative of the rise of David, then such inconsistencies and contradictions were his creation—scarcely an author, we may add, to challenge Herodotus for the title of 'the father of history'! The result is that Van Seters' claim that this author employed a 'literary technique' of the 'repetition of short scenes, motifs, and the like to reinforce the overall theme and unity of the work' is an assertion or, indeed, a piece of theory-driven special pleading to account for the presence of such an assembly of duplicate and conflicting stories and anecdotes within a corpus for which he seeks to claim the genre description 'historiography', an 'analogue', no less, to Herodotus' *Histories*.[27]

Far from demonstrating that the Samuel–Saul–David narrative in 1 Sam. 7–2 Sam. 5 provides evidence that the Deuteronomistic corpus represents 'something that comes very close to what we have in early Greek historiography', it manifests rather that the authors of this corpus 'were not moved by a passion for writing history', as Lothar Perlitt has aptly put it.[28] Such a narrative displays no engagement with *the past as a field of critical study*, as in Hecataeus[29] or Herodotus, and offers nothing that can be compared with Herodotus' pursuit of 'enquiry', 'investigation', in an endeavour to establish *what happened*, or with his many authorial comments that reflect a discriminating attitude towards his sources. Such cannot seriously be said to have been the objective and modus operandi that these supposed ancient Israelite 'historiographers' set themselves.

---

[27] Van Seters, *In Search of History*, 17: 'The analogue to Herodotus in the Old Testament would be the Deuteronomistic historian of Joshua to 2 Kings, seen not simply as a redactor of previously compiled blocks of material ... but rather as a historian who gathered his own material, much of it in the form of disparate oral stories, but some from records and from the royal chronicles.'

[28] For the full quotation, see below, p. 164 and n. 32.

[29] On Hecataeus as 'the first to identity ... the past as a field of critical study', see Peter Derow's essay 'Historical Explanation: Polybius and his Predecessors', in Hornblower (ed.), *Greek Historiography*, 73–90, esp.73 f.

For example, to turn briefly to another series of narratives in the Deuteronomistic corpus, these authors provide a minimalist account of the momentous international power-struggles and shifts that directly and fatefully affected the course of the final years of the Judaean state. Of the fall of Nineveh in 612 BCE to the Babylonians and the beginnings of an international shift in power that this augured there is no mention, and only minimal coverage (one verse, 2 Kgs 23: 29) is given to the international struggle for supremacy that followed between a remnant Assyrian force, which Pharaoh Necho sought in vain to support,[30] and the establishment of the Babylonian empire—events that led within a few years to the sacking of the temple and the royal palace and to the first deportation to Babylonia, and beyond this finally to the cataclysm that engulfed and brought to an end the Judaean state. When, during the unfolding of these events and as part of them, Jehoiakim made and then broke his treaty with Nebuchadrezzar (2 Kgs 24: 1–4), and Judaea was invaded by raiding-parties of Chaldeans, Aramaeans, Moabites, and Ammonites to wreak destruction, this is explained as fulfilment of the purpose of God as foretold by 'his servants the prophets', and because of Manasseh's apostasy and misdeeds.[31] Such a statement, which has many parallels throughout the Deuteronomistic corpus, expresses *in nuce* what most scholars conclude to be the focus and guiding intention of this corpus—theodicy. Thus, to quote in full Perlitt's comment mentioned above: 'The authors of the Deuteronomistic history work were not moved by a passion for writing history but by a need to give a theological explanation of the fall of the two king-doms',[32] or put differently by another recent writer on the topic: 'It [the Deuteronomistic corpus] is one long confession of sin, which is meant to lead to the insight that it is not Yahweh but Israel who is to

---

[30] 2 Kgs 23: 29 erroneously narrates that Necho arrived not, as we now know, to support the Assyrians but *against* them. No explanation is given of why and for what purpose Josiah 'went to meet' Necho at Megiddo (v. 29), who, we are told without explanation, killed him or, since we are not told whether or not there was a military engagement between their armies, had him executed.

[31] MT at 24: 2 reads that YHWH sent these raiding-parties, but it is likely that LXX, which omits 'YHWH' and attributes this action directly to Nebuchadrezzar, is correct. Yet the glossator who attributed the initiative of sending these raiding-bands directly to YHWH by no means injected a meaning into the text that the Deuteronomistic authors would have found theologically unfamiliar.

[32] L. Perlitt, *Bundestheologie im Alten Testament* (Neukirchen-Vluyn, 1969), 7: 'Die Verfasser des DtrG trieb nicht historiographische Leidenschaft, sondern die Nötigung, die Trümmer zweier Reiche theologisch zu deuten.'

blame for the downfall of the state',[33] which echoes Wellhausen's comment upon the leading motif of the Deuteronmistic edition of 1 and 2 Kings:[34]

The writer looks back on the time of the kings as a period past and closed, on which judgment has already been declared. Even at the consecration of the temple the thought of its destruction is not to be restrained; and throughout the book the ruin of the nation and its two kingdoms is present to the writer's mind. This is the light in which the work is to be read; it shows why the catastrophe was unavoidable. It was so because of unfaithfulness to Jehovah, because of the utterly perverted tendency obstinately followed by the people in spite of the Torah of Jehovah and His prophets. The narrative becomes, as it were, a great confession of sins of the exiled nation looking back on its history.

IV

This calls for further comment on the issue of divine causality in human affairs in Herodotus. Van Seters in his essay takes issue with my statement that for 'Herodotus, what happened was not the outworking of a divine will; the claim that for him, as for the Old Testament writers, "history is theodicy" is wholly unjustified'.[35] I acknowledge that it would have avoided any misunderstanding if instead of 'divine will' I had written 'single will', which serves to contrast multi-subjective presentation of causality in Herodotus with the unquestionably characteristic explanation of causality in the thinking of the Deuteronomistic corpus as divinely ordered (see below).[36] What I intended was to reflect Gould's and Christian Meier's[37] analyses. Thus Gould, writing of the features that mark Herodotus' narrative as 'historical', states[38] that 'the answer must

---

[33] R. Albertz, *A History of Israelite Religion in the Old Testament Period*, Vol. II (London, 1994), 389.

[34] *Prolegomena to the History of Israel*, Eng. trans. by J. Sutherland Black and Allan Menzies (Edinburgh, 1885), 278.

[35] See Chapter 7, 'IV', p. 147.

[36] See n. 18.

[37] C. Meier, 'Historical Answers to Historical Questions. The Origins of History in Ancient Greece', *Arethusa*, 20 (1987), 41–57, see esp. 48.

[38] *Herodotus*, 125 f.

lie in those aspects of *his sense of the past* . . . *that is to say, his grasp of the essential role of "enquiry"* and his perception of human experience *not as the working-out of a divine "will" but as a result of the inter-action of multiple and contingent human purposes.* Herodotus . . . asks questions . . . *and he does not see events as the expression of a single will*' (emphasis added). Similarly Meier, to whom Gould in this context refers, writes of Herodotus' *Histories* as 'a multi-subjective, contingency-oriented account' of events and their outcome. In a later essay, 'Herodotus and Religion',[39] Gould writes at further length concerning causality in the *Histories* that 'Herodotus took the possibility of supernatural causation in human experience quite as seriously as he took the involvement of human causation' (p. 93). He draws close attention, however, to Herodotus' studied caution and hesitation 'in admitting such [supernatural] causation and still more so in identifying its source and rationale' (p. 94). He comments also that such caution 'at times may even involve authorial uncertainty and a verdict of *non liquet*', and in any case manifests itself in Herodotus' demand for additional weight of evidence, in his employment of indirect speech when narrating stories of supernatural intervention, or in suggestions of alternative explanations. Gould writes of these expressions of hesitation and uncertainty in questions of divine action in human experience that 'they are no more than the expression of a universal (and among the Greeks universally accepted) implicit acknowledgement of the limitations of human knowledge in such matters', limitations which Herodotus, of course, shared. That is, they 'are not based on specific "historiographical principle" but on the nature of Greek religion' (p. 94).

In his critique of my essay Van Seters has drawn special attention to this essay by Gould,[40] which, I should mention, was not yet published when I was preparing mine. That Herodotus' hesitant handling of divine causation in human affairs did not arise from his 'historiographical method' is not in dispute. None of this, however, seems to me to advance the case that Van Seters seeks to make, for contingency, the effects and eventualities of human responsibility and obligations, and the choices they make for good or ill, remain prominent in Herodotus' presentation of his 'enquiries' in a way that

---

[39] 'Herodotus and Religion', in Hornblower (ed.), *Greek Historiography*, 91–106.
[40] 'Is there any Historiography in the Hebrew Bible?', 10.

they are not in the Deuteronomic corpus.[41] I quote again Meier's succinct depiction of the task in which Herodotus engaged: 'He wanted to know how everything had happened, what had followed what, and what had influenced what. So he showed how the Persian Empire grew up, how Sparta and Athens became powerful, and how it was various chance motives, some of them highly personal, of individual leaders which in a very complicated interaction caused the Ionian conflict with the Persians.' By contrast, a passion such as this for 'enquiry', seeking to discern what happened and the cause or chain of causes thereof, does not seem to have been the motivation and objective of the work of the Deuteronomists.

This contrast requires further comment. Van Seters emphasizes the presence of the 'duality of divine and human causation' in the Deuteronomistic corpus, and compares it with Herodotus' allowance for divine alongside human causation in his investigation of the beginnings of the Greek–Persian conflict.[42] He draws attention, as an example, to the human choices and decisions that brought about the rebellion of the north Israelite tribes against Solomon's successor Rehoboam (1 Kgs 12: 1–20) and the beginnings of the breakaway northern state of Israel, and then, referring to the statement in v. 15 that all this was 'a turn of events brought about by YHWH that he might fulfil his word that YHWH spoke by Ahijah the Shilonite to Jeroboam the son of Nebat' (v. 15), he adds that '[t]he whole scene could have come right out of Herodotus, with the exception of the reference to the specific deity, Yahweh' (p. 14). But could it? Given Gould's observations, of which Van Seters approves, about Herodotus' caution and hesitancy in handling stories attributing events to supernatural agency, it does not seem plausible that he would have taken a report of events that occurred through human choices and decisions and at a stroke transformed it into one of divine design and oversight of the events described and their outcome. By contrast, the leitmotif of the Deuteronomistic corpus is

---

[41] Hornblower, *Thucydides*, 30, observes that though Herodotus allows for the operation of the supernatural in his causal scheme in writing the *Histories*, in the chief subject of his enquiries—the origin and causes of the Greek–Persian conflict— '*the whole economy of his work convinces us that the root cause was late sixth-century Persian expansionism*' (emphasis added), citing *Histories* 5.97, which narrates the dispatch of twenty ships to support the Ionian revolt against the Persians, and Herodotus' comment that this was 'a cause-and-beginning (*archê*) of misfortune for Greeks and non-Greeks alike'.

[42] Van Seters 'Is there any Historiography in the Hebrew Bible?', 13 f.

that YHWH directs the fortunes and misfortunes of Israel, from their deliverance from captivity in Egypt to their exile centuries later in Babylonia, and it is this that runs through and gives coherence to the long unfolding narrative of these authors. This more than anything constitutes a yawning gulf between Herodotus' caution in attributing events to supernatural intervention and the pervasive theme of divine control and direction of history in the Deuteronomistic corpus. These authors wrote from a 'God's eye perspective', as we may put it, and indeed, when they speak *in propria persona* they are in fact saying things that could be known only to God! The comment in 1 Kgs 12: 15, following Rehoboam's acceptance of the ill-judged counsel of the young men, that 'this was a turn of events brought about by YHWH that he might fulfil his word that YHWH spoke by Ahijah the Shilonite to Jeroboam the son of Nebat' is itself an example of this.

The same conviction of divine causality, unqualified by any Herodotean 'enquiry' or circumspection about the dependability of sources, is further evidenced throughout the Deuteronomistic corpus. For example, immediately following the narrative in 1 Kgs 12 of the human choices and scheming that issued in the dissolution of the united monarchy under Rehoboam is the story of 'the man of God' from Judah (1 Kgs 13: 1–10), who confronted Jeroboam I at the newly instituted royal sanctuary of the northern state at Bethel and announced, some 300 years in advance, its destruction, at the same time giving the very name of the king—Josiah—who is later duly recorded as fulfilling this prophecy (2 Kgs 23: 15–18). Similarly, Ahijah's prophecy in the ensuing chapter (1 Kgs 14: 15–16) predicts, two centuries ahead, the uprooting of the people of Jeroboam's kingdom whom YHWH will 'scatter beyond the Euphrates', and Isaiah is narrated in 2 Kgs 20: 12–19 as having foretold to Hezekiah the sacking of the royal palace and the looting of all its treasures and the exile of his descendants by the Babylonians in the early sixth century, that is, a century or more in the future. These events, which drastically reshaped Israel's and Judah's world and future, appear here as the inexorable outworking of a single divine will; the historical content proper of the narratives supplies merely the human *when and how* of their happening; the *why*, however, occupies the foreground and is described as the work of God. Thus, history here seems predetermined, down to precise events, including an individual's name. The presence of such narratives surely places a severe question-mark against Van Seters' claim that the Deuteronomistic corpus 'comes very close to what we have in early Greek historiography'.

Put differently, had Herodotus heard or read such stories and felt it necessary to include them among the *logoi* he records, considers, and reports, he would surely at the least have required—basing ourselves on Gould's observations noted above—additional weight of evidence and expressed authorial uncertainty; or perhaps, indeed, he might even have glossed his narration of such accounts with the comment he makes in 7.152: 'I am obliged to record the things I am told, but I am certainly not required to believe them'! By contrast, the Deuteronomistic author/editor of these stories believed what he wrote. And this reinforces the total impression one has of the Deuteronomists: that their engagement with, and editing of, their sources, and their own compositional contributions were not in the interests of 'historiography' in any meaningful sense of this genre as exemplified, for example, in Herodotus' pursuit of 'inquiry', 'investigation', or, as Van Seters claims on the analogy of Herodotus' work, with the purpose of 'establishing the beginning and cause for the destruction of Israel and Judah by a foreign power' (see below).[43] In short, though some similarities can be identified, there is no plausible 'match' such as Van Seters proposes between Herodotus' *Histories* and the Deuteronomistic corpus—the latter is not an 'analogue' to the former—and the claim that they share the genre description 'historiography' rests upon superficial resemblances. Rather, narratives such as that of 'the old prophet from Judah' and the long-range 'forecast' of Ahijah and of Isaiah reflect what many scholars consider to be the central, guiding motif in the work of the Deuteronomists and what identifies and defines its genre—theodicy.

---

[43] Van Seters, 'Is there any Historiography in the Hebrew Bible?', 8.

V

Van Seters employs this word, claiming that in Herodotus no less than in the Deuteronomistic corpus 'history is theodicy'.[44] This comparison too is flawed, however, and rests upon a misconception of the character and purpose of the genre 'theodicy'. Van Seters writes of the Old Testament as exhibiting 'a dominant concern with the issue of divine retribution for unlawful acts as a fundamental principle of historical causality',[45] and compares this with the theme of 'retribution', 'revenge', in Herodotus. For example, he points to the action of the gods behind the scenes in the wars between the Greeks and Persians, inflicting 'night visions on Xerxes in order to carry out their own retribution on the Persians for the wrongs begun by Croesus and the *hubris* of Persian expansion . . . in order to restore the equilibrium of the world order'.[46] Thus, he seems to define 'theodicy' as 'the notion that the gods are committed to a just world order', maintaining and sustaining it against man's breach of it in whatever way, which they punish. He concludes that 'theodicy seems to be more basic to ancient historiography than Nicholson is willing to recognize'.

This is, however, a curious and idiosyncratic connotation and deployment of the word 'theodicy'.[47] As ordinarily defined and understood, 'theodicy' signifies a defence of God in the face of events that call in question divine justice, for example, and infamously, the Lisbon earthquake catastrophe with its massive destruction of innocent life. In the Hebrew Bible the book of Job, for example, is considered by many scholars to belong to this theological genre: it centres upon the innocent man Job's complaint against the injustice of the tragedies that had befallen him, and upon the attempts of his pious 'comforters' to find the cause of his misfortune in himself and not in God's created order. As more usually understood and defined, that is, theodicy is a defence of God's justice in the face of circumstances that are perceived to deny it. Closely related to this, the term also connotes an endeavour to wrest meaning and coherence in the

---

[44] *In Search of History*, 40.

[45] *In Search of History*, 39.

[46] 'Is there any Historiography in the Hebrew Bible?', 13.

[47] I should comment here that neither in his book on Herodotus nor in his later essay 'Herodotus and Religion', referred to above, does Gould employ the word.

face of circumstances that call in question God's governance of his creation. On such a definition, the Deuteronomistic corpus is correctly regarded by many scholars as belonging to this genre: it seeks to justify the national catastrophes that befell the people of Israel—loss of their ancestral land and deportation into exile—as 'judgement' justly visited by God, but in doing so the purpose of these authors was also to wrest meaning from calamitous circumstances that suggested God's abandonment of his people or his powerlessness to provide them with a future. It is this, rather than any 'historiographical' enterprise, any passion for investigating what happened and questioning the sources available for attempting this, that identifies and characterizes the Deuteronomistic corpus and that differentiates it strikingly from early Greek historiography.[48] To bracket this corpus with Herodotus' *Histories* as a work of ancient historiography is a 'category error', a mismatch.

A further observation prompts the same comment. In his essay, Van Seters writes (p. 7 f.) that much of Herodotus' work is not directly about the Greek–Persian conflict, and that this

is not how Herodotus characterizes his own work. He says that he wants to establish the beginning and the cause of the animosity between the Greeks and the barbarians, of which the Persian Wars is the final phase . . . What is important for Herodotus is the 'cause' or the one responsible for the eventual conflict and the Persian defeat as a consequence of that injustice. If we use a similar analogy to suggest that the Deuteronomist's history is to establish the beginning and cause for the destruction of Israel and Judah by a foreign power, which would be directly comparable to Herodotus' description of his work, and if the biblical history was directly motivated by the most recent disaster, the destruction of Jerusalem, then we do have something that comes very close to what we have in early Greek historiography.

The analogy set out in this paragraph, however, is surely excessively overstated. Where in the lengthy Deuteronomistic corpus is 'the beginning and cause' of the destruction of the northern Israelite state at the hands of the Assyrians and subsequently of Judah by the Babylonians a subject of 'historiographical' attention proper, such as

---

[48] By its nature, it seems, Greek religion would not have conceived or adopted such a genre, since the misfortunes of life could be attributed to an angry and vengeful god, or to 'fate', 'the allotted share' (*moira*) or the Fates (*Moirai*), or to 'what had to be'. On 'fate' see Gould, *Herodotus*, 67–76, and the article on 'fate' in N. G. L. Hammond and H. H. Scullard (eds.), *The Oxford Classical Dictionary*, 2nd edn. (Oxford, 1970).

is represented by Herodotus' 'enquiries'? There is no mention of the Assyrians or of the Babylonians in Deuteronomy, Joshua, Judges, or 1 and 2 Samuel. It is not until 2 Kgs 15 that the Assyrians under Tiglath-pileser (Pul) are introduced, and then abruptly so and without explanation of, or even a reference to, what occasioned this invasion of northern Israel or, rather, two invasions, and the exile of some of the citizens. In 2 Kgs 17, as a result of his vassal king Hoshea's double-dealing, Tiglath-pileser again invades northern Israel, imposing a further exile and now also dismantling the state and constituting its territory a province of the Assyrian empire. Whatever historical annals or state archives or other sources may have been in the possession of the authors of this narrative, there is here but a cursory account of the historical events that brought about this cataclysm, and attention is then focused, in a wordy Deuteronomistic 'sermon', upon these authors' interpretation of why all this befell Israel, which is summed up in its final verse (v. 18): 'The Lord was very angry with Israel, and removed them out of his sight.' No chapter in the Deuteronomistic corpus illustrates more strikingly the main agenda and focus of its authors: the 'sermon', which constitutes the bulk of this chapter, is itself a theodicy, a microcosm, so to speak, of the leading theme of the Deuteronomistic corpus as a whole. Equally striking, however, is the austerity with which, in a mere six verses, these authors record the momentous historical events that brought the Northern Kingdom to its end. To consider such a narrative as 'historiography', comparable to Herodotus' work, strains credulity.

The degree to which, as evidenced in such a chapter, the Deuteronomistic authors were unmoved 'by a passion for writing history' is equally in evidence in the narratives of the devastation of Jerusalem and the destruction of the Judaean state at the hands of the Babylonians in the early sixth century. The first mention of a king of Babylon is recorded in the story of the visit by emissaries of the Chaldean tribal chief Merodach-baladan to the court of Hezekiah in the late eighth century (2 Kgs 20: 12–19), the occasion of Isaiah's prophecy mentioned above. We can surmise, on the basis of what we know of Merodach-baladan from other sources,[49] that behind this

---

[49] On Merodach-baladan (Marduk-apal-iddina) and his encounter with Hezekiah, see H. W. F. Saggs, 'The Assyrians', in D. J. Wiseman (ed.), *Peoples of Old Testament Times* (Oxford, 1973), 156–78; and W. G. Lambert, 'The Babylonians and Chaldaeans', ibid. 179–96.

story lies this king's conspiracy and manoeuvrings to incite rebellion among Assyria's western vassals, including Hezekiah, to whom he 'sent letters and a present [a bribe?]'. The Deuteronomistic author, however, makes no reference to any such wider international context or political rationale of this episode, and in any event the text clearly cannot be construed as marking 'the beginning and cause for the destruction of . . . Judah by a foreign power'. The episode is not mentioned again, unless it is alluded to in the final clause of 2 Kgs 24: 13 which records the looting of 'the treasures of the king's house . . . as the Lord foretold'.

It is only in the final three chapters of 2 Kings that the neo-Babylonian imperial power under Nebuchadrezzar is introduced. Pharaoh Necho's attempt, allying himself with the Assyrians, to thwart Babylon's rise to power is briefly mentioned in one verse (2 Kgs 23: 29), and his short-lived control of Judah is narrated in three further verses (2 Kgs 23: 33–5). One verse (24: 7) is allocated to recording the establishing of Babylonian hegemony over Syria–Palestine, 'from the Brook of Egypt to the river Euphrates', with the concomitant demise of Egyptian control of this region and the consequences of this for Judah's subsequent and catastrophically ill-fated breach of its treaty with Nebuchadrezzar. If there is a note of the 'beginning and cause for the destruction of . . . Judah by a foreign power', 2 Kgs 24: 1 might be regarded as indicating this in recording Nebuchadrezzar's invasion and subjugation of Judah and the imposition of treaty terms upon Jehoiakim, who then rebelled and suffered the consequences. None of this suggests, however, on the analogy of Herodotus' quest to fathom the causes of the Greek–Persian conflict, that the Deuteronomistic authors were in these chapters concerned 'to establish the beginning and cause for the destruction of Israel and Judah by a foreign power'. That is, history is not a governing factor in the selection and presentation of events and their outcome in these chapters. Rather, the calamities which ensued, though they were at the hands of the Babylonians and provoked by political decisions taken at court in Jerusalem, have already been announced:

And the Lord said by his servants the prophets, 'Because Manasseh king of Judah has committed these abominations, and has done things more wicked than all that the Amorites did, who were before him, and has made Judah also to sin with his idols; therefore thus says the Lord, the God of Israel, Behold, I am bringing upon Jerusalem and Judah such evil that the ears of everyone who hears of it will tingle. And I will stretch over Jerusalem the measuring line of Samaria, and the plummet of the house of Ahab; and I will wipe Jerusalem as one wipes a dish, wiping it and turning it upside down. And I will cast off the remnant of my heritage, and give them into the hand of their enemies, and they shall become a prey and a spoil to all their enemies, because they have done what is evil in my sight and have provoked me to anger, since the day their fathers came out of Egypt, even to this day'. (2 Kgs 21: 10–15)

this judgement being reaffirmed, notwithstanding the pious zeal of Josiah:

Still the Lord did not turn from the fierceness of his great wrath, by which his anger was kindled against Judah, because of all the provocation with which Manasseh had provoked him. And the Lord said, 'I will remove Judah also out of my sight, as I have removed Israel, and I will cast off this city which I have chosen, Jerusalem, and the house of which I said, My name shall be there'. (2 Kgs 23: 26–7)

Van Seters' claim, citing Herodotus' work as an analogy, that the Deuteronomists wrote to '*establish the beginning and cause* of the destruction of Israel and Judah by a foreign power' is in the face of the sparse historical content of these narratives, which provide only minimal coverage of the power-struggles of the period and of the political decisions of successive Judaean kings in Jerusalem and the consequential reaction of Nebuchadrezzar. Instead, all is accounted for as the inexorable outworking of a single divine will, which the human actors on all sides unknowingly bring about. As Wellhausen, cited above, put it, the Deuteronomistic writers look 'back on the time of the kings as a period past and closed, on which judgment has already been declared'. This is a far cry from an 'enquiry', 'investigation', into the beginning and cause of the destruction of Judah by a foreign power. To state that, since these authors narrate the destruction of Israel and Judah at the hands of a foreign power, and since they composed their work following the most recent of these two disasters, the destruction of Jerusalem, 'we do have something that comes very close to what we have in early Greek historiography' is manifestly overstated, to the point, indeed, of superficiality.

VI

Van Seters castigates me for focusing exclusively upon Herodotus in my essay,[50] and declares that to make my case I 'must enter into a discussion with the many classical authorities' that he has read, 'to which more could be added, who would strongly dispute' my 'characterization of Greek historiography in general and Herodotus in particular' (p. 23). As to the first of these, an apologia on my part is quite uncalled for, since Van Seters himself, in his *In Search of History*, begins his chapter on 'Early Greek Historiography' thus (emphasis added): 'It would appear to be self-evident and entirely natural for biblical scholars who treat the subject of the origins of history writing in ancient Israel to give some attention to the corresponding rise of history writing in Greece *and to the work of Herodotus in particular*.'[51] In the remainder of this same chapter, apart from one passing allusion to Herodotus' near-contemporary Thucydides (p. 15), and true to his opening proposition, Herodotus is prominently Van Seters' own focus of attention, which issues in the claim, to be elaborated in later chapters, that '[t]he analogue to Herodotus in the Old Testament would be the Deuteronomistic historian of Joshua to 2 Kings' (p. 17). It was this claim that I had mostly in mind when writing my essay, more especially the question it raises of whether the Deuteronomistic corpus, though 'history-like', is properly classified as ancient historiography in the sense that Herodotus' 'enquiries, researches' can be so classified, or whether this long narrative is more accurately described as 'story' rather than 'history', that a 'record' or reconstruction of past events was not the motivation of its authors' endeavours.

In the matter of secondary reading, it would indeed be regrettable for scholarly dialogue if one had of necessity to master the compass of secondary reading—or more!—accomplished by a fellow scholar before one dared to offer some observations and ask some questions of his or her conclusions. As for my 'characterization' of Herodotus 'method', I cannot see that my depiction of what was new in Herodotus' approach to the material he collected, his investigative and *critical* handling of his sources, his sense of the past as a field of

---

[50] 'Is there any Historiography in the Hebrew Bible?', 3.
[51] *In Search of History*, 8.

active 'research', 'enquiry', in order to uncover the causes of what happened, is anything more or less than what Van Seters himself sets out succinctly in his chapter on early Greek historiography in his *In Search of History* (see the opening paragraphs above). Nor, of course, do I consider Herodotus to be 'the very model of a modern critical historian', as Van Seters seems to imply (p. 23), or have 'read back into Greek antiquity the modern critical understanding of what constitutes a narrative as history'.

My purpose in that essay, as in the present chapter, is an attempt to show that Van Seters' main thesis that the Deuteronomistic corpus in significant ways anticipates the genre of early Greek historiography—that it is an 'analogue' to Herodotus' *Histories*—loses conviction when one penetrates behind surface similarities to features in that corpus that stand in obvious and sharp contrast to the critical distance and independence Herodotus maintains towards his sources, his frequent authorial comments on variant versions of the same account and which of them, if any, he thinks may be the more trustworthy, his expressions of doubt about data, his guardedness about informants whose account of events may reflect self-interest or who for some other reason should not be relied upon.

If such is a correct impression of Herodotus' critical method and modus operandi in cross-examining his sources and weighing their testimony, that is, of the kind of reasoning that he considered had to be brought to bear upon the data he had assembled if an informed judgement upon the quality of the information they contain is to be reached, then any supposed substantial similarity between the *Histories* and the Deuteronomistic corpus collapses. The Deuteronomistic authors do not 'enquire', 'investigate', 'research' in the manner of Herodotus; there is no critical assessment of the sources they inherited or collected, no doubts about the veracity of any of them, they offer no comment upon variant accounts of the same event, which they place together as apparently equally valid and true, to be read or listened to in the same sequence of stories, evidently, it seems, without experiencing any sense of anomaly or mutual contradiction. Further, and in contrast to Herodotus' noticeably nuanced perception of the role of the gods in the events he sought to record—and in total contrast to Thucydides' icy silence about any role of the gods in the causes and conduct of the Peloponnesian War—these authors saw the will of God as ordering and controlling the fortunes and misfortunes of Israel, from their deliverance from captivity in Egypt to their exile centuries later in Babylonia, and, related to this, they and their audience could evidently believe that historical events could be accurately foretold centuries in advance, even down the detail of a king's name, a feature surely quite alien to early Greek historiography. History writing analogous to early Greek historiography was evidently not a task that the Deuteronomistic authors undertook or, in terms of method and approach, it seems, even conceived of.

Thus, I am drawn again to the quotation from Wilhelm Vatke, of which Rudolf Smend has reminded us,[52] and with which I ended my earlier essay:

> The Hebrews did not at all raise themselves to the standpoint of properly historical contemplation, and there is no book of the Old Testament, however much it may contain material that is otherwise objectively historical, that deserves the name of true historiography.

More especially, however, I am returned, notwithstanding Van Seters' protests, to the view of James Barr that in the Deuteronomistic corpus 'history is not a governing factor in the selection and presentation of material'.[53] It does not seem that the past was the motivation for these authors' endeavours, and they did not view the past as a field of critical study, which is characteristic of early Greek historiography of a subsequent age and as represented by its earliest writers whose works have survived, Herodotus and Thucydides. Rather, and to a significant extent, the Deuteronmistic writers were evidently concerned to provide patterns of God's dealings with his people in promise, fulfilment, and judgement, that is, paradigms intended for thinking about the present and hoping for the future. In such a way, they sought primarily to provide meaning in circumstances of drastic change—of, indeed, violent disruption—that brought an acute threat to their national and cultural survival.

---

[52] R. Smend, *Elemente alttestamentlichen Geschichtsdenkens*, Theologische Studien 95 (1968), reprinted in his *Die Mitte des Alten Testaments* (Tübingen, 2002), 89–114; see esp. 110 f.

[53] 'Story and History in Biblical Theology', in James Barr, *The Scope and Authority of the Bible*, Explorations in Theology 7 (London, 1980), 1–17, at 7.

Bibliography

Ackerman, S., *Under Every Green Tree: Popular Religion in Sixth-Century Judah*, HSM 46 (Atlanta, GA, 1992).

Albertz, R., *A History of Israelite Religion in the Old Testament Period*, Vols. I and II, London, 1994, trans. by John Bowden from *Religionsgeschichte Israels in alttestamentlicher Zeit*, Vols. I and II (Göttingen, 1992).

—— *Israel in Exile: The History and Literature of the Sixth Century B.C.E.* (Atlanta, GA, 2003), Eng. trans. by David Green from *Die Exilzeit: 6 Jahrhundert v. Chr.* (Stuttgart, 2001).

Alter, R., *The Art of Biblical Narrative* (New York, 1981).

—— *The World of Biblical Literature* (London, 1992).

Anderson, B. W., *The Living World of the Old Testament* (London, 1958).

Assmann, J., *Religion and Cultural Memory* (Stanford, CA, 2006), Eng. trans. by R. Livingstone from *Religion und kulturelles Gedächtnis* (Munich, 2000).

Barr, J., *Old and New in Interpretation* (London, 1966).

—— 'Story and History in Biblical Theology', *JR* 56 (1976), 1–17, repr. in id., *The Scope and Authority of the Bible*, Explorations in Theology 7 (London, 1980), 1–17.

—— 'Historical Reading and the Theological Interpretation of Scripture', in id., *The Scope and Authority of the Bible*, Explorations in Theology 7 (London, 1980), 30–51.

Barstad, H. M., 'No Prophets? Recent Developments in Biblical Prophetic Research and Ancient Near Eastern Prophecy', *JSOT* 57 (1993), 39–60.

—— 'The Understanding of the Prophets in Deuteronomy', *SJOT* 8 (1994), 236–51.

—— *History and the Hebrew Bible: Studies in Ancient Israelite and Ancient Near Eastern Historiography*, FAT 61 (Tübingen, 2008).

Barth, H., *Die Jesaja-Worte in der Josiazeit: Israel und Assur als Thema einer produktiven Neuinterpretation der Jesaja Überlieferung*, WMANT 48 (Neukirchen-Vluyn, 1977).

Barton, J., *Amos's Oracles against the Nations: A Study of Amos 1.3–2.5*, Society for Old Testament Study Monograph Series 6 (Cambridge, 1980).

—— '"The Law and the Prophets": Who were the Prophets?', *OtSt* 23 (1984), 1–18, repr. in id., *The Old Testament: Canon, Literature, and Theology* (Aldershot, 2007), 5–18.

—— *Joel and Obadiah: A Commentary*, OTL (Louisville, KY, 2001).

—— *Oracles of God: Perceptions of Ancient Prophecy in Israel after the Exile*, 2nd revised edn. (Oxford, 2007).

—— *The Theology of the Book of Amos* (Cambridge, 2012).

Baumgartner, W., 'Der Kampf um das Deuteronomium', *ThR* 1 (1929), 7–25.

Beaulieu, P.-A., 'Yahwistic Names in Light of Late Babylonian Onomastics', in O. Lipschits, G. N. Knoppers, and M. Oeming (eds.), *Judah and the Judeans in the Achaemenid Period: Negotiating Identity in an International Context* (Winona Lake, IN, 2011), 245–66.

Becking, B., ' "We All Returned As One!": Critical Notes on the Myth of the Mass Return', in O. Lipschits and M. Oeming (eds.), *Judah and the Judeans in the Persian Period* (Winona Lake, IN, 2006), 3–18.

Berry, G. R., 'The Code Found in the Temple', *JBL* 39 (1920), 44–51.

—— 'The Date of Deuteronomy', *JBL* 59 (1940), 133–9.

Bickerman, E. J., 'The Babylonian Captivity', in W. D. Davies and L. Finkelstein (eds.), *The Cambridge History of Judaism*, Vol. I (Cambridge, 1984), 342–58.

—— 'The Generation of Ezra and Nehemiah', *Proceedings of the American Academy of Jewish Research*, 45 (1978), 1–18, repr. in id., *Studies in Jewish and Christian History*, Vol. II (Leiden, 2007), 975–99.

Blenkinsopp, J., *A History of Prophecy in Israel*, revised and enlarged edn. (Louisville, London, and Leiden, 1996).

—— 'The Age of the Exile', in John Barton (ed.), *The Biblical World*, Vol. I (London and New York, 2002), 416–39.

Braulik, G., 'Das Buch Deuteronomium', in *Studien zum Deuteronomium und seiner Nachgeschiche*, SBAB 33 (Stuttgart, 2001).

Bright, J., *A History of Israel* (London, 1960).

Burchfield, R. W. (ed.), *The New Fowler's Modern English Usage*, 3rd edn. (Oxford, 1996).

Burney, C. F., *Notes on the Hebrew Text of the Books of Kings* (Oxford, 1903).

Childs, B. S., *The Book of Exodus: A Critical, Theological Commentary* (Louisville, KY, 1974).

Clements, R. E., *God and Temple* (Oxford, 1965).

—— *Isaiah 1–39*, NCB (London, 1980).

—— *Isaiah and the Deliverance of Jerusalem: A Study of the Interpretation of Prophecy in the Old Testament*, JSOTSup 12 (Sheffield, 1980).

—— 'The Prophet Isaiah and the Fall of Jerusalem', *VT* 30 (1980), 421–36.

—— 'The Deuteronomic Law of the Centralisation and the Catastrophe of 587 B.C.E.', in J. Barton and D. J. Reimer (eds.), *After the Exile: Essays in Honour of Rex Mason* (Macon, GA, 1996), 5–25.

—— 'The Origins of Deuteronomy: What Are the Clues?', in 'A Dialogue with Gordon McConville on Deuteronomy', *SJT* 56 (2003), 508–16.

Clements, R. E. 'The Davidic Covenant and the Isaiah Tradition', in A. D. H. Mayes and R. B. Salters (eds.), *Covenant as Context: Essays in Honour of E. W. Nicholson* (Oxford, 2003), 44–8.

Coats, G. W. and Long, B. O. (eds.), *Canon and Authority: Essays in Old Testament Religion and Theology* (Philadelphia, 1977).

Cogan, M., *Imperialism and Religion: Assyria, Judah and Israel in the Eighth and Seventh Centuries B.C.E.*, SBLMS 19 (Missoula, 1974).

—— 'Judah under Assyrian Hegemony: A Reexamination of Imperialism and Religion', *JBL* 112 (1993), 403–14.

—— and Tadmor, H., *II Kings: A New Translation with Introduction and Commentary*, Anchor Bible 11 (Garden City, NY, 1988).

Cornill, C. H., *Einleitung in das Alte Testament* (Tübingen, 1891).

Cross, F. M., *Canaanite Myth and Hebrew Epic* (Cambridge, MA, 1973).

Daube, D., 'The Culture of Deuteronomy', in *Orita: Ibadan Journal of Religious Studies*, 3: 1 (1969), 27–52.

Davies, G. I., *Hosea*, NCB (London, 1992).

Derow, P., 'Historical Explanation: Polybius and his Predecessors', in S. Hornblower (ed.), *Greek Historiography* (Oxford, 1994), 73–90.

Dewald, C., 'Narrative Surface and Authorial Voice in Herodotus' Histories', *Arethusa*, 20 (1987), 147–70.

—— 'Introduction' to Robin Waterfield (trans.), *Herodotus: The Histories* (Oxford, 1998), pp. ix–xli.

Dietrich, W., *Prophetie und Geschichte. Eine redaktionsgeschichtliche Untersuchung zum dtr Geschichtswerk*, FRLANT 108 (Göttingen, 1972).

Dohmen, C., *Das Bilderverbot: Seine Entstehung und seine Entwicklung im Alten Testament*, BBB 62 (Frankfurt a.M., 1987).

Donner, H., 'The Separate States of Israel and Judah', in J. H. Hayes and J. M. Miller (eds.), *Israelite and Judaean History* (London, 1977), 381–434.

Douglas, M., *Natural Symbols: Explorations in Cosmology* (Harmondsworth, 1978; first published 1970).

Driver, S. R., *A Critical and Exegetical Commentary on Deuteronomy*, ICC, 3rd edn, (Edinburgh, 1902).

Duhm, B., *Das Buch Jeremia*, KHAT, 9 (Tübingen and Leipzig, 1901).

Eilberg-Schwartz, H., *The Savage in Judaism: An Anthropology of Israelite Religion in Ancient Judaism* (Bloomington, IN, 1990).

Eissfeldt, O., *The Old Testament: An Introduction* (Oxford, 1965), Eng. trans. by P. R. Ackroyd from 3rd edn. of *Einleitung in das Alte Testament* (Tübingen, 1964).

Emerton, J. A., 'Priests and Levites in Deuteronomy', *VT* 12 (1962), 129–38.

Eph'al, I., 'The Western Minorities of Babylonia in the 6th and 5th Centuries B.C.: Maintenance and Cohesion', *Orientalia*, 47 (1978), 74–90.

—— 'On the Political and Social Organization of the Jews in Babylonian Exile', in *Zeitschrift der Deutschen Morgenländischen Gesellschaft*, Supplement Vol. V: Deutscher Orientalistentag XXI, 1980 (1983), 106–12.

Frei, H., *The Eclipse of Biblical Narrative* (New Haven and London, 1974).

Gosse, B., 'Deutéronome 17, 18–19 et la restauration de la royauté au retour de l'exile', *Bibbia e oriente*, 181 (1994), 129–38.

Gould, J., *Herodotus* (London, 1989).

—— 'Herodotus and Religion', in S. Hornblower (ed.), *Greek Historiography* (Oxford, 1994), 91–106.

Gramberg, C. W. P., *Kritische Geschichte der Religionsideen des A.T.*, Vol. I (Berlin, 1829).

Gray, J., *1 and 2 Kings: A Commentary* (London, 1964).

Hagedorn, A., *Between Moses and Plato: Individual and Society in Deuteronomy and Ancient Greek Law*, FRLANT 204 (Göttingen, 2004).

Hale, J. R., *The Evolution of British Historiography from Bacon to Namier* (London, 1967).

Halpern, B., *The Constitution of the Monarchy in Israel*, HSM 25 (Chico, CA, 1981).

—— *The First Historians: The Hebrew Bible and History* (San Francisco, 1988).

Hammond, N. G. L. and Scullard, H. H. (eds.), *The Oxford Classical Dictionary*, 2nd edn. (Oxford, 1970).

Holloway, S. W., *Aššur is King! Aššur is King! Religion in the Exercise of Power in the Neo-Assyrian Empire* (Leiden, Boston, and Cologne, 2002).

Hölscher, G., 'Komposition und Ursprung des Deuteronomiums', *ZAW* 40 (1922), 161–255.

—— *Geschichte der jüdischen und israelitischen Religion* (Giessen, 1922).

—— 'Das Buch der Könige: Seine Quellen und seine Redaktion', in Gunkel *Eucharisterion*, FRLANT 18 (Göttingen, 1923), 158–213.

Hornblower, S., *Thucydides* (London, 1987).

—— (ed.), *Greek Historiography* (Oxford, 1994).

Hossfeld, F.-L., *Der Dekalog: Seine späten Fassungen, die originale Komposition und seine Vorstufen*, OBO 45 (Göttingen, 1982).

—— and Meyer, I., *Prophet gegen Prophet. Eine Analyse der alttestamentlichen Texte zum Thema: Wahre und Falsche Propheten*, Biblische Beiträge 9 (Freiburg, 1973).

Hundley, M., 'To Be or Not to Be: A Reexamination of the Name Language in Deuteronomy and the Deuteronomistic History', *VT* 59 (2009), 533–55.

Irvine, S. A., *Isaiah, Ahaz and the Syro-Ephraimite Crisis*, SBLDS 123 (Atlanta, GA, 1990).

Joannès, F. and Lemaire, A., 'Trois tablettes cunéiformes à l'onomastique ouest-sémitique', *Transeuphratène*, 17 (1999), 17–33.

Joyce, P., 'King and Messiah in Ezekiel', in J. Day (ed.), *King and Messiah in Israel and the Ancient Near East*, JSOTSup 270 (Sheffield, 1998), 323–37.

—— *Ezekiel: A Commentary* (New York and London, 2007).

Knoppers, G. N., 'The Deuteronomist and the Deuteronomic Law of the King: A Reexamination of a Relationship', *ZAW* 108 (1996), 329–46.

Köhler, L., *Theologie des Alten Testaments* (Tübingen, 1936); Eng. trans. by A. S. Todd from 3rd revised edn. (1953), *Old Testament Theology* (London, 1957).

Kratz, R. G., *The Composition of the Narrative Books of the Old Testament* (New York, 2005), Eng. trans. by John Bowden from *Die Komposition der erzählenden Bücher des Alten Testaments* (Göttingen, 2000).

Lambert, W. G., 'The Babylonians and Chaldaeans', in D. J. Wiseman (ed.), *Peoples of Old Testament Times* (Oxford, 1973), 179–96.

—— 'The Historical Development of the Mesopotamian Pantheon: A Study in Sophisticated Polytheism', in H. Goedicke and J. J. M. Roberts (eds.), *Unity and Diversity: Essays in the History, Literature, and Religion of the Ancient Near East* (Baltimore and London, 1975), 191–200.

—— 'A Document from a Community of Exiles in Babylonia', in Meir Lubetski (ed.), *New Seals and Inscriptions, Hebrew, Idumean, and Cuneiform* (Sheffield, 2007), 201–5.

Lemaire, A.: see under Joannès, F.

Levinson, B. M., 'The Reconceptualization of Kingship in Deuteronomy and the Deuteronomistic History's Transformation of Torah', *VT* 51 (2001), 511–34.

Levtow, N. B., *Images of Others: Iconic Politics in Ancient Israel* (Winona Lake, IN, 2008).

Lipschits, O., Knoppers, G. N., and Oeming, M. (eds.), *Judah and the Judeans in the Achaemenid Period: Negotiating Identity in an International Context* (Winona Lake, IN, 2011), 265–77.

Liverani, M., 'The Medes at Esarhaddon's Court', *JCS* 47 (1995), 57–62.

Lohfink, N., '2 Kings 22–23: The State of the Question', in D. L. Christensen (ed.), *A Song of Power and the Power of Song: Essays on the Book of Deuteronomy* (Winona Lake, IN, 1993), 36–61.

—— 'Zur Dekalogfassung von Dt 5', *BZ* 9 (1965), 17–32.

—— 'Die Sicherung der Wirksamkeit des Gotteswortes durch das Prinzip der Gewaltenteilung nach den Ämtergesetzen des Buches Deuteronomium (Dt 16, 18–18, 22)', in H. Wolter (ed.), *Testimonium Veritati* (Festschrift Wilhelm Kempf), Frankfurter theologische Studien 7 (Frankfurt a.M., 1971), 144–55, repr. in id. *Studien zum Deuteronomium und zur deuteronomistischen Literatur* I, SBAB 8 (Stuttgart, 1990), 305–23; Eng. trans. 'Distribution of the Functions of Power: The Laws Concerning Public Offices in Deuteronomy 16: 18–18: 22', in D. L. Christensen (ed.),

A Song of Power and the Power of Song: Essays on the Book of Deuteronomy (Winona Lake, IN, 1993), 336–52.

Lohfink, N. 'The Cult Reform of Josiah of Judah: 2 Kings 22–23 as a Source for the History of Israelite Religion', in J. M. Miller, P. D. Hanson, and S. D. McBride (eds.), *Ancient Israelite Religion: Essays in Honor of Frank Moore Cross* (Philadelphia, 1987), 459–75.

Long. B. O.: see under Coats, G. W.

López, F. García, 'Le Roi d'Israel: Dt 17, 14–20', in N. Lohfink (ed.), *Das Deuteronomium: Entstehung, Gestalt und Botschaft*, BETL 68 (Leuven, 1985), 277–97.

Lowery, R. H., *The Reforming Kings: Cults and Society in First Temple Judah*, JSOTSup 120 (Sheffield, 1991).

Lust, J., Eynikel, E., and Hauspie, K., *A Greek–English Lexicon of the Septuagint*, 2 vols. (Stuttgart, 1992 and 1996).

McBride, S. Dean, 'Polity of the Covenant People: The Book of Deuteronomy', *Interpretation*, 41 (1987), 229–44.

McConville, J. G., 'King and Messiah in Deuteronomy and the Deuteronomistic History', in J. Day (ed.) *King and Messiah in Israel and the Ancient Near East*, JSOTSup 270 (Sheffield, 1998), 271–95.

Machinist, P., 'Mesopotamian Imperialism and Israelite Religion: A Case Study from the Second Isaiah', in W. G. Dever and S. Gitin (eds.), *Symbiosis, Symbolism, and the Power of the Past: Canaan, Ancient Israel, and their Neighbours from the Late Bronze Age through Roman Palestine* (Winona Lake, IN, 2003), 237–64.

Macintosh, A. A., *Hosea*, ICC (Edinburgh, 1997).

McKane, W., *Jeremiah*, Vol. I, ICC (Edinburgh, 1986).

—— *Jeremiah*, Vol. II, ICC (Edinburgh, 1996).

—— *The Book of Micah: Introduction and Commentary* (Edinburgh, 1998).

Mason, R. A., *Preaching the Tradition: Homily and Hermeneutics after the Exile* (Cambridge, 1990).

Mayes, A. D. H., *Deuteronomy*, NCB (London, 1979).

—— 'Deuteronomy 4 and the Literary Criticism of Deuteronomy', *JBL* 100 (1981), 23–51.

—— 'Deuteronomy 14 and the Deuteronomic World View', in F. García Martínez *et al.* (eds.), *Studies in Deuteronomy in Honour of C. J. Labuschagne on the Occasion of his 65th Birthday* (Leiden, New York, and Cologne, 1994), 165–81.

Meier, C., 'Historical Answers to Historical Questions: The Origins of History in Ancient Greece', *Arethusa*, 20 (1987), 41–57.

Mein, A., *Ezekiel and the Ethics of Exile* (Oxford, 2001).

Mettinger, T. N. D., *The Dethronement of Sabaoth: Studies in the Shem and Kabod Theologies*, ConBOT 18 (Lund, 1982).

Meyer, I., *Jeremia und die falschen Propheten*, OBO (Fribourg and Göttingen, 1977). See also under F. L. Hossfeld.

Meyers, C. L. and Meyers, E. M., *Haggai, Zechariah 1–8: A New Translation with Introduction and Commentary* (Garden City, NY, 1987).

Milgrom, J., *Leviticus 1–16: A New Translation with Introduction and Commentary* (New York, 1991).

Momigliano, A., *The Classical Foundations of Modern Historiography* (Berkeley, 1990).

—— *Essays in Ancient and Modern Historiography* (Oxford, 1977).

Montgomery, J. A. and Gehman, H. S., *A Critical and Exegetical Commentary on the Books of Kings*, ICC (Edinburgh, 1951).

Murray, O., 'Greek Historians', in J. Boardman, J. Griffin, and O. Murray (eds.), *Greece and the Hellenistic World* (Oxford, 1988).

Nelson, R. D., *The Double Redaction of the Deuteronomistic History*, JSOT-Supp 18 (Sheffield, 1981).

—— *Deuteronomy: A Commentary*, OTL (Louisville and London, 2002).

Nicholson, E. W., *Deuteronomy and Tradition* (Oxford, 1967).

—— *Preaching to the Exiles: A Study of the Prose Tradition in the Book of Jeremiah* (Oxford, 1970).

—— *God and His People: Covenant and Theology in the Old Testament* (Oxford, 1986).

—— 'Story and History in the Old Testament', in S. E. Ballentine and J. Barton (eds.), *Language, Theology, and the Bible: Essays in Honour of James Barr* (Oxford, 1994), 135–50.

—— *The Pentateuch in the Twentieth Century: The Legacy of Julius Wellhausen* (Oxford, 1998).

—— ' "Do not dare to set a foreigner over you": The King in Deuteronomy and "The Great King" ', *ZAW* 118 (2006), 46–61.

—— 'Josiah and the Priests of the High Places (II Reg 23, 8a, 9)', *ZAW* 119 (2007), 499–513.

—— '*Traditum* and *traditio*: The Case of Deuteronomy 17: 14–20', in D. A. Green and L. S. Lieber (eds.), *Scriptural Exegesis: The Shapes of Culture and the Religious Imagination. Essays in Honour of Michael Fishbane* (Oxford, 2009), 46–61.

—— 'Deuteronomy 18.9–22, The Prophets and Scripture', in J. Day (ed.), *Prophecy and the Prophets in Ancient Israel*, Library of Hebrew Bible/Old Testament Studies 531 (New York and London, 2010), 151–71.

—— 'Deuteronomy and the Babylonian Diaspora', in J. K. Aitken, Katharine J. Dell, and Brian A. Mastin (eds.), *On Stone and Scroll: Essays in Honour of Graham Ivor Davies*, BZAW 420 (Berlin, 2011), 269–85.

—— 'Once again Josiah and the Priests of the High Places (II Reg 23, 8a, 9)', *ZAW* 124 (2012), 356–68.

—— 'Reconsidering the Provenance of Deuteronomy', *ZAW* 124 (2012), 528–40.

Noth, M., *Die Gesetz im Pentateuch (Ihre Vorraussetzungen und ihre Sinn)* (Halle, 1940); Eng. trans. 'The Laws in the Pentateuch: Their Assumptions and Meaning', in id., *The Laws in the Pentateuch and Other Essays*, trans. D. R. Ap-Thomas (Edinburgh and London, 1966), 1–107.

—— *Überlieferungsgeschichtliche Studien* (1943; 2nd edn. Tübingen, 1957); Eng. trans. by H. G. M. Williamson from *The Deuteronomistic History*, JSOTSup 15 (Sheffield, 1981).

—— *Überlieferungsgeschichte des Pentateuch* (Stuttgart, 1948); Eng. trans. by B. W. Anderson from *A History of Pentateuchal Traditions* (Englewood Cliffs, NJ, 1972).

—— *Geschichte Israels* (Göttingen, 1950; 2nd edn. 1954); Eng. trans. by Peter Ackroyd from 2nd edn., *The History of Israel* (London, 1960).

—— 'Die Bewährung von Salomos "göttliche Weisheit"', in M. Noth and D. Winton Thomas (eds.), *Wisdom in Israel and in the Ancient Near East: Essays Presented to Professsor Harold Henry Rowley*, VTSup 3 (Leiden 1955), 225–37.

Oestreicher, T., *Das Deuteronomische Grundgesetz* (Gütersloh, 1923).

Pearce, L. E., 'New Evidence for Judeans in Babylonia', in O. Lipschits and M. Oeming (eds.), *Judah and the Judeans in the Persian Period* (Winona Lake, IN, 2006), 399–411.

—— '"Judean": A Special Status in Neo-Babylonian and Achemenid Babylonia?', in O. Lipschits, G. N. Knoppers, and M. Oeming (eds.), *Judah and the Judeans in the Achaemenid Period: Negotiating Identity in an International Context* (Winona Lake, IN, 2011), 265–77.

Perlitt, L., *Bundestheologie im Alten Testament*, WMANT 36 (Neukirchen-Vluyn, 1969).

—— 'Der Staatsgedanke im Deuteronomium', in S. E. Ballentine and J. Barton (eds.), *Language, Theology, and The Bible: Essays in Honour of James Barr* (Oxford, 1994), 182–98.

—— 'Ein einzig Volk von Brüdern': Zur deuteronomischen Herkunft der biblischen Bezeichnung "Bruder"', in *Deuteronomium-Studien*, FAT 8 (Tübingen, 1994), 50–73.

—— 'Hebraismus—Deuteronomismus—Judaismus', in *Deuteronomium-Studien*, FAT 8 (Tübingen, 1994), 245–60.

Pritchard, J. (ed.), *Ancient Near Eastern Texts Relating to the Old Testament*, 3rd edn. (Princeton, 1969).

Rad, G. von, *Das formgeschichtliche Problem des Hexateuch*, BWANT 26 (Stuttgart, 1938); Eng. trans. 'The Form Critical Problem of the Hexateuch', in id., *The Problem of the Hexateuch and other Essays*, trans. E. W. Dicken Trueman (Edinburgh, 1966), 1–78.

Rad, G. von, 'Der Anfang der Geschichtsschreibung im alten Israel', *Archiv für Kulturgeschichte*, 32 (1944), 1–42, repr. in *Gesammelte Studien zum alten Testament* (Munich, 1958), 14–88; Eng. trans. 'The Beginnings of Historical Writing in Ancient Israel', in id., *The Problem of the Hexateuch and other Essays*, trans. E. W. Dicken Trueman (Edinburgh, 1966), 166–204.

—— 'Die deuteronomistische Geschichtstheologie in den Königsbüchern' (1944), repr. in id., *Gesammelte Studien zum Alten Testament* (Munich 1958), 189–204; Eng. trans. 'The Deuteronomistic Theology of History in I and II Kings', in id., *The Problem of the Hexateuch and Other Essays*, trans. E. W. Dicken Trueman (Edinburgh, 1966), 205–21.

—— *Deuteronomium-Studien*, FRLANT 58 (Göttingen, 1947); Eng. trans. by D. M. G. Stalker, *Studies in Deuteronomy* (London, 1953).

—— *Theologie des Alten Testaments*, Vol. I, *Die Theologie der geschichtliche Überlieferungen Israels* (Munich, 1957); Eng. trans. by D. M. G. Stalker, *Old Testament Theology*, Vol. I, *The Theology of Israel's Historical Traditions* (Edinburgh, 1962).

—— *Theologie des Alten Testaments*, Vol. II, *Die Theologie der prophetischen Überlieferungen Israels* (Munich, 1960); Eng. trans. by D. M. Stalker, *Old Testament Theology*, Vol. II, *The Theology of Israel's Prophetic Traditions* (Edinburgh, 1965).

Ratheiser, G. M. H., *Mitzvoth Ethics and the Jewish Bible: The End of Old Testament Theology*, Library of Hebrew Bible/Old Testament Studies 460 (New York and London, 2007).

Römer, T., 'L'École deutéronomiste et la formation de la Bible hébraïque', in T. Römer (ed.), *The Future of the Deuteronomistic History*, BETL 147 (Leuven, 2000), 179–93.

Rüterswörden, U., *Von der politischen Gemeinschaft zur Gemeinde: Studien zu Dt 16, 18–18, 22*, BBB 65 (Frankfurt a.M., 1987).

Saggs, H. W. F., 'The Assyrians', in D. J. Wiseman (ed.), *Peoples of Old Testament Times* (Oxford, 1973), 156–78.

Schaper, J., *Priester und Leviten im achämenidischen Juda: Studien zur Kult- und Sozialgeschichte Israels in persischer Zeit*, FAT 31 (Tübingen, 2000).

Schmidt, W. H., 'Das Prophetengesetz Dtn 18:9–22 im Kontext erzählender Literatur', in M. Vervenne and J. Lust (eds.), *Deuteronomy and Deuteronomic Literature. Festschrift C. H. W. Brekelmans*, BETL 133 (Leuven, 1997), 55–69.

—— *Das Buch Jeremia, Kapitel 1–20*, ATD 20 (Göttingen, 2008).

Scullard, H. H.: see under Hammond, N. G. L.

Smend, Rudolf, 'Das Nein des Amos', *EvT* 23 (1963), 404–23, repr. in id., *Die Mitte des Alten Testaments* (Tübingen, 2002), 219–37.

—— '*Elemente alttestamentlichen Geschichtsdenkens*', Theologische Studien 95 (Zürich, 1968), repr. in *Die Mitte des Alten Testaments* (Tübingen, 2002), 89–114.

—— 'Das Gesetz und die Völker. Ein Beitrag zur dtr Redaktionsgeschichte', originally published in *Probleme biblischer Theologie. Gerhard v. Rad zum 70. Geburtstag*, ed. H. W. Wolff (Munich, 1971), 494–507, repr. in id. *Die Mitte des Alten Testaments* (Tübingen, 2002), 148–61.

Smith, D. L., *The Religion of the Landless: The Social Context of the Babylonian Exile* (Bloomington, IN, 1989).

Smith-Christopher, D. L., *A Biblical Theology of Exile* (Minneapolis, 2002).

Soggin, A., *A History of Israel from the Beginnings to the Bar Kochba Revolt*, AD 135 (London, 1984), Eng. trans. by John Bowden of *Storia d'Israele, dalle origini alla rivolta di Bar-Kochba* (Brescia, 1984).

Spieckermann, H., *Juda unter Assur in der Sargonidenzeit*, FRLANT 129 (Göttingen, 1982).

Staerk, W., *Das Deuteronomium: sein Inhalt und seine literarische Form* (Leipzig, 1994).

Stavrakopoulou, F., *King Manasseh and Child Sacrifice: Biblical Distortions of Historical Realities*, BZAW 338 (Berlin, 2004).

Steck, O. H., *Israel und das gewaltsame Geschick der Propheten*, WMANT 23 (Neukirchen-Vluyn, 1967).

Steuernagel, K., *Der Rahmen des Deuteronomiums* (Halle, 1894).

Štrba, B., *Take Off Your Sandals from Your Feet! An Exegetical Study of Josh 5, 13–15*, Österreichische Biblische Studien 32 (Frankfurt a.M., 2008).

Stulman, L., 'Encroachment in Deuteronomy: An Analysis of the Social World of the D Code', *JBL* 109 (1990), 613–32.

Sundberg, A. C. Jr., 'The Bible Canon and the Christian Doctrine of Inspiration', *Interpretation*, 29 (1975), 352–71.

Sweeney, M. A., *Zephaniah: A Commentary* (Minneapolis, 2003).

Tadmor, H.: see under Cogan, M.

Tengström, S., 'Moses and the Prophets in the Deuteronomistic History', *SJT* 8 (1994), 257–66.

Tollington, J. E., *Tradition and Innovation in Haggai and Zechariah 1–8*, JSOTSup 150 (Sheffield, 1993).

Tucker, Gene M., 'Prophetic Superscriptions and the Growth of a Canon', in G. W. Coats and B. O. Long (eds.), *Canon and Authority: Essays in Old Testament Religion and Theology* (Philadelphia, 1977), 56–70.

Uehlinger, C., 'Was There a Cult Reform under King Josiah? The Case for a Well-grounded Minimum', in L. L. Grabbe (ed.), *Good Kings and Bad Kings*, Library of Hebrew Bible/Old Testament Studies 393 (London, 2005), 279–316.

Van Seters, J., *In Search of History: Historiography the Ancient World and the Origins of Biblical History* (New Haven and London, 1983).

—— *Prologue to History: The Yahwist as Historian in Genesis* (Louisville, KY, 1992).

—— 'Is there any Historiography in the Hebrew Bible? A Hebrew–Greek Comparison', *Journal of Northwest Semitic Languages*, 28: 2 (2002), 1–25.

Vaux, R. de, *Ancient Israel: Its Life and Institutions* (London, 1961), Eng. trans. by John McHugh of *Les Institutions de l'Ancien Testament*, I–II (Paris, 1958–60).

Veijola, T., 'Die Deuteronomisten als Vorgänger der Schriftgelehrten. Ein Beitrag zur Entstehung des Judentums', in id., *Moses Erben. Studien zum Dekalog, zum Deuteronomismus und zum Schriftgelehrtentum*, BWANT 149 (Stuttgart, 2000), 192–240.

Vermeylen, J., *Du prophète Isaïe à l'apocalyptique. Isaïe I–XXXV, miroir d'un demi-millénaire d'expérience religieuse en Israël*, Vols. I–II, Études Bibliques (Paris, 1977–8).

'L'École deutéronomiste aurait-elle imaginé un premier canon des Écritures?', in T. Römer (ed.), *The Future of the Deuteronomistic History*, BETL 147 (Leuven, 2000), 223–40.

Weinfeld, M., *Deuteronomy and the Deuteronomic School* (Oxford, 1972).

Wellhausen, J., *Prolegomena to the History of Israel* (Edinburgh, 1885), Eng. trans. by J. Sutherland Black and Allan Menzies from *Prolegomena zur Geschichte Israels* (Berlin, 1883).

—— *Die Composition des Hexateuchs und der historischen Bücher des AT*, 3rd edn. (Berlin, 1899).

deWette, W. M. L., *Dissertatio critica-exegetica, qua Deuteronomium a prioribus Pentateuchi libris diversum, alius cuiusdam recentioris auctoris opus esse monstratur* (Jena, 1805), repr. in his *Opuscula* (Berlin, 1833).

Williamson, H. G. M., *The Book Called Isaiah: Deutero-Isaiah's Role in Composition and Redaction* (Oxford, 1994).

Wilson, R. R., *Prophecy and Society in Ancient Israel* (Philadelphia, 1980).

Wolff, H. W., *Hosea* (Philadelphia, 1974), Eng. trans. by G. Stansell from *Dodekapropheton 1 Hosea*, 2nd edn., BKAT 14.1 (Neukirchen-Vluyn, 1965).

—— *Joel and Amos* (Philadelphia, 1977), Eng. trans. by W. Janzen, S. Dean McBride, and C. A. Muenchow from *Dodekapropheton 2: Joel und Amos*, BKAT 14.2 (Neukirchen-Vluyn, 1969).

—— *Micah the Prophet* (Philadelphia, 1981), Eng. trans. by R. D. Gehrke from *Mit Micha reden: Prophetie einst und jetzt* (Munich, 1978).

—— *Micha*, BKAT 14.4 (Neukirchen-Vluyn, 1982).

Zadok, R., *The Earliest Diaspora: Israelites and Judeans in Pre-Hellenistic Mesopotamia*, Publications of the Diaspora Research Institute 151 (Tel Aviv, 2002).

Zimmerli, W., *Ezekiel 1: A Commentary on the Book of Ezekiel, Chapters 1–24* (Philadelphia, 1979), Eng. trans. by R. E. Clements from *Ezechiel 1*, BKAT 13.1 (Neukirchen-Vluyn, 1969).

—— *Ezekiel 2: A Commentary on the Book of Ezekiel Chapters 25–48* (Philadelphia, 1983), Eng. trans. by J. D. Martin from 2nd German edn., *Ezechiel 2*, BKAT 13.2 (Neukirchen-Vluyn, 1979).

Index of Authors

Index of Sources